Open University Press
New Directions in Criminology series

Series Editor: Colin Sumner, Lecturer in Sociology,
Institute of Criminology, and Fellow of
Wolfson College, University of Cambridge

Current and forthcoming titles include:

Imperial Policing
Philip Ahire

Lawyers' Work
Maureen Cain and Christine Harrington

Feminist Perspectives in Criminology
Loraine Gelsthorpe and Allison Morris (eds.)

The Enemy Without: Policing and Class Consciousness in the Miners' Strike
Penny Green

Regulating Women in Wartime
Ruth Jamieson

Black Women and Crime
Marcia Rice

Criminal Justice and Underdevelopment in Tanzania
Leonard Shaidi

Censure, Politics and Criminal Justice
Colin Sumner (ed.)

Reading the Riot Act
Richard Vogler

Reading the Riot Act

The magistracy, the police and the army in civil disorder

Richard Vogler

Open University Press
Milton Keynes • Philadelphia

Open University Press
Celtic Court
22 Ballmoor
Buckingham
MK18 1XW

and
1900 Frost Road, Suite 101
Bristol, PA 19007, US

First Published 1991

British Library Cataloguing-in-Publication Data

Vogler, Richard
  Reading the Riot Act: The magistracy, the police
  and the army in civil disorder. – (New directions
  in criminology)
  I. Title   II. Series
  322.4

  ISBN 0–335–15184–1 (pbk)
  ISBN 0–335–15185–X

Library of Congress Cataloging-in-Publication Data

Vogler, Richard, 1951–
    Reading the Riot Act : the magistracy, the police, and the army in
  civil disorder / Richard Vogler.
      p.   cm. — (New directions in criminology series)
    Includes bibliographical references and index.
    ISBN 0-335-15185-X (hb)   ISBN 0-335-15184-1 (pb)
    1. Law enforcement—England—History.   2. Riot control—England—
  History.   I. Title.   II. Series.
  HV8196.A3V64   1991
  363.3'2—dc20   91-10574
                                                              CIP

Typeset by Inforum Typesetting, Portsmouth
Printed in Great Britain by Biddles Limited, Guildford and Kings Lynn

Contents

Series editor's introduction

This series is founded upon the socialist and feminist research carried out in the Institute of Criminology over the last decade. It is, however, concerned more broadly to publish any work which renews theoretical development or opens up new and important areas in criminology. Particular attention will be paid to the politics and ideology of criminal justice, gender and crime, crimes of state officials, crime and justice in underdeveloped societies, European criminal justice, environmental crime, and the general sociology of censure and regulation. The series will centre upon substantial empirical research informed by contemporary social theory, and will be unusually international in character.

Behind the series is a belief that criminology cannot be limited to policy-oriented studies and must retain its integrity as an area of independent, critical enquiry or interest to scholars from a variety of disciplinary backgrounds. A criminology that wants to remain dynamic and worthy of its complex subject matter must therefore constantly renew theoretical debate, explore current issues, and develop new methods of research. To allow itself to be limited by the often narrowly political interests of government departments or the funding agencies' need for a parochial 'relevance', especially in an age when 'realism' is so often defined by short-run philosophies, is to promote its own destruction as an intellectual enterprise. A criminology which is not intellectually alive is useless to everybody. We live in increasingly international societies which, more than ever, require a broad, non-parochial vision to ensure their viability and health. The various kinds of administrative criminology may be necessary for wise government, but they can be of general value only if they remain closely connected to an independent, intellectually rigorous criminology, which, even now, actually provides them with ideas, topicality, drive, depth and legitimacy. The latter, equally, must retain a close connection with political reality if it is to achieve real insight and sharpness. Both, we believe, must be committed to a general drive towards increased democratization and justice, and the indivisibility of freedom, truth and justice, if they want to avoid a drift into the twin culs-de-sac of 'police science' and political propaganda.

Some might argue that 'criminology' is an outdated term in that very few people believe any more that a positive science of crime and criminal justice administration is possible. Indeed, some of the studies in this series will look more like studies in the sociology of law, or in political socio-logy, and their view of science is never positivistic. We have decided to retain the term criminology, however, because we intend this series to contribute to redefining its meaning, so that it clearly includes sociology of law, political sociology, social history, political economy, discourse analysis, and so on. Criminology merely refers to any kind of study concerned with crime and criminal justice. It is an umbrella term covering a multitude of topics and approaches. The task for all of us is to give it a meaningful substance to meet the emerging and exciting challenges of the 1990s. The cold war is almost over; now, we enter a phase which will demand a new clarity on fundamental social values, and a stronger vision of the substance and form of social censure and regulation necessary to promote peace, health, growth, equity and co-operation on an interna-tional scale.

This book by Richard Vogler exemplifies the character of the series in many ways. Expressing an interdisciplinary perspective combining so-ciology, law, social history, and politics, the book contains an authorita-tive study of the changing balance of power between the magistrates, police and the army as evidenced in the regulation of civil disorder over the last two centuries. In so doing, it documents in detail the regulation of public disorder during this period. Tracing the earlier dominance of the magistracy through a historical analysis of 'reading the Riot Act' in a number of incidents of public disorder, and documenting, through so-ciological fieldwork into the 1981 'riots', the contemporary power of the police to 'clear the streets' with the aid of a more subordinate magistracy, this study combines detailed empirical research with an exploration of Poulantzas's theory of the state. Quite uniquely, it also combines a law-yer's inside knowledge of the workings of the lower courts with a socio-logist's sense of the workings of the social formation as a whole.

It demonstrates, in particular, the importance of looking at the relations between the central and the local state, within the context of the general class relations of the time, in order to understand the concrete political realities of the state. With its sensitivity to the historically changing character of social classes and of the form of state itself, the study is a timely reminder of the political importance of the local state in the formation and operation of what we have come to know as liberal democracy. Too often, in the past, Marxist studies of the state have treated it as monolithic entity with no significant internal or local relations. Recent devolutionary movements in the Soviet Union, alongside the frequent attacks on the power of local authorities in the UK, have taught us that the state is neither an empty abstraction nor a single concrete entity. They have also demonstrated the crucial role the local state has to play in the maintenance of democracy, however one understands that mischievously ambiguous phrase.

Richard Vogler's book, emerging in the UK shortly after the massive resistance against the poll tax and the concomitant increasing central-state control of local budgets, is eloquent testimony to the important historical role of the magistracy, and other local authorities, as legal intermediaries between central state and local people. His conclusion, that the post-1945 magistracy has rendered itself immune to democratic pressure, only reinforces our belief that one of the central tasks of a socialist criminology in the 1990s must be to sustain a critical awareness of the value of creating independent local justice agencies which proportionately represent the full range of local interests.

Colin Sumner

Preface

This is the tenth anniversary of the street fighting which overwhelmed the cities of England in 1981. Perhaps sufficient time has by now elapsed to permit a clearer perspective on what was undoubtedly the most extensive national breakdown of civil order since the General Strike. This book is not the 'missing' history of those terrible days a decade ago. Although it is hoped to provide as lucid an account of them as possible, they are viewed here as merely one incident, albeit a significant and climactic one, in the long historical development of the control agencies in England and Wales. This is a book not about rioters or the causes of civil disorder, but about forms of control. The events of 1981 are placed alongside a number of other similar crises in public order over the previous 160 years, as a means of illustrating some of the radical changes which have taken place during that time in the agencies of the state involved in the repression of disorder. These changes have important implications, it will be argued, for the form of the state itself. What is more, a crisis, particularly one which threatens public order, reveals hidden tensions and stresses and brings out into the open conflicts which may be concealed in less demanding times. It throws a flood of light upon the material structures of the state.

The book is therefore concerned with the developing relations between the three principal agencies of the state involved in the repression of civil disorder – the magistracy, the police and the army. It combines narrative accounts of specific historical incidents with structural analysis of the development of relations between the agencies themselves and it begins with a consideration of the theory of the state. For reasons of space, some of the academic debates in this area have been condensed more than would otherwise be desirable, and for my necessarily schematic approach I apologize wholeheartedly.

My sources for the historical material have been a heterogeneous collection of eye-witness accounts, newspapers, memoirs, state papers and academic references. For the 1981 material I was fortunate enough to be able to interview many of the lawyers, court officials, prosecutors and defence committee workers involved and to examine the court registers in a number of city magistrates' courts. I am profoundly grateful to all those who gave their time and effort to help me in the research, as well as to my colleagues at the Institute of Criminology at Cambridge and Sussex University.

My daughter, Katherine, arrived in this world on the day after the manuscript was delivered and her wonderful sense of timing justifies me, I hope, in dedicating the book to her.

1 Reading the Riot Act: local state power and social class

Commanding with a loud voice

> Our Sovereign Lord the King chargeth and commandeth all Persons, being assembled, immediately to disperse themselves, and peaceably to depart to their Habitations, or to their lawful Business, upon the Pains contained in the Act made in the first year of King *George*, for preventing Tumults and riotous Assemblies.   God Save the King.[1]

This is the proclamation which justices, in cases of 'Tumult and riotous Assemblies', were required to read 'with a loud voice'. 'Reading the Riot Act' has entered our language to denote the exercise of ultimate authority. It is expressive of command and domination; the overwhelming power of the central state, applied by its minor functionaries.

The Act itself was among the first measures of the Hanoverian regime, faced with military rebellion from the Jacobites and the disaffection of the existing provincial authorities (Speck 1977, p. 80; Collison 1983, p. 2; Bennett and Ryan 1985, p. 178). It was drafted by Sir Edward Northey and Lord Raymond, in the panic which arose from 'the prodigious riots that were then in the City'.[2] The Act provided the sanction of felony against persons remaining assembled an hour after the reading of the proclamation. In contrast to previous offences of riot and unlawful assembly, it was not necessary to prove a specific act or intention; mere presence was enough to hang the accused. More importantly, it represented a message to the justices of the peace themselves, warning them of 'neglect or misbehaviour'[3] and demanding a vigorous exercise of their authority.

To this end, justices and their servants engaged in efforts to 'disperse, seize or apprehend' rioters were 'free, discharged and indemnified' for the 'killing, maiming or hurting of any such Person or Persons' who resisted (s.iii).

The Riot Act was, in many senses, a law to abolish law; a kind of modified martial law against rioters. In General Sir Charles Napier's (1837, p. 43) view, this should be established by a solemn tolling of church bells during which the magistrate would hand over authority to the military, saying: 'Sir, the law is at an end; the public safety is no longer protected by it.'

The extraordinary effect of the Act was to convert, by mere command, every person who chanced to be in the vicinity of the reading after the expiry of an hour, into a felon. A closer reading of the Act however, reveals that although it creates a new *felony*, its penal sections refer explicitly to *treason*: 'by such rioters his Majesty and his Administration have been most maliciously and falsely traduced, with an Intent to raise Divisions, and to alienate the affections of the People from his Majesty' (s.i). Thus the proclamation served not only to transform rioters into felons but by implication (if not by law) also into traitors and therefore outside the King's Peace. It is this aspect of the legislation which justified the suspension of laws and the exercise against rioters of the ultimate lethal force of the state. It is for this reason that actual prosecutions were hardly ever founded on the Act (Collison 1983, p. 192), which was concerned above all with the immediate defence of authority.

The concept of guilt by proclamation was a familiar characteristic of early Hanoverian legislation (Thompson 1975, p. 174), but it was a doctrine which subsequently caused considerable difficulties. Napier (1857, pp. 71–2) describes a familiar scene during the Chartist disturbances of the 1840s:

> I rode out, ordering dragoons to follow me. Mr N. and I found the mob, which would not notice us and marched on. Old N. put on his spectacles, pulled out the riot act and read it in an audible voice – to who? Myself and about a dozen old women, looking out at their doors to see what we were at! We came back, found another mob and ordered it to disperse. No. N. told me to disperse it. I laughed, the dragoons laughed, the young women of the mob laughed, and then old N. laughed, and so the second act of folly passed.

Efforts by a police constable in 1887 simultaneously to translate the proclamation into Welsh as it was read by an English magistrate during the tithe riots provoked more amusement.[4] James Sexton described the equally absurd procedures adopted during disorders in Belfast in the Edwardian period for the present farcical, if I may call it so, attitude adopted by the military magistrates, or any other magistrates, in holding up a piece of paper and pretending to read it to a crowd of these dimensions. And that constitutes reading the Riot Act. Nobody hears it, nobody knows what it is about, except the magistrate who reads it.[5]

The last reading of the Act was in 1919, although the town clerk of Stockport gave serious consideration to a further reading during the Roberts-Arundel dispute in February 1967.[6] It would have been the final opportunity. Later that year, after a lifespan of 250 years, the Act was repealed by Schedule 3, Part III of the Criminal Justice Act 1967. But the legislation could not be forgotten so easily. In 1981, in the aftermath of the inner-city riots, the chief commissioner of the metropolitan police argued vigorously for its re-enactment,[7] a view shared by Evelegh (1978, p. 157) who felt that its repeal in 1967 had been a 'grave error'.

This book is not about the Riot Act itself, but about the people who read it and those who enforced its provisions. Throughout the lifetime of the Act and into the 1990s, the major agencies involved in the suppression of riot have been the *magistracy*, the *police* and the *military*. This study will examine these three agencies, the relations between them and the contributions which they have each made to the formation and development of the state. The right to 'read the Riot Act', to exercise the ultimate authority of the state in the last instance of disorder, is a crucial aspect of state power. It will be argued in the following pages that this distasteful duty, therefore, brought with it enormous authority. The constantly changing relations which existed between the agencies involved in the suppression of disorder provide not only an important indication of their respective power but also, and more importantly, an insight into the developing character of the state itself. In short, this study is a sustained attack on the idea that the state remains unchanging and monolithic in its exercise of authority.

'By the authority aforesaid': the state and its agencies

If we ask what is the authority wielded by the magistrate, the police or army officer in suppressing a riot, the obvious answer is that they are all exercising power associated with the state. But the concept of the 'state' is not self-explanatory. It conceals an elision of structure and agency which has provoked endless theoretical debates and which is neatly exemplified by Gramsci's (1971, p. 470) troublesome army recruit:

Thus one could imagine a recruit explaining to the recruiting officers the theory of the State as superior to individuals and demanding that they should leave in liberty his physical and material person and just enrol that mysterious something that contributes to building that national something known as the State.

Marxist theory in particular has become deeply polarized between capital-theoretical and class-theoretical accounts of the state. The one suggests a logical and often complex connection between the abstract categories of Marxist political economy and surface forms such as the state. The other interposes between state and economy an intermediate level of 'civil society', composed of interacting groups, classes and class factions.

Briefly, a capital-theoretical analysis might seek to derive the necessity of the form of the state as a separate institution from the nature of the relations between capitals. There are several variations on this 'state-derivationist' approach, depending on the point of departure in each case (Holloway and Picciotto 1977; 1978; Jessop 1982), but the crucial issue in many of these analyses is the question of the separation of the economic and political levels and the apparent neutrality of the state form; that is, its ability to stand aside from the struggle of competing capitals. Jessop (1982, p. 121) has accordingly criticized form-theory for 'essentialism' and 'functionalism' and, in particular, for its failure to develop any analysis of social process or class struggle.

Class-theoretical accounts, on the other hand, seek to locate the state within the configuration of class forces. The state is here usually seen as the location of the apparatuses for the organization of the twin functions of coercion and education. In their most extreme forms, these groups of theories bear more than a passing resemblance to pluralist bourgeois sociologies and, in particular, the social interaction school. They are concerned primarily with the adaptation of Marxist categories in the light of empirical analysis of contemporary social formations.

The tension between these two bodies of theory is unresolved and both have serious drawbacks for an analysis of the three subordinate state agencies referred to above. First, they have not, in general, addressed themselves to an analysis of component institutions within the national state. Second, there is no readily available working basis for examining the dynamic character of the state over a period of time under the impact of class and other forces. Finally, there has been no sustained account of the spatial characteristics of the modern state and the dispersal of its institutional structure over a geographical territory. Such problems, although not always central to the more widely ranging debate, are very relevant to any consideration of locally based agencies, such as the magistrates and police, with a constantly changing class character and jurisdiction. To meet these defects, I have drawn on the work of Nicos Poulantzas.

There were several reasons for this approach. Although Poulantzas's work extends across theoretical terrain associated with all the major traditions of Marxist state analysis,[8] for too long he has been regarded as merely a disciple of Althusser (Jessop 1985, p. 82) or a source of useful quotations on the 'strong state'. It will be argued here that his work is of far greater significance. As Hall (1980a, p. 67) puts it, some parts of his later writings

> begin to break that knot in Marxist theory which has retarded the development of an adequate conception of the state for so long – best represented in terms of the opposed poles of the state as 'functional to the needs/logic of capital', and the state as 'nothing but the product of class struggle'.

Three of Poulantzas's major theoretical departures will be discussed briefly here in terms of their usefulness in resolving the special problems outlined above.

The first of these innovations is concerned with what Poulantzas called the 'institutional materiality' of the state. He begins by asking why it is that certain *particular* forms of state correspond to bourgeois political domination (Poulantzas 1978, p. 52). His answer implies that class divisions are redrawn within the state itself and thus the state is seen as a complex institutional ensemble of agencies acting in relation to each other. In this way Poulantzas indicates the broad outline of a Marxist theory which answers to the complexity and differentiation of activities characteristic of the bourgeois state. The materiality of the state, he argues, is not exhausted by the apparatus necessary for the organization of coercion or intervention on behalf of individual or collective capitals. Moreover, the state must not be seen as merely the instrument of the dominant class, but as reflecting and 'condensing' all the contradictions of a class-divided society and thereby constituting a strategic terrain for class struggle (Jessop 1985, p. 61). The state, in short, is a social relation, just as much as capital is a social relation.

Here we must pause to consider the obvious parallels with the 'institutional differentiation' school of non-Marxist theorists such as Smelser and Durkheim, who argued that structural arrangements were elaborated in an evolutionary process (Poggi 1978, pp. 13–15). This should sound a first warning of the tendency of this approach to slide into pluralism.

However, provided the primacy of productive relations is accepted there is no reason why the concept of 'institutional materiality' may not provide a crucial tool of analysis of state power and practice. In particular, it opens up to scrutiny specific sub-units of the state which have been regarded hitherto only in functionalist terms. These sub-units appear in this study not as mere channels for class or state authority, but as material institutions with distinctive ideological characters sustaining complex relationships with other such institutions and class groupings.

The second major area of advance is the stress upon the dynamic quality of state composition. Poulantzas regarded the state as the site of 'the political condensation of class struggle' and thus neither class division nor class struggle can be regarded as logically prior to its formation.

State and economy cannot be separated either in chronology or in causality.

Poulantzas's model of class relations is considerably more complex than those of his predecessors. Since the state is grounded in such class relations, Poulantzas opens up the possibility of a more sophisticated 'relational' analysis which may take account of the 'fissured, contradictory nature of the capitalist state' (Jessop 1982, pp. 157–8). Under the hegemony of the leading bourgeois factions the power block is unified and organized politically through the state apparatus (Jessop 1982, p. 156). The flexibility of the state structure is such that shifts in the relation of forces between dominant classes and dominating factions can be accommodated by institutional reorganization and changes within the location of power within the state. In his earlier work Poulantzas had illustrated the relation between class struggle and both the 'exceptional' forms of state (1976) and those characteristic of monopoly capitalism (1975). In *State, Power, Socialism* he goes on to demonstrate the potential of internal state dissension for popular struggles as the state moves deeper into intervention (1978, pp. 140–4).

The struggle for class authority around such institutions as the magistracy, police and the army is seen here as one important aspect of a wider confrontation. We should expect, therefore, to see the successive reorganization of institutional relations between the three agencies as in some way reflecting changes in the mode of production and the balance of class forces. The problem therefore arises of how best to represent these reciprocal relations in a manner which indicates their complexity.

It was evident at once that the narrative mode (the reconstruction of 'links in a series of occurrences') could not take account of simultaneous shifts in inter-institutional relations. In its place, therefore, it was decided to adopt Thompson's alternative formulation, which is based on the analysis of 'links in a lateral series of social . . . political . . .' (institutional) relations (1978, p. 221). In other words, the answer was to construct a *relational* history.

Before doing so, however, it is necessary to introduce a caveat. Sugarman (1983, p. 239), with evident enthusiasm for the theory of institutional relations in connection with the history of criminal justice, has written:

> once the problems of ordering and organisation become viewed pluralistically – that is, once it is recognised that certain aspects . . . are . . . outside the state proper . . . or connected to the state's coercive powers in complex and indirect ways . . . these reductionist characterizations become untenable.

Poulantzas (1978, p. 37) echoes this concern, pointing out that 'the State spreads out into the tiniest vein . . . All the same, class powers – and not just economic ones – still stretch beyond the State.' Such remarks serve to

indicate the tendency of relational work to shrug off 'untenable character-
izations' and to incline towards an atheoretical pluralism. For example,
the boundaries of each agency will be defined here in terms of its ability
to invoke the juridical power of the Crown for its actions. There are
obvious difficulties with this approach and it must be conceded at once
that legal and institutional relations are not conterminous with relations
of production. However, it must not be forgotten, equally, that the former
are constructed and reconstructed not in any neutral space but in a social
context, under the organizing pressure of productive relations.

Much academic analysis of particular agencies has been concerned
with the development of professional status (see, for example, Reith 1943;
1956; Reader 1966; Harries-Jenkins 1970; 1977). A great deal of this work,
however, has suffered from a tendency to reproduce professional self-
images (Johnson 1972; Roth 1974) and to construct developmental models
based upon internal structure and regulation. However, in the context of
the shifting composition of inter-institutional relations, the terms of professionalization theory are simply inappropriate. In order to describe and
analyse relations with both the central and the local states we must look
outside the boundaries of each agency.

As a working plan, therefore, three broad concepts (two of which are
familiar) will be adopted. The first is that of *dependency*, by which is
signified a relation in which one agency relies for its material support and
direction and its ideological frame of reference upon others. The second,
which is derived from professionalization theory, is the notion of *autonomy*, consisting in the ability to exercise internal self-regulation and
discipline and to monopolize the use of certain resources or activities. In
order to move beyond this type of theory, a third concept will be introduced, that of *incorporation*, which is here used to designate the relation
existing between the state and an autonomous agency which nevertheless
exercises authority on behalf of the state.[9] Behind this notion, of course,
lies the idea that the state is 'constructed and fought over' (Corrigan 1980,
p. 17) by agencies representing (in different ways) the material forces of
the economy:

> Rather than facing a corps of state functionaries and personnel
> united and cemented around an unequivocal political will, we are
> dealing with fiefs, clans and factions: a multiplicity of diversified
> micro-policies . . . and the policy of the State essentially consists in
> the outcome of their collision rather than in the (more or less success-
> ful) application of the global objectives of the state apex.
>
> (Poulantzas 1978, pp. 135–6)

Four characteristics distinguish an agency incorporated within the structure of the state, as follows: the achievement of professional autonomy in
the conventional sense; the ability to establish links with other state

agencies at all levels; exclusive access to material forces necessary for the continued survival of the state in its present form; the ability to formulate and carry into effect state policy.

The third innovation considered here concerns Poulantzas's interest in the spatial and territorial aspects of the materiality of the state. The need for historical periodization is well established (see, for example, Mandel 1975, pp. 108–46; Poulantzas 1975, pp. 14–20, 109–55). What has not yet become sufficiently clear, despite the proliferation of analyses which depend on the internationalization of productive relations, is the geographical specificity of particular state forms. As Poulantzas (1978, p. 104) puts it: 'The modern State materializes this spatial matrix in its various apparatuses . . . patterning in turn the subjects over whom it exercises power.'

Although this insistence on the importance of the spatial matrix clearly owes much (through Foucault) to liberal theories of political authority,[10] the self-definition of the bourgeois state (that is, its ability to control and organize physical space within fixed boundaries) cannot be ignored. For Poulantzas, national divisions play an important role in the dual movement of disorganization/unification which is central to his theory of hegemony. However, if we are to provide an adequate account of particular fragments of the larger institution we must move beyond the concept of the state as a simple geographical unity. It is at this stage that we must introduce the idea of an organic relationship between the central state (within the national area) and the local state (within the local area).

The concept of the local state has been current in Marxist theory for some considerable time but there has only recently been any sustained attempt at explanation.[11] Indeed, the obsession with the central state has led to a certain historical myopia with regard to local courts, authorities and policing arrangements. The field of study has, in short, been determined by the self-image of the bourgeois state. Thus while, on the one hand, the local state has been conceptualized as merely a scaled-down version of the central state (Dearlove 1973, p. 11; Cockburn 1977, p. 46), on the other, the central state has been displaced entirely in favour of the micro-structures of authority (Foucault 1977).

It is important to ask, for example, whether the local state represents merely the projection of state authority into the localities (see Griffith 1966; Broadbent 1977, p. 128), or whether it enjoys autonomy; whether the local state and central states stand in differing relations with the economy and the relations of production (see Broadbent 1977; Nairn 1977, pp. 306–28; Dear and Clarke 1978, p. 180; Saunders 1985); and whether the centre represents more than the sum of the peripheral authorities (see, for example, Saunders 1979; 1986; Duncan and Goodwin 1988, pp. 32–44). These questions are crucial and can be answered only by a consideration of particular political and economic relations within a historical dimension (see Duncan and Goodwin 1988, pp. 32–44). As Hogg (1979, p. 7) and

Sugarman (1983, p. 242) argue, the local–centre dichotomy within the state structure supplies a crucial axis along which conflicts over law, state and society are to be understood.

If we may consider the local state, in the same way as the central state,[12] as a social relation and the condensation of class forces, then its operation becomes susceptible to a more sensitive mode of analysis. The material institutions of the local state (and by this is meant the formal agencies of quarter sessions, local boards, poor law guardians, local councils, magistrates courts, police force area bureaucracies, and so on) are all permeable by class interests. This is not to suggest that the local state, in any of its historical configurations, is merely a neutral terrain. Quite the reverse is true. Its institutional character bears the imprint of continuing class conflict, not to mention the influence of the central state. As we shall see, a local state agency such as the magistracy serves to magnify the power of dominant class fractions. It also provides a 'spatial fix' for existing interests in a rapidly and unevenly developing economy (Duncan and Goodwin 1988, pp. 61–71). Questions of jurisdiction will therefore be crucial to an examination of these agencies.

By ignoring these issues, a number of otherwise excellent histories of control agencies in civil disorder have been forced to rely on rather unwieldy and atheoretical structural analogies. Blake (1979, p. 253) talks of alternating 'cycles' of police and army authority, Geary (1985, p. 25) of 'pivotal periods' and Morgan (1987, pp. 73, 147) has presented the police and army as expanding and retracting 'arms' of the state. The sequential mode simply cannot accommodate the interplay of spatial and historical relationships. As Gramsci (1971, p. 178) has put it:

> A common error in historico-political analysis consists in an inability to find the correct relation between what is organic and what is conjunctural. This leads to presenting causes as immediately operative which in fact only operate indirectly, or to asserting that the immediate causes are the only effective ones . . . The distinction between organic 'movements' and facts and 'conjunctural' or occasional ones must be applied to all types of situation . . . The dialectical nexus between the two categories of movement, and therefore of research, is hard to establish precisely.

This study, therefore, focuses on ten specific incidents of public disorder over the period 1831–1981 and provides a number of 'freeze-frame' accounts of the balance of authority between the agencies in particular historical conjunctures and geographical locations. By presenting this material in parallel with an examination of developments in relations between the agencies it is hoped to establish more clearly the 'dialectical nexus' to which Gramsci refers.

In respect of these 'freeze-frame' histories, Chapter 3 deals with the problems faced by the unreformed magistracy in Bristol during the riots of 1831 and the conduct of the stipendiaries and Metropolitan Police during the London disorders in Hyde Park in 1855. Chapter 5 considers the disorders at Trafalgar Square in 1887, Featherstone in 1893 and Tonypandy in 1910. Chapter 8 is an extended examination, based on original fieldwork, of five incidents of disorder during the inner-city riots of 1981, including Brixton (April and July), Southall, Liverpool and Manchester. Prominence is given to the disorders of the early 1980s which were the most serious breakdown of state authority for half a century and produced momentous shifts, not only in the strategy of policing (Reiner 1984, p. 52; Northam 1988, pp. 36–41) but also in relations with the magistracy, police authorities and other agencies (Spencer 1985b, p. 5; Weatheritt 1986, p. 104). As Reiner (1985, p. 167) puts it, 1981 was a 'climacteric' for the control agencies which was to have far-reaching effects throughout the 1980s and beyond.

The intervening chapters consider in more detail the structural changes in the balance of authority between the agencies illustrated by the conjunctural accounts. Since the relations between agencies in the 'freeze-frame' histories will be seen in class terms, some schematic overview of developments in productive relations during the period is necessary. Clearly a delineation of 'the distinctive total trajectory of modern British society since the emergence of capitalism', proposed by Anderson (1964, p. 28) as a prerequisite for an understanding of contemporary conditions, is well beyond the scope of this account and a broad periodization must suffice.

Chapter 2, for example, considers the approaches adopted by the representatives of early, small-scale enterprises (locally centred capitals) towards a magistracy dominated by the landed interest. The onset of industrialization (by which is meant the organization and control of labour by capital)[13] coincided with demands for a state magistracy. Why this project was ultimately unsuccessful outside the metropolis is a question which has important implications. It was not, as Anderson (1964) suggests in another context, the English bourgeoisie failing to perform its historical task, but part of a gigantic accommodation between industrial and landed capitals. It is argued here that traditional forms of magisterial authority and gentry paternalism were retained almost intact and adapted by new personnel for revolutionary new ends.

Chapter 4 examines the consolidation of magisterial power in the mid-nineteenth century. However, the relentless pressure of declining rates of profit in the late Victorian period and the amalgamation of local capitals into new corporate (nationally centred)[14] forms, capable of organizing extended production, were to have a disastrous effect upon magisterial authority. The impact of these developments on relations with the army and police are considered in Chapters 6 and 7, respectively.

As we shall see when we come to examine the disorders of the 1980s in Chapter 8, further shifts in the composition of class forces during a period in which new, internationally centred forms of capital were developed, have once again been reflected in the relations between the control forces. The final chapter will draw out the significance of these events in the current period.

2 The magistrate as state servant

The Riot Act was a recognition of the crucial role of the justices in the maintenance of central authority. No pre-industrial national regime could survive without the support or acquiescence of the landowning interest and, until 1888, the county justices represented that interest and constituted in their collective organizations the local state itself. Meeting in quarter session (with a county jurisdiction), petty session (with a local jurisdiction) and on local boards, they superintended local taxes, price control, employment, poor relief, road and bridge building, the prisons, policing and the militia. In short, they undertook all the functions which were later assumed by the local councils, and a good deal more (Page 1947; Osborne 1960; Glassey 1979). This, however, was an enlarged concept of the local state which embraced many powers which subsequently devolved upon the central state.

The passage of the Riot Act opened the way for a yet more remarkable concentration of power. By 1768 the justices had established the unfettered personal right to call upon and to deploy the military forces of the Crown without the prior sanction of Parliament or of any other central or local institution (Clode, 1869, pp. 125–37). Until well into the twentieth century, therefore, they were able to control the material forces of repression with a freedom almost as extensive as that enjoyed by an absolutist regime.

In 1831 we find the Merthyr Tydfil strikers complaining that 'the masters [in their capacity as justices] have brought the soldiers against us' and that 'the soldiers there were no more than a gooseberry in their hands to squeeze'.[1] The occurrence of a riot acted in many senses as a liberation for employer justices. One Lancashire magistrate in 1839 expressed it as follows:

> I passed yesterday with the Grand Jury shovelling in bills against the rioters and orators by dozens: I am happy to think we have been suddenly transformed to an absolute despotism as to speaking or arming. A copper cap or a piece of wadding are sufficient evidence against anybody.[2]

In the last instance of insurrection, their powers were indeed despotic. According to statute:

> Justices of the Peace shall have power to restrain offenders, rioters and all other barrators, and to pursue, arrest, take and chastise them according to their trespass or offence, and then cause them to be imprisoned and duly punished.[3]

Such authority seems extensive enough but, in addition, a single magistrate enjoyed the following additional powers:

(a) to forbid the holding of meetings by notice;
(b) to call upon the assistance of the militia, the military, the yeomanry or the constabulary, to enrol military pensioners (Mather 1959, p. 54) and to command any of these in action against rioters;[4]
(c) to call out the power of the county (the *posse comitatus*) to suppress rioting;[5]
(d) from 1831 to swear in special constables (two justices required);[6]
(e) to arrest those riotously assembled and to bind them over to keep the peace;
(f) to authorize others to arrest rioters without a warrant;
(g) from 1715 until 1967, where 12 or more persons were 'unlawfully, riotously and tumultuously assembled', to read the Riot Act, in which circumstances those who remained after the expiry of an hour would be deemed guilty of felony;[7]
(h) to imprison rioters failing to provide good bail;
(i) to convict and sentence rioters for a range of summary offences or to commit them for trial.

However, none of the standard manuals (for example, Nelson 1718) gave any coherent guidance on the practical approach to repression. Although the classic exposition of magisterial duty by Littledale J. in *R* v *Pinney* (1832) is restrictive – 'he is bound to hit the exact line between an excess and doing what is sufficient'[8] – we may believe that the powers were in practice, 'liberally construed' (Wise 1907, p. 171). It is only where the exercise of magisterial authority was the subject of pre-existing political conflict that contested proceedings were likely.[9]

The magistracy represented the only means by which the power of the central state could be projected into the local areas. Since the beginning of the Georgian period, it was no longer possible to enforce central authority by purges of local justices (Glassey 1979, p. 265). It had become customary, therefore, to circulate legislation to the quarter sessions for vetting before consideration in Parliament (Osborne 1960, p. 210). Webb and Webb (1963, p. 554) have gone so far as to assert that, in respect of legislation which affected the localities, the House of Commons was no more than a clearing house for the several courts of quarter session.

When the Manchester magistrates in 1819 had unleashed the yeomanry and hussars upon an unarmed crowd in St Peter's Fields, the Home Office had no option but to sanction their conduct without question. To have done otherwise would have been to jeopardize the power base of the central state. Lord Sidmouth considered it absolutely essential 'to acquire the confidence of the magistracy . . . by showing a readiness to support them . . . without inquiring too minutely whether they might have performed their duty a little better or a little worse' (Pellew 1847, p. 262).

The Georgian magistracy represented the unmediated class power of the landowning classes. The Duke of Wellington, for example, counselled magistrates in time of riot

> to put themselves on horseback, each at the head of his own servants and retainers, grooms, huntsmen, game-keepers, armed with horse-whips, pistols, fowling pieces and what they could get, and to attack in concert, if necessary, or singly, these mobs, disperse them and take and put in confinement those who would not escape . . . it is astonishing how soon the country [is] tranquillised and that in the best way, by the activity and spirit of the gentlemen.[10]

Bentham, Blackstone and the contest over the state magistracy

Wellington's view represents a practical (if perhaps rather highly coloured) representation of the Blackstonian jurisprudence which dominated the legal thinking of most provincial benches. William Blackstone (1723–80) was the chief exponent of the eighteenth-century cult of legalism, a doctrine closely linked to Georgian property relations and the ascendancy of the landed interest expressed through the magistracy and the jury. His major critic, Jeremy Bentham (1742–1832), 'the oracle of the commonplace bourgeois intelligence',[11] may be regarded as the founding father of English summary jurisprudence, an antithetical view of law which depended upon the rational and benevolent action of a state-appointed magistracy. It is the dialogue between these two which provided the language and grammar in which the struggles over the role of the magistracy between 1785 and 1888 were fought out. In the sense that the compromises achieved remain enshrined in the material structures of the modern magistrates courts, the debate remains of relevance.

The system of law delineated by Blackstone is deeply informed by the writings of Locke and Montesquieu, from both of which he quotes freely. At the core of his argument lies the familiar enlightenment concept of the hypothesized pre-social contract as a material alternative to divine command. This contract is, of course, represented explicitly in the terms of the English common law. The *Commentaries* were designed both to instruct and to panegyrize the landed aristocracy as well as to serve as a textbook for justices of the peace (Lucas 1962).

Central state power, the power of the single judge, was deflected by a 'strong and two-fold barrier, of a presentment and a trial by jury' (Blackstone 1830, vol. IV, p. 349). The direct personal involvement of the propertied classes in the conduct of criminal proceedings was crucial. In short, Blackstonism stood for the entrenchment of the values of the landed elites into the common law. Personal and propertial rights were the means of legal defence against new forms of economic power.

In 1776, only seven years after the appearance of the final volume of the *Commentaries*, Bentham published his *Commentary on the Commentaries* (I, pp. 221–96)[12] in which he endeavoured to state, 'with some degree of precision, the grounds of that war which for the interests of true science and of liberal improvement, I think myself bound to wage against this work' (I, p. 229). Law, for Bentham, was an expression of the rational, sovereign will of the legislator and it had little relation to the immemorial customs of the common law mediated by the judiciary. This responsiveness to direction was the key to Bentham's idea of state organization. His entire enterprise was concerned with 'making the subordinate officials and other resources, quickly, completely and economically responsive to the superordinates' commands' (Hume 1981, p. 5). He asserted the authority of the state to intervene to break up the circuits of power monopolized by the landed aristocracy.

For example, Bentham differed significantly from previous command theorists in his disdain for the concept of 'order' (Rosenblum 1978, pp. 89–90). This was sharply dissociated from 'security' (I, pp. 309, 311) in Bentham's mind and connected with the absolutist state and subjective anti-rationalism. In his vilification of the massacre carried out by the magistrates at Peterloo (II, p. 345; III, p. 559) Bentham indicates the complexity of his version of command. Burke and Blackstone would doubtless have commended the magistrates.

Although his enthusiasm in principle for a state magistracy was long-standing, Bentham produced two major practical schemes. The first was entitled *Draught of a New Plan for the Organisation of the Judicial Establishment in France* (IV, pp. 285–406) and was published in March 1790. This proposed to dispense with legal formalities to enable the judge to act as *ex post facto* policeman (Burns and Hart 1970, p. 198) directing an investigation upon inquisitorial principles as a 'public accuser clothed with the character of a magistrate' (I, p. 559).

By the time the second major structural scheme, the *Constitutional Code* (IX, pp. 1–662) was published, Bentham had been 'radicalised' (Himmelfarb 1968, pp. 73–4) and was prepared to contemplate the 'euthanasia of the establishment'. Bentham's criticisms of the unpaid magistracy which he described as 'a class of judges' were scarcely muted. It was 'an institution against which and with so much force and justice, so much of late has been urged . . . the country which is the scene of it . . . swarms with evils of the greatest magnitude: with oppression and depredation' (IX, p. 524). His solution was the appointment of a quasi-judicial, quasi-administrative functionary, the 'headman', a local agent of the central state. In discarding the Justice of the Peace in favour of a paid local headman who would have administrative duties which included 'effecting the cessation of any casual riot' (IX, p. 617) Bentham was proposing a radical new departure: 'Their function in his scheme was to complete the network of control over the community and to leave no gaps in the means for "giving effect to the will of government in all its several main branches" ' (Hume 1981, p. 225). In these proposals we can see quite clearly the groundplan for a system of stipendiary magistracy which was to cover the entire country. The call for summary justice administered by a state magistracy was to Bentham just as important as parliamentary reform: 'To regular, substitute summary procedure everywhere. Seldom has change so important been found expressible in so few words' (III, p. 321).

Two schemes for a Benthamite state magistracy were brought forward in London in 1785 and 1792, respectively. They were heavily influenced by the Bow Street system of executive/judicial authority pioneered by the Fieldings[13] and at once ran into the vigorous opposition of those whose political outlook rested upon the Blackstonian concept of direct class action by the county elites.

The first experiment: the London and Westminster Police Bill 1785

The London and Westminster Police Bill 1785 represented the first and certainly the most radical attempt to create an integrated police magistracy under the control of the Home Office. Although the proposals were eventually abandoned by the Pitt administration, their importance as a model for the London stipendiary system cannot be overestimated (Critchley 1978, p. 36). Lord Beauchamp predicted that the system would be adopted around the country: 'the time would come when the magistrates of Manchester, of Bristol, and Birmingham, and all large and populous places . . . would expect to be paid.'[14] Briefly, the Bill contemplated the creation of a single 'District of the Metropolis' for London, policed by resident stipendiaries operated from three public offices located in separate divisions. Each office would maintain its own force of 25 armed and equipped constables who would be empowered to arrest and detain persons whom they had 'probable grounds to suspect were in possession of stolen articles'.[15] The magistrates would be directly responsible to three commissioners of police, appointed by the Home Secretary, who would have the power to discipline them for failure to act in certain circumstances.

Modern historians in the Whig tradition, such as Radzinowicz, have tended to dramatize the self-interest and corrupt practices of the eighteenth-century Middlesex bench in order to demonstrate the apparent inevitability of the creation of a centralized system of summary power. In this argument the emergence of a state magistracy in London is generally related to a supposed 'sudden deterioration' in the standards of Middlesex justices after 1780 (Babington 1969, p. 170).

Stevenson (1977a) and Philips (1980) have pointed to the effects of demographic change upon traditional links of deference and control. They argue that the process of urbanization created a huge and largely transient population in the commercial districts which was beyond the control of the old parish and county authorities. Worse still, the accumulation of the labouring classes in slum areas was undermining the stratification of class:

> there were many parts of London which were predominantly lower class in population [which] were also the sort of area in which gentlemen were unlikely to want to take on the burdensome task of all the magisterial business in such a neighbourhood.
>
> (Philips 1980, p. 163)

It is generally assumed that the tactless mishandling of the City interest, which led ultimately to the abandonment of the Bill by the Tories, merely delayed the necessary creation of 'an instrument for keeping the peace in the Metropolis' (Radzinowicz 1956b, p. 109; Critchley 1978, pp. 35–7; see also Beattie 1986, p. 66) which was an inevitable consequence of industrialization and the decline in standards of the magistracy.

Despite the insistence of the sponsors of the Bill[16] and many subsequent Whig historians that this was a *crime*-control rather than a *crowd*-control measure, the legislation must be seen as a direct response to the cataclysmic events of the 1780 Gordon uprising. As the Solicitor-General admitted on the withdrawal of the Bill, his major objective had been 'to keep the bayonet out of employ' in London.[17]

The extent to which the bayonet had become the last argument of the Georgian state was impressed on a severely traumatized parliament when the mob supporting Lord Gordon's petition for the abolition of the Catholic Relief Act launched a furious onslaught on the Palace of Westminster. Both Dickens and de Castro (1926, p. 32–41) have described the manner in which peers and bishops attending the House were abused and assaulted while members drew their swords to defend the entry of the Chamber against the besieging crowd. No more dramatic representation of the political impact of the London crowd on the central state can be imagined.

Faced with the failure of the magistrates to maintain order, the King, acting through the Privy Council, had directed the military to use force to suppress the riots without recourse to the civil power. In order to obviate the necessity for an Act of Indemnity which would amount, in the eyes of the opposition at least, to an admission of illegality, Lord Mansfield, and later the Solicitor-General, both argued forcefully that the troops had acted merely as private individuals in accordance with their common-law duties and it was 'no matter whether their coats be red or brown'.[18] The effect of Lord Mansfield's doctrine among the troops themselves seems to have given some cause for concern:

> To such a pitch of vanity did the common soldiers arrive in June last from being told they were magistrates and being clothed in fact with the powers of magistracy, that he (Townshend) had heard them frequently address each other by the title of 'Your worship'.[19]

What is clear above all is that the driving force behind the reform movement came from the sense of vulnerability felt by the central state administration to the actions of the London crowd. 'Direct attempts to influence and intimidate the legislature in the heart of the metropolis' (Radzinowicz 1968, p. 116) were not an uncommon feature of metropolitan Georgian life, and the position of the magistracy was crucial. Magistrates aware that energetic action against the mob would lead to the looting of their own property tactfully withdrew and left not only the streets of London but also the organs of criminal justice to the crowd. In short, the London magistracy, occupying a pivotal position with regard to the regulation of the political power of the lower orders, could not, in a crisis, be relied upon to exert their influence in favour of the central administration.

It was to be the police commissioners, therefore, who would take over final responsibility for the maintenance of order, with the justices as their subordinates:

> The justices . . . are . . . hereby required, upon Requisition made in writing under the hands and seal of the Commissioners . . . attend in person together with a sufficient number of constables . . . at such time and place as the said Commissioners shall direct as aforesaid

and then and there dispose of themselves and the said constables and act in such a manner as shall seem best to the said Commissioners.[20]

The complaint of the administration that the justices owed their allegiance elsewhere and 'could not easily be called to account'[21] was here met with a vengeance.

The Middlesex magistrates were not slow to recognize the Bill as a threat to their independence and an attempt to relegate them to the position of subordinates within a police hierarchy. When the proposals were produced before the quarter sessions at Hicks Hall, 'everyone viewed [them] with an eye as much to his present situation as to his future prospects'.[22] What was the Bill, it was argued, but 'a total subversion of the established system of the administration of justice in the metropolis'.[23]

In the face of a vigorous counter-attack by the City and the justices themselves, Pitt was obliged to intervene to halt the Bill, referring in terms to the Middlesex justices and petitions from the City.[24] For the time being, therefore, with the defeat of the Bill, the criminal justice system in London remained as it had been, in a state of uneasy truce between these forces. In Dublin, proposals approximating to the 1785 Bill were shortly enacted by way of experiment,[25] and the amalgamation of police and magisterial functions within a single hierarchy became a common feature of British colonial practice. No such radical concentrations of central state authority were possible in the atmosphere of intense class hostility of eighteenth-century London. Indeed, even the relative period of truce among dominant class fractions occasioned by the revolutionary panic of the 1790s was to permit only a partial surrender of magisterial authority to the state.

Threats of revolution: the Middlesex Justices Act 1792

By 1792, however, the further disintegration of the Whig Party and the widening rift between Fox and Burke over the events in Paris ensured a large majority for Pitt in the House of Commons. The Middlesex Justices Act of that year, which established the first 'local judiciary' of the type envisaged by Bentham, was facilitated by, and was to some extent a response to, the revolutionary aspects of Jacobinism.

Patrick Colquhoun (1806, p. 364), one of the first stipendiary magistrates nominated under the Act and a close friend of Bentham, warned appointees to

> look with a jealous eye on the several thousand miscreants . . . which now infest London: for they too upon any fatal emergency (which God forbid!) would be equally ready as their brethren in iniquity were in Paris to repeat the same atrocities, if any opportunity offered.

In February 1792, with the foundation of the London Corresponding Society (LCS) which pledged itself to a policy of mass meetings and demonstrations, the government was made painfully aware of its reliance upon the magistracy for the suppression of political dissent. The incompetence and partiality of the Birmingham bench in dealing with the Priestley rioters (Stevenson 1979, pp. 138–40) caused considerable unease.[26] As a prelude to the long campaign against sedition, a Royal proclamation of 21 May commanded all magistrates to

> make diligent inquiry in order to discover the Authors, and Printers of . . . seditious Writings . . . take the most immediate and effectual care to suppress and prevent all Riots, Tumults and other Disorders . . . to transmit to One of Our principal Secretaries of State due and full Information of such persons . . .[27]

Three days before the Royal proclamation, a Private Member's Bill, originally intended to abolish the payment of fees to London justices and establish five permanent police offices on the Bow Street model, was returned to the House of Commons in a much amended form by the Home Secretary, Henry Dundas. The Bill, as drafted, had been taken over by a committee of Pitt's closest allies, which had increased the number of offices proposed to seven. Each 'public' or 'police' office was to be situated within existing parish boundaries and was to be staffed by three professional magistrates (who automatically, on appointment, became justices within the metropolitan counties). 'Watch and ward' (preventive policing) was to be retained by the parishes, 'hue and cry' (reactive policing) taken over by the stipendiaries. They were to be paid an individual stipend of £300 and were to be assisted by a force of six constables at each office under the direct command of the magistrates. All staff (including the magistrates themselves) were to be appointed and dismissed by and subject to the discipline of the Home Secretary.

The adoption and enlargement of the Middlesex Justices Bill by the Pitt administration must be seen as a first and logical step in its campaign of repression in the metropolis which was to intensify in the so-called 'reign of terror' between 1794 and 1797. Under the Seditious Meetings Act 1794[28] all 'public meetings of over fifty persons convened for the discussion of public grievances or for the consideration of any petition remonstrance or address to King or Parliament' were subject to the discretionary control of the magistrates and any popular resistance to their orders was to be punishable by death. The reliance placed upon the magistracy for control of political dissent was underlined by Fox: 'Behold, then, the state of a free born Englishman! Before he can discuss any topic which involves his liberty, he must send to a magistrate who is to attend the discussion.'[29]

There is no doubt that the newly appointed stipendiary magistracy was active in the employment of its powers in conjunction with those given under the Riot Act. As Fox had predicted in 1792, the use of the salaried magistrate 'under influence' from the government 'might be extended infinitely under various pretexts'.[30] One such pretext came in July 1797 when a LCS meeting at St Pancras was broken up by Sir William Addington, the Chief Magistrate, but not before one of the speakers had announced from the tribune: 'I conjure you to depart, and I believe it will shortly be seen whether Bow Street magistrates are to be the interpreters of the Laws of England.'[31] Just how misplaced was his optimism, the speaker was to discover before the Bow Street bench. What is important, however, is that such discretionary powers could never have been entrusted to a magistracy composed of trading justices or men such as those who connived at mob rule in 1780. It was only when their loyalty to the administration could be put beyond doubt that their discretionary powers could begin to grow. After 1792, therefore, the London paid magistracy became more and more an instrument of the Home Office and an object of its patronage.

Whatever the protestations of the Act's supporters that it was intended to succour the 'indigent and the ignorant' (Colquhoun 1806, p. 519) and to 'serve the poor'[32] it was clearly the business community which greeted it with the most enthusiasm. In 1793 the Spitalfields manufacturers were petitioning the Home Secretary in praise of the 'correct and regular manner' in which the 'Magistrates of the Police' dealt with business.

Nevertheless, relative to other parts of the country, London was not advanced in the development of manufacturing industries and the establishment of a Thames police office in 1800[33] was a mercantile initiative promoted by a gift of £500 from some West India merchants to Colquhoun. In no sense, then, could the establishment of the police offices be regarded as a direct response to industrialization. What was important was the *political* threat to the embryonic central state from the London crowd, which, in the 1790s at least, had aligned itself behind the democratic radicals. The controversy over the first appointees illustrates the point.

Radzinowicz (1956b, p. 133), relying perhaps on the not entirely disinterested views of Colquhoun,[34] has argued that the social status of the new government appointed justices after 1792 was much improved:

> a class of people very different from those who used to fill the offices. Among them were a former Lord Mayor of London, two City Councillors, a former Lord Provost of Glasgow, two ex-Members of Parliament, a clergyman, three or four barristers and . . . the Poet Laureate . . .

Contemporary supporters of the new state magistracy made much of the alleged shift from 'justices of mean degree' to 'persons of opulence'

(Lambert 1806, p. 524) and men of business (Colquhoun 1806, p. 517; Bentham 1825, p. 14). This seems, however, to have been wishful thinking. As Peel remarked in 1825: 'When the police magistrates were first appointed, it was the practice to select individuals to fill the office, who, he must say, were utterly incompetent to discharge the duties which devolved upon them.'[35]

Nor were the personal reputations of the newly appointed justices all that Radzinowicz has maintained. Their number included the execrable Sir Richard Birnie, 'an unscrupulous and dissolute Scotchman', the illiterate Nicholas Bond and George Norton, precursor of Dickens's Mr Fang (Milton 1959, pp. 35–7). The whole system, argued Melville Lee (1901, p. 173), was 'conceived in too parsimonious a spirit, and the right sort of men did not come forward'.

Many observers felt that the government had deliberately insisted on low remuneration for the stipendiaries (as it was later to do for the police) to ensure their complete submission to the Home Department. As Bird (1828, p. 100) put it: 'this trust (the Commission of the Peace) when slighted by gentlemen, falls of course into the hands of those who are not so, *but the mere tools of office*'.

According to a Tory barrister, John Adolphus (1824, p. 74), the justices of Middlesex should have been of 'the most respectable character' in order to correspond to constitutional principles. However:

> The plan was degraded, in the first place, by considering the offices merely as police stations, and not investing them with a more evidently judicial appellation. As mere agents of police, the justices were placed below those of other counties . . . Parsimony and jealousy of the influence of the Crown lent their aid in frustrating any benefit that might be expected of an enlarged scale.

In 1801 the number of offices had been increased to ten, still within the parochial jurisdictions.[36] By 1820 the value of the patronage available to the Home Office through the police offices had escalated to £50,000 (without taking into account the secret service salaries) while the Bow Street establishment had doubled since 1800 (Adolphus 1824, p. 98). Various attempts were made by the government to improve the status of the public offices. By recruiting justices from the junior bar and increasing salaries in 1825 to £800, Peel hoped that the stipendiaries would take on a quasi-judicial status[37] without breaking their links with the Home Office. Adolphus (1824, p. 75) lamented the lack of respect for the new stipendiary system in legal circles:

> Had the views respecting the establishment been less ungenerous, the remuneration more liberal, and the duration more certain, it is not to be doubted that many gentlemen of considerable standing in

the law . . . would have embraced these offices as an honourable retirement from the bustle of courts.

The critical difference, however, between the newly created corps of London magistrates and the professional judiciary lay in the relations of dependency of the former towards the Home Office. Whereas the judiciary looked to their Inns as their centre of authority and government patronage was filtered through an existing professional structure of great durability, the stipendiaries had no such alternative apparatus. The gravitational pull of the Home Office was for them irresistible, and advances in status or power had to be co-ordinated with the intentions of government. Adolphus (1824, pp. 75–6) has well described the uncertainty of the offices, which he terms 'a detached set of police establishments with justices ever seeking to change their stations from the extremity to the centre as opportunity might permit'.

The net effect was to ensure that collective ambition was expressed uniquely through the championship of ministerial interest. Thus as the movement to 'judicialize' the police offices gathered momentum in the 1830s it was limited to matters of form and appearance rather than the substance of judicial independence. Nevertheless, Colquhoun (1806, p. 516) talked enthusiastically of a national network, pointing out that 'not merely to the Metropolis but to many large Provincial Towns . . . stipendiary justices have become indispensably necessary'.

By the 1830s the conflict between the two models of magisterial power – on the one hand, the magistrate as independent representative of the local oligarchy, and, on the other, the magistrate as a channel of central state power – had coalesced into two distinct systems of criminal justice.

It was not simply that (until the revolutionary changes of personnel after 1835) the county benches represented undiluted Toryism, whereas the London stipendiaries adopted a Whig perspective, since the paid magistracy owed not only their very existence but also their entire patronage to the Tory ministry. The essential difference between the two systems lay in the nature of the authority they represented.

The new public offices were chronically underfunded (Colquhoun 1806, p. 509), the social status of new appointees was dubious and they possessed no constabulary forces on the scale even of the existing watch. They were weakened by the 'pronounced enmity' (Melville Lee 1901, pp. 189–90) of the parochial authorities onto whose jurisdictions they had so unceremoniously been grafted, and only the Bow Street stipendiaries had the material forces and an undisputed mandate to operate throughout the metropolis.

As a result, the stipendiaries proved to be incapable of exercising sufficient authority over the military and the constabulary to establish themselves as a reliable locus of authority in civil disorder. In short, they constituted a dependent agency of the central state which nevertheless lacked the freedom of action and independence from local influence to make it serviceable.

Institutional separation in London: police and police magistracy to 1840

The creation of a second professional agency in competition with the stipendiaries was a direct result of their failure in the area of civil disorder. In 1821 Sir Robert Baker, the chief stipendiary magistrate at Bow Street, was dismissed for his disastrous mishandling of Queen Caroline's funeral. Although the Riot Act was not read, the Horse Guards, acting on their own initiative, fired on the crowd and killed two demonstrators before Sir Robert capitulated. Deviating 'grossly from his instructions',[38] he dismissed the troops and allowed the mob to redirect the procession through the City (Pellew 1847, pp. 358–66, Stevenson 1977b, pp. 136–8; 1979, p. 203; Palmer 1988, pp. 172–8). During the catastrophic events of the day, some of the Guards mutinied against Sir Robert's authority (Reith 1943, p. 27) and the records of most of his stipendiary colleagues in controlling the material forces of repression were equally dismal.

The decisive loss of control by the magistrates of police forces in London began in 1829 with the appointment of two non-judicial justices, Rowan and Mayne, as commissioners of police and the recruitment of an independent force of nearly 1,000 officers under their command (Reith 1943; 1956; Critchley 1978, pp. 47–57). The London reorganization, which was not completed until 1839, may be regarded more as a realignment of the police and magistracy in their hierarchical relations with the central state, or, as Mayne put it, their 'due comparative position',[39] than a complete division between them.

Peel's 1829 reforms deprived the Bow Street magistrates of their foot patrols but allowed them to retain their mounted forces. These, together with the small force of plain-clothes constables attached to the police offices, survived under magisterial control until 1839. Throughout the decade, the separate forces, under the authority of the metropolitan magistrates and the police commissioners respectively, operated within the same jurisdictions. Naturally there was considerable hostility between magisterial and non-magisterial forces, especially in relation to the financial perquisites of policing (Radzinowicz 1956a, pp. 194–201).[40] Peel clearly intended his new protégés to assume, in time, all the non-judicial powers of the stipendiaries, but the change of ministry in 1830 left Rowan and Mayne temporarily exposed to counter-attack by the magistrates. The resulting contest for authority between the new police commissioners and stipendiaries was not resolved until the end of the 1830s.

Sir Frederick Roe, a stipendiary and chief magistrate at Bow Street between 1832 and 1839, organized the professional magistrates into a formidable pressure group in support of their privileges and, in particular, of their right to issue direct orders to the police. On behalf of his colleagues, he complained bitterly of exclusion from the new police chain of command: 'The system of subordination, I may almost say military discipline . . . [ensured that] . . . the corps at large consider themselves as being in no way subject to the authority of the magistrates.'[41] The guerrilla campaign conducted by the stipendiaries to reverse this state of affairs included the refusal by the Bow Street magistrates to issue warrants direct to the new police.[42] In concert with the other stipendiaries, they also subjected these officers to relentless hostility in the conduct of prosecutions (Reith 1943, pp. 82–3; 1956, p. 151). This hostility was not diminished by the eventual loss by the stipendiaries of their own forces in 1839, but persisted into the mid-century. As late as the 1860s and 1870s, the stipendiary magistrates were still seeking to assert their authority against the police by subverting their campaigns against costermongers and prostitutes (Davis 1984, p. 328).

In his evidence to the 1834 Select Committee, Roe proposed that the commissioners should be deprived of all responsibility for the metropolitan force except for 'distribution, clothing, lodging and organisation'. Instead, the force should be organized around the existing magisterial police offices and the stipendiaries themselves should have 'immediate direction and control'.[43] Failing that, officers of superintendent rank should be placed under the direct authority of the stipendiaries and posted to each police station.[44] Needless to say, these proposals did not meet with the approval of the committee.

However, it was the crucial question of the control of forces in disorder that produced the most violent antagonism between the two agencies. As Reith (1956, p. 144) puts it, Peel

> gave [the commissioners] duties which usurped the powers of the Chief Magistrate and others and was adamant in refusing to give a ruling that on occasions of riots the magistrates were to take orders from the Commissioners or that these were to take orders from the magistrates.

Clashes over authority began almost at once. In November 1831 Roe was ordered by Lord Melbourne to attend with another magistrate, Laing, at White Conduit House, the site of a threatened disorder. He found there between 600 and 700 new police under the command of a superintendent who refused to communicate to the magistrates the details of his dispositions and appeared, as Roe put it,

> reserved as to taking orders from us; at last he was asked 'Do you consider yourself here under the authority of the magistrates?' The

man hesitated a little, and then he said 'Yes he did' but a reluctant 'Yes'. . . . Mr. Laing and I might have the responsibility, while the men did not understand they were to look to us for directions; on such grounds, I think the constables should be bound to attend to the magistrates . . .[45]

In response, Mayne petitioned the Home Secretary with a demand that the stipendiaries be confined to judicial duties (Reith 1943, pp. 99–101). The last attempt by a metropolitan stipendiary to exercise direct authority over the forces of repression at the scene of a disorder was by Mr Bennet of Queen Square office in March 1832. Bennet apparently sought to give orders to the police and was censured subsequently by the commissioners who were also present.[46]

Despite these significant setbacks, Roe continued his campaign of harassment towards the commissioners until his retirement in 1839. According to Reith (1956, pp. 191–4), 'final success' in excluding the stipendiaries from any exercise of direct authority over the new police was achieved in 1837, following an unseemly squabble over the control of forces at the funeral of William IV. During the 1848 Chartist demonstrations (Reith 1956, pp. 168–94) the stipendiaries were confined to the police offices (Keller 1976, p. 108). It was nearly half a century before the county magistracy was similarly withdrawn from the control of forces on the streets.

The success of the police commissioners in achieving organizational supremacy over the stipendiaries in London relates not only to the numerical strength of their forces, but also to the single unified jurisdiction which they enjoyed over almost the entire metropolitan area. The new police area, unlike the jurisdictions controlled by the stipendiaries, was constructed without reference to the existing parish system and the divisions and beats were laid out independently of existing authority. In contrast to the stipendiaries, who were still subject to the local influence of the vestries, the new police were responsive only to central control. They were a dependent agency of the central state in a much more complete sense than the 1792 stipendiaries.

However, the stipendiaries had not been entirely deserted by their allies in the Whig ministry. As so-called 'satellites of Whig patronage', they still enjoyed close links with the Home Office. Sir Frederick Roe claimed:

My duties in addition to those of the other police magistrates are to attend at the Home Office frequently, I will not say daily, because I use my discretion about it, whether I think the Secretary of State will want to see me.[47]

While the Whigs would never contemplate any increase in the summary powers of the county benches, they were willing to introduce legislation in February 1839 to extend the jurisdiction of London stipendiary magistrates sitting alone to include larcenies up to £2. Significantly it was proposed also to amalgamate the hitherto autonomous constabularies of the City of London, the Thames and Bow Street into the Metropolitan Police.

The campaign in favour of the new jurisdiction was waged in the 1837–8 Select Committees on the Metropolis Police Offices[48] and represents the last significant attempt by the stipendiaries to establish the concept of a state magistracy. It was undertaken largely by the stipendiaries themselves and, in particular, by James Traill and his colleagues at Union Hall, who produced lengthy and detailed letters and pamphlets in support of their case. The proceedings of the heavily packed Committee illustrate vividly the creation and demarcation of a special area of forensic skill supposedly unique to the stipendiaries. Significantly, they were presented as unmoved by popular tumults (Traill 1839, p. 30) and were 'Sensible men, conversant with judicial enquiries'.[49]

What was critically important for the stipendiaries was an elevation of the status of their office. What barrister of successful practice would consider joining the 'weak, worn out, imbecile old fixtures at Worship Street and Queen Square'?[50] A radical change was needed 'to raise the character of the court in the estimation of the public . . . by practically maintaining the analogy between the higher and the inferior functionaries of justice'.[51]

The exercise was to be cosmetic only and would involve dressing the stipendiaries in bar dress and refurbishing the public offices which apparently were 'undignified and unworthy places for a gentleman to be in: it rather disgraces a man to be huddled in a crowd in such places'.[52] Henceforth (despite the parliamentary protests of the Recorder of London, Mr Law [53]) their offices were to be designated 'courts' and the committee, in its wish to 'elevate the character of the Police Magistrate in the Metropolis' made a point of referring to them as 'Judges of [the] Police Courts'.[54]

The proposal for a wider jurisdiction as a trial court foundered on the continuing demand for control over executive forces. A 'very great outcry' from the City of London[55] about the potential loss of control of its police force, coupled with a vigorous campaign in the Tory press against the loss of jury trial and the centralizing tendencies of the metropolitan reforms[56] soon disposed of the proposals.

The London stipendiaries took their revenge against Charles Law, the Tory Recorder of London, who had led the opposition to the Bill in the House of Commons. As if 'they had a trade meeting for the express purpose' the stipendiaries acted in concert to commit all available cases to Mr Law's court so that the unfortunate Recorder was deluged with work, whereas the Middlesex Quarter Sessions had only two cases in the entire session:

The obvious and disgraceful truth is that the Police Magistrates in committing cases for trial have made a dead set at the Recorder of London. Instead of distributing the petty criminal business as heretofore . . . these vindictive gentlemen have devolved the entire disposal of it upon the shoulders of Mr. Law – whether the Home Office may have some share in this conspiracy . . . we are unable to say. The thing is by no means unlikely.[57]

This little plot neatly exemplifies the ability of the London stipendiaries to act together as a pressure group. The defeat of the 1839 Bill, however, marked the end of the attempt to create a model for the national system of stipendiary justices favoured by Bentham. Although the London stipendiary courts continued to exercise a wide jurisdiction (including poor relief) throughout the mid-century, their decline in status (Davis 1984, p. 310) relative to the police must date from this period. Their authority had derived entirely from the central state. They were therefore unable to resist the organizational ascendancy of the police which had rapidly established a professional competency in crowd control which contrasted sharply with that of the stipendiaries. With no local resources of power, their independence of action was lost at least a half century before that of the provincial benches. By 1855, as we see in the response to the Hyde Park riot, the stipendiaries were confined to a peripheral, supporting role to the police and were unable to contemplate any challenge whatsoever to the operational policies of the latter.

The new borough magistracy in 1835

The events in Bristol in 1831 were to reveal the extent to which a municipal corporation and its magisterial bench could be dominated by oligarchical factions whose economic interests did not coincide with those of the nascent industrial bourgeoisie. The latter were prepared to enlist both popular disorder and the authority of the central state as weapons against the close corporations.

Following the success of Parliamentary Reform, the Whig administration was able to bring more assistance to its municipal allies. Under the Municipal Corporations Act 1835,[58] elective municipal corporations were established in 178 boroughs on the basis of a franchise limited to ratepayers of three years' standing. These corporations had no judicial functions (see, for example, Laski *et al.* 1935; Finer 1945, pp. 63–5; Smellie 1963, pp. 28–33; Keith-Lucas 1977).

In the debate over the Act, the House of Lords refused to consent to the nomination of borough justices by the proposed municipal corporations, and, as a result, the right of nomination fell to the Crown (s.93). The significance of this compromise was that the office of borough justice,

unlike that of county justice, was not to be in the gift of the Lords Lieutenant. The Lord Chancellor, in making appointments, had little alternative
but to consult the local Member of Parliament who, in the boroughs,
might well be a Whig or Radical. Moreover, the property qualification
was not to apply to the new borough justices (s.101) and hence these
benches might be expected to take on a very different class character from
the county ones. According to the *Quarterly Review*, the Russell administration then embarked upon 'a flagrant and extensive prostitution of
magisterial appointments for mere party purposes'.[59]

Indeed, the figures extracted from the Commons debate on 5 May 1842
(Table 2.1) do seem to indicate a determined Whig campaign to ensure
political domination of the new borough magistracy. The dismay of the
Tory press at the appointment of the 'too notorious Frost' at Newport or
Anti-Corn Leaguers in Lancashire was evident. Such magistrates, they
argued, not only threatened to protect the mob from the military, but
refused to be answerable for public order unless the government was
prepared to 'do something for the people'. They even encouraged the
'capture of Manchester, Stockport and Bolton by an *unresisted* mob'.[60]

> We have shown that the *Magistrates* who belonged to these societies,
> instead of maintaining the tranquillity of their respective jurisdic-
> tions, were amongst the most prominent and violent promoters of
> every species of agitation . . . [volunteering] declarations which those
> inclined to disturb the public peace might reasonably consider as
> promises of at least impunity.[61]

In the temporary alliances of the 1830s, it was not to the county elites
that the new municipal justices turned for support. Indeed, by 1837, the
Commission had become deeply polarized and, according to Napier
(1857, p. 7):

> The magistrates are divided into Whigs, Tories and personal en-
> mities; and every mother's son of them ready to go to any length for
> his sect and creed. The town magistrates are liberal for fear of the
> populace; the county bucks are too old and too far gone Tories . . .

Surrender to the cotton lords, he argued, might well make a paid magistracy inevitable (1857, p. 51).

Throughout the winter of 1838–9 the Home Office was receiving reports of increasing Chartist agitation, including drilling, arming and mass
rallies consequent upon the publication of the 'People's Charter' in May
1838.[62] In early June 1839, attempts to suppress the Chartist Convention
at Birmingham resulted in several days' rioting and, on 16 July, the House
of Lords met to discuss the critical situation amid accusations that Whig-
appointed magistrates were encouraging the disorders for political purposes. The Tory Earl of Warwick, Lord Lieutenant of Warwickshire,

Table 2.1 Summary of nominations to the borough magistracy, 1835–42

(a) Towns affected by anti-Corn Law agitation

	Whig and Radical	Tory		Whig and Radical	Tory
Birmingham	27	6	Liverpool	25	6
Bolton	11	3	Macclesfield	6	0
Carlisle	10	1	Manchester	29	4
Coventry	12	0	Nottingham	12	4
Derby	8	0	Newcastle	13	3
Kendal	4	0	Pontefract	4	0
Kidderminster	6	2	Richmond	4	0
Hull	18	3	Stockport	12	4
Lancaster	5	1	Sunderland	10	0
Leeds	17	4	Walsall	6	1
Leicester	11	1	Warwick	5	1
Lichfield	6	0	Wigan	13	1
carried over	135	21	Total	274	45

(b) Towns not affected

	Whig and Radical	Tory		Whig and Radical	Tory
Bath	9	2	Oxford	5	1
Boston	5	6	Plymouth	7	2
Bridgwater	7	2	Poole	8	1
Canterbury	8	0	Portsmouth	11	0
Flint	8	0	Rochester	4	1
Grimsby	7	0	Shrewsbury	5	2
Hereford	6	1	Truro	2	0
Ipswich	8	2	Worcester	8	1
Lincoln	7	1	Yarmouth	19	1
carried over	65	14	Total	134	23

Source: 3 *Pltry Debs.* lxii, 5 May 1842, 116–91.

insisted that the new magistracy no longer consulted with him with regard to their actions but reported directly to the Secretary of State:

> he could not help expressing his surprise, that as the Lord Lieutenant
> of the county he had no communication made to him by the [Bir-
> mingham] magistrates on that subject . . . The magistrates also that
> had recently been appointed under the new corporation in that town
> were, many of them, taken out of the class connected with the Char-
> tists, to fill those most responsible and respectable situations, and
> some of them were actually Political Unionists and Chartists . . . He
> could give, if it were necessary, a list of the names of the parties he

alluded to . . . six or eight of these new magistrates were political unionists . . .[63]

Lord Wharncliffe went so far as to accuse one so-called 'Chartist magistrate' (Muntz) of 'agitating the people up to the very moment of his appointment'.[64]

It is significant that, only three days after Lord Russell had been roundly accused of appointing the new magistrates on party grounds and conniving at the disorders, the Tories mounted their first attack on the Metropolis Police Courts Bill. The issue of Whig patronage was clearly much in their minds. Recorder Law maintained:

> Whether Her Majesty's Government had been induced to seek this power from having seen the wretched appointments which, from time to time, they had made, and feeling the consequences which had arisen from the way other magistrates of their selection had conducted themselves, he knew not. It might be they had looked at Birmingham and [seen] how their friends had acted there . . .[65]

It was argued with some force that the promoters of the Reform Bill were now launching a fresh attack on the social order by creating a new class of petty functionaries (or, as *The Times* would have it, 'Whig ridden nominees')[66] under the direct supervision of the Home Office. If the control of the local judicial process in the counties, like that of the Poor Law, was to be eventually removed from the landed interest and brought within the direct ambit of government, the results would be disastrous:

> Mr Canning said that if they superseded the local magistracy, that connecting link between the higher and poorer classes, they would do more by that single blow to destroy the constitution of the country than could be accomplished by all the efforts of the Radical reformers.[67]

The catastrophes in Bristol in 1831 and in Birmingham in 1839 demonstrated clearly that, without some resolution of the class conflict around the composition of the magistracy, the existing control apparatus would be completely paralysed. Whether this resolution would encompass a Benthamite state magistracy on the London model, remained in doubt. The next chapter considers in detail the collapse of existing arrangements between the magistracy and the army in Bristol and attempts to coordinate the new police and the state magistracy in London in 1855.

3 Two versions of magisterial authority: Bristol and Hyde Park

Bristol 1831

Much of the critical attention devoted to the Bristol riot of 1831 has focused on three related areas: the reasons for the breakdown in order (Hamburger 1963, p. 173; Thomas 1974, pp. 5–6); the relative importance of local (i.e. corporation) and national (i.e. Reform) issues in the conflict (Eagles 1832, p. 64; Little 1967, pp. 237–8; Thomas 1974, pp. 1–2, 26); and the social and economic composition and the motivations of the crowd (Cole and Postgate 1961, pp. 244–5; Thompson 1963, p. 80; Halévy 1972, p. 51; Thomis and Holt 1977, pp. 93–6).

A consideration of the position of the magistracy in the disorders, however, leads us into a different kind of analysis. The questions to be asked here are the following: What was the class character of the Bristol magistracy? Why was political support from the central state denied it at a crucial juncture? And what permanent effects did these events have upon the balance of economic and political forces as represented in the control of the judicial and coercive agencies within the city? These questions are important because, in many respects, the Bristol riots were dominated by the question of the legitimacy of legal action in the criminal courts.

On 29 October 1831 the Recorder of Bristol, Sir Charles Wetherell, an ardent Tory anti-Reformer, was due in the city to preside over the assizes. As *The Times* observed: 'although the magistrates were aware of his [Wetherell's] outrageous conduct on the liberties of the people, they chose to let him come here as a Judge'.[1] Wetherell's offence was to have claimed to speak against Reform in Parliament on behalf of a city with which his connections were purely legal. He was met on arrival by a huge crowd. Shouting 'Give us the b . . . . y Recorder. We'll murder him!' (Eagles 1832 p. 74) They interrupted the assizes and besieged the judge, the mayor and the magistrates in the Mansion House before proceeding to make their own gaol delivery by sacking the city's prisons. Two troops of the 14th Dragoon Guards seemed incapable of co-ordinating their activities with those of the civil power, and order was restored only with much blood-shed and after quantities of corporation property (including the Mansion House) had been destroyed.

In order to understand the inability of the bench to act, it is necessary to look at its political history. The twelve magistrates (including Wetherell) who comprised the active portion of the common council personified the 'West India aristocracy' which had dominated the corporation for 150 years. With the exception of the mayor[2] they were all Tories. A *Sun* correspondent wrote:

> I herewith send you a list of the Bristol magistrates, the whole of whom are Tories or anti-Reformers. . . . Your readers may judge from this what confidence the inhabitants may have in such a *junto*. They are a self-elected body . . . not more than one of them (Barrow) with the mayor, resides in the city.[3]

According to Somerton (1832, p. 6), the exclusive system – as exemplified by the self-perpetuating 'close corporation' – was more strongly de-veloped in Bristol than anywhere else in England, and this view was echoed by Webb and Webb (1963, p. 470) who have shown how political power was narrowed down to the mayor and the aldermanic magistrates at the expense of the corporation (1963, p. 464).

Although this coterie swung from the old Whig party to the Tories in 1812, they remained consistent in their support for the interests of the West India aristocracy. Indeed, according to Marshall (1975, p. 3), a quar-ter of the membership of the Bristol West India Association had seats also on the common council. This interest, however, no longer represented the real sources of wealth within the city. Until the 1830s local finances had been based upon the exploitation of plantation slave labour (Little 1967, p. 159) and nearly all local industry and a large proportion of the shipping were oriented towards the supply and maintenance of this kind of colo-nial economy. In the words of a broadsheet produced by the Tory candi-date for the violent 1830 election:

> You are no doubt aware, fellow citizens, that BRISTOL owes ALL her prosperity, nay, I had almost said her existence with the WEST IN-DIES. Without it she must sink to rise no more. Picture in your imagination her now crowded streets, grass-grown and desolate . . .[4]

This was no mere hyperbole. The long revolutionary wars had interrupted the triangular Caribbean trade and a series of banking crashes in 1825 (Little 1967, p. 155), the disastrous loss of shipping to the deeper-water ports of Liverpool and Glasgow, and, finally, the prospect of slave emancipation (Marshall 1975) all indicated a terminal decline in the Bristol West India interest.[5]

As mortgagees and bankers for the plantation owners, the West India aristocrats were cut off by many thousands of miles and degrees of subordination from the forces of production from which their wealth was derived. As magistrates for the city of Bristol, however, they exercised direct control over the productive classes in whose economic capacity they had no immediate financial interest. Outside this dislocated power bloc, however, there were those whose incomes depended upon non-slave shipping, the smaller plantation owners and mortgagors and the growing number of copper and brass founders and glass manufacturers who exploited the profitable combination of Kingswood coal and Bristol's central position in the network of communications (Little 1967, pp. 166–80).

One of the chief grievances expressed by these men against the corporation was the heavy rate which was imposed upon shipping operated by non-freemen and driving trade away to other ports. Although the city dues were reduced by a third in the face of falling revenues in 1825 (Webb and Webb 1963, pp. 448–9), it was still felt that the West India monopoly was operating at the expense of other species of trade, especially that carried on by the flourishing coastal fleet. At a public meeting held to censure the magistrates for their failure to control the riots, the American consul summed up the major source of resentment: 'an enormous rate was impending over the inhabitants – a rate calculated to crush their energies'.[6]

Unable to gain entry into the corporation itself, the Liberals had endeavoured to organize alternative centres of power within the city. Webb and Webb (1963 pp. 464–5) have shown in detail how the 'corporation of the poor', the 'bridge authority', the 'dock company' and the 'gaol corporation' all developed as a kind of displaced local state in exile and in opposition to the Tory magistracy.

Exactly the same process was apparent in the development of policing in the city. In the course of the riots of 1831 we see clearly the traditional crime-control apparatus first boycotted and then superseded by a new organization of extra-legal authority. This was not a case of 'licence' being given to the rioters by terrified magistrates, as Thompson (1963, p. 80) contends, but the appropriation of the forces of control out of their hands. The most striking feature of the first few days of the riot was the refusal of the 'respectable classes' to assist the magistrates. Faced with the failure of the call for special constables, the sheriff was obliged to hire 119 'bludgeon men' to act for the corporation (Manchee 1832, p. 13; Hamburger

1963, p. 169; Thomas 1974, p. 3); these men distinguished themselves by the brutality and random nature of their arrests.[7]

While the crowds were acting vigorously throughout Saturday and early Sunday against the persons and property of the corporation,[8] there is abundant evidence of indifference and even encouragement from respectable bourgeois Bristolians.[9] Brereton and the 3rd Dragoon Guards (who had been quartered in Bristol for some time (Hamburger 1963, pp. 164–5)) seemed to display exactly the same feelings, waving their gloves and shouting with the mob 'the King and Reform!' It was the mayor himself and his constables who were the chief targets for these '*sans-culottes* who have taken their degrees from the University of Paris and who may read the *Edinburgh Review*'.[10] Evidence was certainly forthcoming at Pinney's trial that the 3rd Dragoons released prisoners and attacked the special constables. The magistrates suspected that their power was being subverted by the government in collusion with the Bristol Liberals. At the height of the Mansion House siege the town clerk 'thought it necessary to ask [Brereton] if he had any secret instructions from the government which conflicted with the orders of the magistrates' (Eagles 1832, p. 76).

The last attempt to salvage some vestiges of corporation authority was made on the morning of Sunday 30 October with an appeal to church congregations to attend at the Guildhall to defend the city. A sparse 150 assembled and milled up and down the stairs in confusion before returning home. In sharp contrast to this civic impotence, the political unions had long boasted of their ability to deploy large numbers of supporters in a peace-keeping role. It was only on Sunday night that Herepath, chairman of the Bristol Political Union, offered a force of men to the aldermen (Thomas 1974, p. 8).

By this time, the mob had turned its attention away from the property of the 'tax-eaters' to that of private citizens. As the class composition of the crowd began to change, a 'thrill of horror' (Eagles 1832, pp. 130–1) went through the city. Even the 'Bloody Blues', the 14th Dragoons who had been sent away by Brereton as a result of their energetic commitment to the civic authorities, were now welcomed back by the bourgeoisie:

> By this time a marked change had been produced in public feeling; the troops which had been treated with every mark of *popular* indignity, and were finally sent away in obedience to popular dictation, were received on their return with cheering as deliverers.
>
> (Eagles 1832, p. 141)

In justification of the sobriquet, the 14th soon cleared the streets with their sabres of the '*lumpen* of the quay',[11] killing and maiming at least as many as at Peterloo. There was no outcry from the Liberals and Radicals who now flocked to tie on the white linen armband of the special constabulary. As the *United Services Journal* put it: 'The Unionists . . . armed with white favours suddenly swarmed in the streets like butterflies after a shower.'[12]

2,819 men, of whom at least 300 were provided directly through the political unions, joined the special constabulary (Hamburger 1963, p. 169n) and patrolled the city jointly with the army. They set about scouring the working-class and Irish districts of Marsh Street, St James' Back and the Dings for 'suspects' (Eagles 1832, p. 155), who were arrested in large numbers. On the morning of 1 November, 60 people, including 10- and 11-year-old children, had been confined to the New Gaol[13] and by 4.00 p.m. the number had risen to 150.[14] *The Times* reported that 206 'rioters' had been captured by the following Sunday and were to be paraded in the gaolyard 'for the purpose of identification'.[15] The frigate *Saturn* was ordered out from Milford Haven to serve as a floating prison for those condemned. With some satisfaction, the Reform press reported that two-thirds of those arrested were Irish and that none, significantly, were £10 householders.[16]

At this stage the involvement of the magistracy could not be avoided. The laxity of the Bristol bench in its judicial functions had long been notorious. As the *Bristolian* had pointed out four years earlier:

> Two or three or four magistrates walk up to a string of prisoners, prosecutors and witnesses and each proceeds in the interrogation of a case. The confusion of Babel is admirably imitated, but the appearance of cool and deliberate justice dispensed with in a most unseemly (not to say, indecent) manner.[17]

The mass arrests presented work for which the justices were thus well fitted. Examinations began in private[18] in rooms in the council house, with constables 'flocking in with prisoners'.[19] Later in the week proceedings were transferred to the gaol itself, where an observer found that 'officials and demi-officials, having recovered their confidence had also resumed their wonted importance'. The committals, he judged, were 'but loosely conducted. For instance, prisoners had been released in compliance with the solicitations of citizens who spoke to [their] character . . . and soon after they were enlarged, constables went in quest of them upon distinct charges.'[20]

Both the Annual Register and *The Times*[21] maintained that, within four days, the justices had committed 180 defendants. Since only 117 defendants appear eventually in the trial calendar, and 36 of these were discharged by grand or petty juries, the standard of judgment shown by the magistrates could not have inspired confidence. The attrition rate of discharges/acquittals against committals stood at 55 per cent. In these circumstances the desire of the Bench to have a corporation member, Sir Charles Wetherell, as a presiding judge, is understandable. The government, however, would not agree and a Special Commission was appointed. In his charge to the grand jury, Tindall LCJ noted that the government had deliberately avoided leaving 'the investigation and punishment of such charges to the ordinary course and stated periods of the administration of criminal jurisdiction within the city'.[22] The words were significant. The liberal press had feared that Wetherell would return 'in triumph' to sit in judgement, and on 8 November a group of 'respect-able inhabitants' met to express their concern that 'the judicial functions [might] . . . be entrusted to a political partisan'.[23] Wetherell, on the other hand, was incensed that proceedings should have been taken out of the hands of the city authorities: 'In two former Special Commissions for similar purposes, the Recorder's name had been included, and so had [those of] the local magistrates'.[24]

The completeness of the takeover is evidenced by the huge presence of government troops. A squadron of artillery, 450 infantrymen and 250 cavalry were encamped in the city during the trials to give support to the 4,000 special constables on duty around the court. The proceedings were opened on 3 January and were concluded after nine days. Five so-called 'ring-leaders' were sentenced to death and were immediately disowned by the bourgeois Reformers (Hamburger 1963, p. 260). As in the trials of the 'Swing' rioters, the Special Commission proved to be a very blunt instrument of retribution. Thirty-one per cent of cases had to be dismissed by grand or petty juries and, whereas over a quarter of those committed were sentenced to death, only four were left for execution (see Table 3.1). Bearing in mind the large numbers already released for want of evidence strong enough for indictment, the results of excluding summary process were all too clear.

The alleged rioters were not the only ones on trial. Meetings were called to examine the conduct of the magistrates and to consider means of taking the control of the criminal justice apparatus out of their hands. A secret enquiry was empanelled and collected depositions for forwarding to the Attorney-General. The Tories reacted bitterly:

> It is a fearful state of things if such local inquisitions are to be set up by, and in secret correspondence with a government . . . this secretly working tyranny – this formal denunciation and degradation of the magistracy . . . these new Star chambers.[25]

In response to intense pressure from the Bristol Liberals, the Attorney-General proceeded on an information against Pinney and his fellow magistrates for criminal negligence. The case was not dealt with at *nisi prius* but removed to the more exalted sphere of King's Bench. In the event, Lord Denman's prosecution (unlike that he had unleashed against the rioters) was half-hearted and Pinney and the others were acquitted. However, it is noteworthy that all proceedings arising from the riot were displaced from their natural local jurisdictions.

Table 3.1 Defendants arrested in Bristol riots of 1831: Disposals of cases by special commission, January 1832

Offence	Death	Death recorded	Transportation			Hard labour					No Bill	Acquitted	NEO†	Total
			14 yrs	7 yrs	2 yrs	1yr	6 mo.	4 mo.	3 mo.	1 mo.				
Demolishing buildings	5*	19	–	–	–	–	–	–	–	–	10	3	–	36
Burglary	–	5	–	–	–	–	–	–	–	–	–	–	–	5
Theft	–	–	1	6	2	10	6	3	3	2	2	12	3	49
Riotous assembly	–	–	–	–	9	7	1	–	–	–	–	6	–	23
Robbery	–	2	–	–	–	–	–	–	–	–	–	–	–	2
Total	5	26	1	6	11	17	7	3	3	2	12	21	3	117

* 1 pardoned.
† NEO – No evidence offered.

The riots also provided a sharp incentive to the campaign for a stipendiary magistracy. At a meeting on 22 November, Thomas Manchee spoke of the necessity for a paid magistracy. The existing magistrates, he added:

> were willing to lend their sanction to a Police Bill with one proviso only – that the police should be under their own care (laughter). For his part he would not consent to place the police of Bristol under the control of a body of irresponsible magistrates (immense cheering).[26]

Indeed, the Bristol MPs introduced local legislation modelled on the London system, but this fell victim to the government's wider plans.

The Bristol riots of 1831 represented a crisis in the lengthy three-cornered struggle for control of the institutions of the local state between the magistrates, the anti-corporation bourgeoisie and the government. In 1831 the central state decisively withdrew military and judicial support from the West India aristocracy and put them on trial with the same prosecutor (and a similarly constituted bench) as the rioters themselves. The city was handed over to the physical control of the local bourgeoisie who patrolled the streets and reported back to London on their own authority. As Pinney's counsel, Sir James Scarlett put it: 'at that period the magistrates were deserted, nobody would act with them'.[27] The state had entered into a coalition with the Bristol bourgeoisie in order to deprive a particular economic class of its access to administrative and judicial power. It permitted the establishment of new agencies of criminal justice to replace those which were dying with the West India trade.

The crime of the magistrates was not that they had been 'accomplices with the incendiaries'[28] but that they had no direct class interest in either the policing of the labouring population or in the maintenance of boundaries with the casual workers and residuum. The assault by the special constabulary on the Dings and Marsh Street was class action at its most open, given force by the restraint and frustration so long imposed by the absentee magistrates.

Hyde Park 1855

Bristol demonstrated the paralysing effect of contradictions within the ruling-class power bloc on the local forces of repression. In London, however, as we have seen, the central state had intervened to appropriate control of the magistracy and the police. These two dependent agencies were both involved in the 1855 Sunday trading riots in Hyde Park and their actions there provide a striking contrast to the events in Bristol. The riots were, in the first place, unusual because they took place in one of the London parks which had become a meeting ground for the classes, where the aristocracy paraded in their coaches, and bourgeois and working-class families picnicked. It was a riot in which elements of all classes were involved. Barristers and wealthy businessmen, troops from the Crimea, MPs, dukes and even Karl Marx were present.[29] When the police charged the crowd, 'well dressed women' were forced ankle deep into the Serpentine,[30] and respectable gentlemen were arrested for shouting 'Shame!'

The meeting in Hyde Park had been called to protest against the Sunday Trading Bill. This was a measure inspired by radical evangelicalism and designed to prohibit trading on Sundays. Opposition, sponsored by the Chartists, who regarded this as a class measure, was fierce. As Marx (1980, p. 303) put it:

> This new coercive measure . . . was sure to receive the votes of big capital, because only small shopkeepers keep open on Sunday and the proprietors of the big stores are quite willing to do away with the Sunday competition of the small fry by parliamentary means . . . The workers get their wages late on Saturday: it is for them alone that trading is carried on on Sundays.

It was decided to hold a mass meeting in Hyde Park of 'artisans, workers and the "lower orders"' to 'see how religiously the aristocracy keeps the Sabbath'. On 24 June and again on 1 July, large crowds (estimated by the police to number 50,000)[31] hooted and jeered at the passing carriages, shouting 'Go to church' in at their windows. But the second meeting had been prohibited by a notice issued by the chief commissioner acting with the approval of the Home Office.[32] This notice was of dubious legality and when it was read to the crowd it was ignored. Both meetings were essentially good humoured and festive (Harrison 1965, p. 233) although there was a large police presence.[33] However, at 3.30 p.m. on 1 July, Superintendent Hughes, a veteran of Calthorpe Street,[34] mindful of the fact that the prohibition had been treated with contempt, ordered a charge with batons to clear the carriageway and some distance back from the rails. Seventy-two people were eventually arrested. As a barrister witness put it, 'it was a truncheon riot'[35] and the Commissioners of Inquiry were forced to confess: 'We have deemed it our duty to report misconduct on the part of various members of the police'.[36] *The Times* was more robust: 'We pay the police to protect our houses and our pockets and not to break our heads. They are our servants and not our masters.'[37] No magistrate was present with the police at Hyde Park during the disorder, and the commissioner with the powers of a justice was in his office at Scotland Yard. No attempt was made to read the Riot Act. Here was a clear indication that, in London at least, the justices had withdrawn from the streets.

The military were said to be involved with the rioters (Marx 1980, p. 326) and calls for military repressive action were met with alarm.[38] As Harrison (1965, p. 234) put it:

Many observers did not appreciate that the police were trying to develop systematic techniques of riot control . . . Shaftesbury noted in 1867 that no minister would now dare to use the fire of the military against civil disturbances like those in Bristol in 1831.

While this may have been true of London, in the counties the magistrates had a wider discretion, as the events in 1893 (see Chapter 5) were to show.

A second interesting feature of the riot, clearly connected with the first, was that it had an immediate effect upon the legislature. Within 24 hours the Bill had been withdrawn by Lord Grosvenor, who felt himself 'mobbed and bullied out of [the] measure'.[39] The *Spectator* considered this to be a case of 'mob legislation'.[40] Harrison (1965, pp. 227ff.) has argued that the government had received intelligence reports which indicated the possibility of a large-scale insurrection. As *The Times* put it:

> The House of Commons has been driven from a course which they had deliberately adopted by the voice of a mob and what is worse than this, the mob were in the right and the House of Commons in the wrong.[41]

Having conceded the justice of the cause, the government was in a somewhat difficult position with regard to the 72 prisoners. The history of these unfortunate individuals demonstrates clearly the government's dilemma. First they were taken to the yard of the Dairy Lodge near the Receiving House in the Park, and then marched or driven in cabs to Vine Street police station, which was hopelessly inadequate for their accommodation. At one time, 43 prisoners were shut up in an airless basement cell measuring only 24ft by 8ft and inches deep in foul water. The Commission of Inquiry was sufficiently shocked to write: 'The sufferings of the forty three inmates or of the thirty three who ultimately remained there during a sultry night may be imagined.'[42] By this time, the police and Sir Richard Mayne, the commissioner, took the view that charges of felonious riot would be appropriate in most cases, and it was on this ground that bail was refused to all as a matter of policy. Under the Metropolitan Police Act 1828[42a] police bail could not be granted except to persons who were 'liable to be summarily convicted by a magistrate'. The decision that the prisoners should be indicted for felony and bail refused was taken by Mayne that night at 10.00 o'clock at his own house.

The next morning the government was clearly in a state of alarm with regard to the consequences of the riot, and a large crowd was gathering at Marlborough Street magistrates' court (Lock 1980, pp. 174–82). Mr Hardwick, the stipendiary, was stoned as he arrived and during the day 28 windows in the court were smashed. Two Frenchmen were arrested for calling out 'Bravo Englishmen, a Republic! A Republic!'[43] and elsewhere

Marx (1980, p. 303) was writing hopefully to his newspaper 'The English Revolution began in Hyde Park yesterday'.

Three hours passed but no prisoners were produced. William Ballantine, a barrister who was prepared to act for the prisoners, demanded to know what was happening: 'They are in custody and again I say that they may at once be brought into court unless, indeed, the Inspector does not wish them to be brought before an impartial tribunal.'[44] In the meantime, at the Home Office, there was considerable activity. Mayne, in evidence to the Commissioners, insisted that the delay was occasioned merely by the inability of the Treasury Solicitor to find Henry Bodkin[45] and that the law officers were not consulted at all.[46] Since Mayne was not present at these transactions his opinion does not, perhaps, count for much. As Harrison suggests, directions in this matter were coming from a much higher source, and at some time in the morning it was decided that Mayne should be overruled and that indictments would not be appropriate. It is quite clear that the decision to proceed in the summary courts was directly related to the desire to avoid further disorder. As Mayne put it, the question was not one of 'law' but of 'prudence':[47]

> all that I know is that in the morning it was considered by me as well as by others that it was very desirable with a view to put an end to the irritation and to allay the popular excitement . . . to dispose of the cases by summary conviction rather than by committing for trial.[48]

Ballantine suspected that the government also wanted the cases moved from Marlborough Street to its own home territory at Bow Street: 'All sorts of tricks and traps have been resorted to to get the cases to Bow Street, as if an independent magistrate was not to be trusted.'[49]

At 4.45 p.m. two rioters were finally brought in and the court spent the last hour and a quarter of the day listening to an *exparte* and highly coloured account of the disorder from Superintendent Hughes (Lock 1980, p. 176) and in discharging an elderly ecclesiastical estate agent and in adjourning a further case part-heard. About 18 of the prisoners now charged merely with obstruction were bailed and the rest returned, 'almost suffocated with the heat', to the horrors of Vine Street.

The logic of the government's position was that all bailable summary offenders should be released that night. Had the cases been unconnected with the riot, and had the government not been involved, that is doubtless what would have happened.[50] Clearly, however, there was now face to be saved.

The next morning, the government announced the abandonment of proceedings against ten people charged with obstructing the police. However, the remaining defendants were left to be dealt with 'in the ordinary way, according to the evidence'.[51] During the course of the day, Mr Hardwick, working under enormous pressure and conscious of the volatility of the crowd outside, disposed of 60 further cases, acquitting nine, binding over ten and imprisoning 28, mostly for a week. All the cases were dealt with summarily, nearly half without the imposition of any criminal penalty.

Hardwick, who had successfully delayed proceedings until the arrival of the prosecutor and resisted, on his behalf, the attacks of the defence barrister Ballantine, took the view that 'he could not refuse to convict on the evidence on oath of the police'.[52] Ballantine, on the other hand, was quite prepared to put the case for the defence in overtly political terms, asserting that: 'The silly manner in which an obnoxious measure has been brought into the House of Commons made people justly anxious.'[53] In the same way, Mr Clarkson, for the government, asserted that the withdrawal of proceedings against ten of the defendants was the result of 'what had passed in the House of Commons last night'.[54]

Clarkson's admission did not, however, chime with the announcement made the previous day in the House of Commons by Sir Charles Gray. When asked about the liberation of 'persons in gaol for having assembled . . . legally and properly yesterday in the park', he replied:

> The remainder belong to that large class of persons always assembled upon occasions of this kind – pickpockets – and I suppose that it is not desired that the prerogative of mercy of the Crown should be exercised to release these prisoners from the consequences of any offences with which they are charged.[55]

Here, then, were two contradictory images of the arrested rioters. The latter, given on the Monday, describes them as criminal; the former, by the Treasury Solicitor the next day, refers to them in political terms. It was as if, as counsel to the Inquiry put it, there had been a change in the law between one day and the next[56] in order to extract the Home Office from its scrape.[57] On the first two days we see the defendants confined in appalling conditions, refused legal advice,[58] denied bail, threatened with indictment for capital felony, and finally kept from the courts. Immediately the government had become aware of the danger of further disorder in the streets and had pressurized Grosvenor into withdrawing his Bill, it was forced to acknowledge the politicality of the arrests and to release many of the defendants and reduce the charges against the rest. All this had taken place within a matter of three days.

In contrast to the proceedings in Bristol, 24 years earlier, both magistrates and police acted with co-ordination under a central direction. The ease of communication and the flexibility of procedure enabled the agencies to respond quickly and with sensitivity over a matter of hours to the smallest changes of policy.

4 Provincial magistrates and local power

The growth of judicial authority 1835–88

The Benthamites had long envisaged a network of local courts, staffed by a paid state magistracy which would administer rapid and effective summary justice on the model of the London police courts. They would also control the material forces of repression under the direction of the Home Office. Influential supporters of this vision included the reformer Chadwick and the Home Secretary Sir James Gordon (Palmer 1988, p. 462). The main obstacle to its realization, however, was the entrenched power of the Tory county magistracy. It was towards this target, therefore, that the Benthamites directed much of their attention in a succession of attacks throughout the first half of the century. The county benches were roundly condemned as feudal in character, unaccountable, class-ridden and incompetent.[1] As Mill (1972, p. 349) put it: 'The institution is the most aristocratic in principle which now remained in England; far more so than the House of Lords.' Although s.99 of the Municipal Corporations Act 1835 provided for the appointment of stipendiary magistrates (responsible to the local rather than the central state) in provincial cities, only a handful had been appointed by mid-century (Emsley 1987, p. 158) and it is clear that this was almost the only success in the campaign for a universal paid magistracy outside London.

Why was the project left unfinished? Why were the extensive judicial powers which the Benthamites sought, conceded after the 1850s, not to a network of state functionaries, but to the much derided, unreformed magistracy of the counties and boroughs? A number of reasons will be put forward for this compromise. However, it is important first to note that the breakdown of the indictable system under pressure of numbers left a vacuum to be filled.

Throughout this period it was becoming increasingly obvious that existing arrangements to deal with civil disorder were inadequate. Almost two-thirds of those arrested during the Wilkite riots of 1763 were released without any punishment other than pre-trial remand, and the proportion was even higher for those charged with serious felonies. The figures for the 'Swing' disturbances 70 years later reveal again the unwillingness of juries to convict those charged with capital offences arising from civil disorder. In this case 40 per cent of all defendants were acquitted and even among those sentenced to death, only 4 per cent were actually left for execution (Hobsbawm and Rudé 1969). In the Bristol riot of 1831 (see Chapter 3) the failure rate was equally high. As a means of criminalizing and punishing groups of defendants *en masse* the indictable system of justice, even when fortified by Special Commission, was clearly not an effective weapon. Again, following the Coldbath Fields riots of 13 May 1833 the only defendants to be convicted and punished from among the 28 arrested, were the six charged with the summary offence of 'assault on constable' who were foolish enough to plead guilty before Sir Frederick Roe, sitting at Bow Street. In 1833 Sir Frederick and his colleagues were still working under the constraints imposed by a system of criminal process based largely on indictment.

The transfer of magisterial authority from direct policing to adjudication seemed to be a solution which addressed both the low arrest rate and the low conviction rate in civil disorder and other offences. The ending of the justices' exclusive authority for policing in the 1850s coincided with further diversification of the executive powers of the magistracy under the Poor Law and in respect of their authority over gaols and beerhouse licensing (Osborne 1960, pp. 221–2).

As executive authority was drained away from the benches, so the magistracy of the shires successfully renewed the agitation, begun by the Whig stipendiaries, for an extension of their judicial role as a trial court. Throughout the first half of the century, the rhetoric of Blackstonism had been marched out to defeat legislation which contemplated a Benthamite system of summary justice. By 1847, however, a new consensus seems to have emerged. Even Lord Brougham, who had vilified previous proposals, now felt able to move for a Lords Select Committee which, under his chairmanship, reported in favour of summary jurisdiction for juveniles.[2] *The Times*, which in 1839 had attacked as 'perilous and unconstitutional, suppression of trial by jury, the main safeguard of British justice',[3] now took the view that the jury could be cast off as 'effete, unprofitable and dangerous to public safety'.[4] An explanation for this shift must lie in the profound realignment of the class character of the magistracy which was taking place in mid-century.

The domination of the county benches by the Tory Party had ensured an uninterrupted succession by the landed (as opposed to the trade) interest throughout the first half of the nineteenth century. Recruiting itself, in effect, by co-option[5] and enjoying almost complete autonomy from the central state, this resilient provincial oligarchy was determined to resist any incursion by the 'blue-aproned':

> The country gentlemen set their faces against the admission of any person engaged in trade . . . they were prejudiced against any unconventionality in opinions, tastes or conduct even in men of their own class; they resented any expression of Radical or even Whig politics and they extremely disliked any active association with the Methodists or other dissenters.
>
> (Webb and Webb, 1963, pp. 383–4)

However, with the ending of the long parliamentary ascendancy of the Tories in 1830 we see the beginning of a dramatic change in the composition of the county benches. The efforts of the Whig administration to nominate its supporters was not confined exclusively to the new municipal borough benches. In his study of the Black Country magistracy from 1835 to 1860, Philips (1976, p. 166) has noted a radical shift in its class composition:

> Before 1836, appointments were dominated by the landed classes, and coal and iron masters were not appointed at all; by the late 1850s coal and iron masters dominated the appointees, and the landowners had shrunk to just over one tenth . . .

This change did not occur accidentally, but as a result of direct pressure by Lord John Russell on the Lord Lieutenant (Philips 1976, p. 169). During the disorders arising from the colliery strikes of 1842 the new magistrates were able to act directly in their own interests:

> Having cut the wages, these same men, acting as magistrates . . . [were enabled to] repress the disorder which followed their action . . . In these instances, the iron master-magistrates were able to exercise their responsibility to preserve public order in a way which coincided with their own economic interests . . .
>
> (Philips 1976, p. 177)

Since the magistracy in the counties was no longer the exclusive preserve of one political party and class, measures designed to increase its authority were now more likely to find favour with wider sections of the county elite.

With the winding up of the Anti-Corn Law League in 1846, the demise of

Chartism after 1851 and the end of the successive social crises of the 'hungry forties', the local magistracy was no longer in the front line of political and street-level confrontation. This 'prolonged, catatonic withdrawal' (Anderson 1964, p. 36) engendered in the working class after the collapse of Chartism, has been linked in many accounts to the embourgeoisement of sections of the labour leadership in the context of the buoyant economic conditions of the early imperialist period (Hobsbawm 1954; Hinton 1965; Foster 1974; Gray 1976). However, as Stedman-Jones (1975) and Moorhouse (1978) have pointed out, explanations for the ebbing of class struggle in the 1850s must take account of a more complex realignment of class forces. In particular the relationship between different factions of the bourgeoisie and the aristocracy has been regarded as a significant factor in these developments (Anderson 1964; Thompson 1965).

Whatever the case, it is clear that, in the pre-Victorian period, the institution of the magistracy had occupied a crucial position in the conflict between industrial and landed capital. Provincial magistrates, for example, were active in the opposition to the 1830–2 Reform legislation (Osborne, 1960, p. 171; Fraser 1982b) and the new Poor Law (Rose 1982, p. 84). John Adolphus (1824, p. 85), no doubt remembering his work for Mainwaring in the 1804 Middlesex election, commented:

> It must be truly edifying at the time of an election for the people to be informed that, if with one colour in their hats they carry bludgeons in their hands, they will be sent to the house of correction; but if they wear the adverse favour, his good Worship will do them no harm.

By 1850, however, the rigid class-exclusive structure of the provincial Georgian magistracy had been altered almost beyond recognition. The commission of the peace now represented a framework within which the various dominant classes of early Victorian society could be assimilated and their power concerted. In short, it had become a major mechanism of ruling-class alliance. Two factors favoured this process.

The first was the patchwork of county and municipal jurisdictions which, since 1835, had permitted the bench to reflect the class structure of dominant groups involved in particular types of production in a rapidly developing economy. The entry into the commission of large sections of the industrial bourgeoisie in the municipal boroughs after 1835 successfully stabilized the urban magistracy and put an end to the unseemly squabbles which had been evident in Bristol in 1831.

In the agricultural counties, the Lords Lieutenant and chairmen of quarter sessions continued to be recruited almost exclusively from the landed aristocracy (Zangerl 1971, p. 116; Quinault 1974, p. 186) which retained complete control over magisterial appointments until as late as 1910. Even in this context, the 'open structure' (Gramsci 1971, p. 83) of the English aristocracy allowed new sources of wealth to be assimilated.

This new permeability was not confined to the bench itself. Constellations of statutory and *ad hoc* committees, on which the justices were usually represented, brought outside participants into administration.[6] Their presence served 'to give new life . . . to an oligarchic office' (Redlich 1958, p. 210).

The second factor was the effective combination of the principles of financial eligibility and nomination. The property qualification by now was low enough to admit the least exalted sections of the bourgeoisie.[7] Under the system of nomination, wealthy Radicals could be effectively excluded whereas the institutional mechanism allowed the co-option of professionals and representatives from other classes to strengthen the bench in particular areas without abandoning control.

> As an increasing number of names was added to the Commission of the Peace between 1846 and 1886, a much greater proportion of the total consisted of mill-owners, bankers and businessmen . . . after 1860 the number of mill-owners in the [Cheshire] County Commission of the Peace was greatly increased . . . The names which were added to the Commission during the 1860s and 1870s . . . represent the most important revolution of county society, the merging of the landed and business interests.
>
> (Lee 1963, p. 30)

Zangerl (1971, p. 125) makes essentially the same point, asserting that: 'The circle of landed allies on the county bench merely expanded to include bourgeois individuals as well as (professionals).'

This social reorganization of the magistracy in the mid-nineteenth century was in no sense a take-over, more an uneven amalgamation of fresh capital and professional interests into the existing landed hierarchy. The effect of this union was a magnification of the magistracy's collective social authority (Zangerl 1971, p. 116; Harries-Jenkins 1977, p. 252) and, as Keith-Lucas (1977, p. 8) puts it, the magistracy in this period 'constituted in a very real sense a ruling class'. *Blackwood's Magazine* summed up their power: 'In short [they] superintended and set in motion, either in whole or in part, the entire administrative machinery established in the English Counties.'[8]

Between 1835 and 1888, on the basis of these powerful infusions, the magistracy enjoyed a period of unrivalled ascendancy in the counties and qualified ascendancy in the municipal boroughs which stood like quasi-democratic archipeligos in an ocean of oligarchy. For the first time, in the 1840s, the new powers to try offences were to be conferred not only on the metropolitan professional magistracy but also on the county oligarchs who sat on the shire benches.

Whereas in 1840 a Kentish magistrate might fear that the Constabulary Act would 'go far to complete that principle of centralisation . . . [would]

interfere with the administration of law by the unpaid magistracy . . . and is bound to be followed by a paid magistracy',[9] by 1855 there was no such possibility. There would be no new magistrates on the 1792 or 1835 models and the Benthamite conception had been dismantled sufficiently for the constitutionalist defences of the county justices to be redundant.

The Criminal Justice Act 1855[10] was to work 'a revolution in the criminal law',[11] empowering magistrates to try smaller larcenies themselves. The number of committals for trial halved almost immediately (Jackson 1937). The Summary Jurisdiction Act 1879[12] established a more comprehensive system of summary jurisdiction and shifted the magistrates' courts yet further from a registry for guilty pleas and an executive pretrial review of indictable cases, to a trial court in its own right.

Therefore, in the period 1847–79 we see the magistracy constituted as a petty judiciary. Further legislation added to magistrates' jurisdiction obtaining goods by false pretences and some types of malicious damage in 1899,[13] and in 1914 the larceny limit was raised to £20.[14] In 1925, a whole list of further offences was made summary[15] and by this stage magistrates had accrued to themselves something like 90 per cent of all criminal business (Jackson 1937, p. 137).

The development of a new 'judicial' role for the magistrates coincided with the loss of most of their executive powers within the local state to the new elective county councils established by the Local Government Act 1888. Around the country, special meetings of quarter sessions were held to examine the legislation[16] which was 'sweeping away' the 'ancient constitution of the country'[17] together with the squirearchy itself. Such sentiments were 'the predominant note of alarm wherever two or three Tories have been gathered together'.[18] On 10 April the Society of Chairmen of Quarter Sessions held a meeting at The Magistrates' Club in London at which 50 attended. This appears to have been the only attempt by the justices to resist the change. With no permanent county bureaucracy (Ensor 1935, p. 429) the justices had to rely on a disorganized group of county MPs to defend them. The profound changes in the nature of the justices' authority at this period were to have a serious impact upon their relations with the other agencies.

The loss of authority by provincial benches from 1888

In one particular the county interest was successful in its campaign of defence. The justices were to comprise half the members of the new joint standing committees to supervise the police, and they retained their powers in riot. Lord Herschell could 'hardly imagine that it could ever have been intended to take away the powers of justices in regard to riot and disorder'.[19] While freeing the chief constables generally from the direct control of the magistrates, Lord Salisbury was careful to reserve magisterial power to command the absolute obedience of the police in cases where it was necessary 'to prevent occurrence of riot and disorder'.[20]

It has been argued here that the London stipendiary magistrates, who from their inception were heavily dependent upon the Home Office, had come by degrees during the mid-nineteenth century within the sphere of influence of the chief commissioner. We have also seen how from a much earlier period they were withdrawn from the streets. At the Clerkenwell riot in 1833 and Hyde Park in 1855 the magistrates awaited the leadership of the Home Office. By 1887, however, the authority of the commissioner had increased to the point that the ultimate control of both physical and, to a certain extent, judicial repression was in his hands.

It has been a common assumption that the original appropriation of the London magistracy by the central state from 1792 was reflected by a similar process of assimilation which supposedly took place throughout England and Wales during the nineteenth century. According to Stevenson (1977a, p. 39):

> imperceptibly the Home Office acquired a vastly expanded range of activities. It tightened its control over the forces in London under its direct command and increased in importance for peacekeeping in the country at large, acting as the clearing house for information, co-ordinator of forces and source of military support.

Evidence from an examination of the involvement of the magistrates in the repression of provincial disorder does not, however, support this view. On the contrary, we see the coercive forces more firmly in the hands of local magistrates/industrialists in 1893 at Featherstone than we do in 1831 in Bristol where contemporary shifts in the balance of economic forces had neutralized their power. As late as 1901, Sir William Harcourt was still able to argue that, in respect of troop requisitions: 'The Home Office is not in itself a magisterial body, the Home Secretary is not himself *ex officio* a magistrate; but it is from the local magistracy that the authority in this transaction should come.'[21] Mr Balfour agreed that neither the Home Office nor the War Office had any power to interfere with a magistrate's requisition.[22] The justices (and occasionally non-magisterial members of their class) therefore continued to call upon and to use the military on numerous occasions throughout the century, often to the acute embarrassment of the Home Office.

Unlike the London stipendiaries who suffered 'relentless' control by the Home Office (Stevenson 1977a, p. 38), the local justices were as free to encourage, for example, the mobbing of the Salvationists (Bailey 1977, pp. 243–7) in the nineteenth century as they were forestallers (Thompson 1971, pp. 95–6) or Methodists (Hayter 1978, p. 38) in the eighteenth. However, after the disaster at Featherstone in 1893 and the demand by the Committee of Inquiry for a closer integration of military and civil powers in riot, Asquith was obliged to convene a further inter-departmental committee to define 'the several and relative responsibilities of the civil and military authorities in cases of riot'.[23] The report of this committee, adopted *in toto* in 1894, was of enormous significance in terms of the relationship between the magistracy and the chief constables in civil disorder. It did not, however, advocate any enlargement of the role of the Home Office.

Under new regulations, magistrates were forbidden (save in an 'emergency so pressing that a direct requisition is imperative')[24] to send directly for troops. All requisitions would henceforth have to be channelled via the chief constable who was entitled to exercise his professional discretion in deciding whether or not they should be transmitted. Previously, such direct requisitions from the police had been refused point-blank by the military.[25]

In 1908 Charles Troup at the Home Office commended this arrangement, contrasting the 'panic stricken' magistrate sending off unnecessary demands for troops with the cool and professional chief constable anxious to preserve his autonomous command.[26] Unlike the magistrates, the police from 1890 had the advantage of being able to operate under mutual aid provisions outside (or on the borders of) county jurisdictions. Further operational control was withdrawn from the magistrates with the insertion of a provision in Queen's Regulations requiring that an army officer, having been given the simple command to 'take action', could dispose of his forces as he thought fit.

Although the fundamental changes made between 1888 and 1908 were of enormous organizational significance in terms of the relations between magistracy, police and military, it is clear that traditional links of deference preserved the old system for some considerable time. Thus in 1908 the Chief Constable of Nottingham insisted (erroneously) that, in a riot, 'I should hardly like to claim anything superior to what any magistrate could do, who of course are my masters in that respect.'[27]

However, with the growing power of the police establishment after 1888 and the relative decline in importance of local industrial capital, the magistrates were slowly eased out of even this residual role. Changes in personnel played an important part in this process. The Conservative stranglehold on appointments was ended in 1906 and thereafter the Liberal Chancellor, Lord Loreburn, appointed nearly 2,800 supporters of his party within three years. Moreover, the abolition of the property qualification and the creation of 'politically balanced' advisory committees to assume responsibility for nominations in 1910, opened the Commission of the Peace up to the Labour movement. A vigorous campaign orchestrated by the Labour Party General Secretary, J.S. Middleton, ensured a significant increase in the number of working-class magistrates and for the first time positions on the bench were being filled from outside the land-owning and property-owning classes (Vogler 1990). Troup complained at the lack of vigour shown against strikers by the Liberal magistrates in South Wales, Lleufar Thomas and Llewellyn Williams, adding 'but we cannot get rid of them' (Morgan 1987, p. 196). Clearly, the reconstituted benches after the reforms of 1906–10 could no longer be relied upon to support employers' interests without question.

Perhaps more significantly, the geographical structure of the provincial magistracy had been superseded by developments in productive relations. The industrial interests of the new joint stock companies which represented amalgamated or nationally centred forms of capital, now extended far beyond the confines of the petty sessional jurisdictions. As a result, no individual magistrate had the authority to deal with industrial action which occurred throughout the network of a railway company or across a coalmining area.

In 1893 the Law Officers concluded that a justice of the peace was not competent or bound to read the proclamation under the Riot Act outside his own county.[28] Such restricted powers were, of course, of very little use to corporate industries experiencing disorder and strike action over a wide geographical territory. Attempts to deal with the problem by the creation of strategic county sub-committees of justices met severe parliamentary opposition.[29] Ultimately, the national co-ordination of the military was a much more appropriate resource, provided that it could be freed from the control of the local justices. As General Sir Redvers Buller put it: 'a magistrate here would telegraph for men, a magistrate three miles away would telegraph at the next moment to York, and a magistrate three miles further would telegraph somewhere else. He wanted some central authority.'[30]

Bitter disputes between the military authorities and the justices as to the necessity for military assistance in a particular locality were common.[31] Therefore, during the disputes of this period between nationally centralized capital and the amalgamated unions, the power devolved *de facto* upon the central representatives of industrial concerns. Direct requisition for the military by non-justice corporate officers seems to have occurred during strikes throughout the 1890s. In the Taff Vale dispute in 1890, two railway companies sought military protection[32] and the Wilson line tried to requisition gunboats during the 1893 Hull dock strike.[33] The practice of direct communication was common in the 1893 miners' strike (see Chapter 5). In 1901 Keir Hardie, noting that the troops had been requisitioned in the Penrhyn dispute by a group of slate-owning magistrates from another petty sessional jurisdiction, demanded that the law be amended to prohibit interested magistrates from calling directly for the army.[34] According to James Sexton, the Secretary of the National Union of Dockers, 'troops were requisitioned (in Belfast in 1906) on the application of the manager of the Midland Railway Company',[35] without recourse either to the justices or to the government.

Put briefly, it was evident by 1910, when selection of county justices by the Lords Lieutenant alone was abolished, that the magistracy and the elected mayors represented institutions which were no longer cohesive in terms of class interest, had no collective identity at a national level, and could not be expected to respond to the demands of new amalgamated forms of capital. The danger had arisen that 'sectional interests' might prevail over those of the new industrial complex.

Churchill's response at Tonypandy in 1910 was to sideline the justices entirely and impose central authority upon the local police through a military nominee (see Chapter 5). In August 1911, during the national railway strike, Churchill swept the local authorities yet further into the background by dividing Britain into areas under the command of military officers 'charged with general duties for protecting the property of the railways and for securing law and order'.[36] Railway companies and other super-corporations dealing with simultaneous disruptive action around the country could call directly on the military chiefs (Blake 1979, p. 122; Morgan 1987, p. 52).[37] Despite the quiescence of the major part of the magistracy in the face of this attack, Churchill came into direct conflict with those representatives of the local state who owed their positions not to enfeebled local capital interests but to the nascent labour movement.

George Lansbury and the Poplar councillors were incensed to learn that troops were occupying the local power station without their permission and ordered them out. The mayors of Manchester, Sheffield and Liverpool woke to find that, despite their protests and the absence of disorder, their cities were under military occupation. Churchill, at this juncture, was moved to offer the following explanation:

> the regulation which has hitherto restricted their [the military's] employment in places where there was disorder until there had been a requisition from the local authority *was only a regulation for the convenience of the War Office and generally of the government, and has in the circumstances necessarily been abrogated* . . .[38]

With members of the House calling out 'They have all gone mad' and 'Martial law', Ramsay MacDonald denounced Churchill's curious assertion as a 'new doctrine'[39] and Keir Hardie contrasted the careful discussion of relations with the magistracy made in 1894 and 1908 with the reality of 1911:

> On this [current] occasion, before a single man had gone on strike, troops were ordered out, ball cartridge was supplied to the troops, machine guns were lined up behind the regiments, and the military authorities – we have this statement from the Home Secretary

himself – were given an absolute free hand to act where they pleased and to do as they pleased in what they called the preservation of order. Talk about revolution! The law of England has been broken in the interests of the railway companies of the country.[40]

It is suitably ironic that this last rearguard action on behalf of the power of the magistracy in civil disorder should have been fought by the representatives of organized labour.

Although magistrates appeared dutifully to read the Riot Act at Tonypandy and Mansfield, there was no question that their strategic authority was now extinguished by the new police/military establishment. In 1919 in Liverpool one of the last street appearances was made: 'an extremely nervous local magistrate arrived in an armoured car flanked by soldiers with fixed bayonets . . . gabbled through the Riot Act . . . then made a quick escape under a shower of bricks and abuse' (Reynolds and Judge 1968, p. 163). *Justice of the Peace* magazine in 1920 described the position of the magistrate in a riot as a 'peculiar' legacy of historical executive duties. In the past, it noted, the justice of the peace

> was expected to take charge of the whole situation. The fact that in present times he will have the constant assistance and advice of specialists such as experienced police officers used to handling crowds and military commanders conversant with the effects of modern weapons, *greatly modified and simplified his position.*[41]

In 1926 the position of the magistrates on the streets was simplified almost out of existence in the disorders arising from the General Strike. Half-hearted attempts were made by the police to contact magistrates in case they might be needed to accompany convoys. One London superintendent complained:

> Many justices are not on the phone, others were out or retired for the night, some resented being called out at that late hour or pleaded prior engagements. It can therefore be realised the difficulty and sometimes uncertainty there was getting a justice.[42]

The rota of justices, a colleague pointed out, 'could not be relied upon'[43] and 50 Labour magistrates were themselves involved in allegations of intimidation and seven imprisoned (Morgan 1987, p. 211). In general, the magistrates served only to process the 7,000–8,000 defendants summonsed for offences in connection with the strike.[44] Some justices, however, refused to co-operate despite protests from their chief constables and the Home Office (1987, p. 222). Almost all the strike cases were dealt with summarily although regional policies were still significant. The questionable sympathies of the South Wales benches, for example, ensured that most cases in that region were dealt with on indictment and 900 charges of riot and unlawul assembly were heard (1987, p. 210). Labour and Liberal representation on the Welsh benches after the 1906–10 reforms ensured that the indictment of demonstrators was used on a scale hardly seen since the eighteenth century (1987, p. 224).[45] What is remarkable is that there was no longer any real sense of deference towards the justices and certainly no leadership exercised by them. Their role was that of support: 'Police were well supported by the magistrates before whom charges in connection with the strike were taken and severe sentences imposed in many cases.'[46] It was the police who, from this period, organized the rota of justices to attend on them.[47] The lay magistracy therefore had come by the period of the General Strike into a relation with the police and military which was the exact reverse of that of 1887. It was now the magistrates who were required to support the police and military and not vice versa. As Troup rather condescendingly put it in the *Police Journal* in 1929, the magistrate's 'support almost always strengthens the chief constable's hand'.[48] This slide into dependency, which was accomplished without statutory provision of any kind, had serious implications which will become apparent in the detailed examination of the proceedings arising out of the disorders of the 1980s.

The growing police domination of the magistracy in the late nineteenth and early twentieth centuries was accelerated by the decline (particularly after 1906) in the social status of appointees to the commission. It was evidenced by the extension to benches outside London of the term 'police court', a usage which was general by 1920.[49] Moreover, the practice initiated by Ingham and Vaughan during the Trafalgar Square disorders (see Chapter 5) of inviting senior police officers to sit with them on the bench seems to have been reproduced, with some modifications, in provincial courts as late as 1932:

> Far too many courts are dominated by the police. In some courts it is the practice of the Chief Constable or Superintendent, as the case may be, to order witnesses out of court without any direction from the justices. It is a common thing to hear a police officer direct a witness to take his hands out of his pockets or to stand up properly. It is not unusual for a police officer of rank to sit immediately beneath the magistrates, facing the body of the court . . .[50]
>
> (Solicitor 1932, p. 93)

The decline in the standing of the justices is also indicated by their exclusion from participation in the counter-espionage and internment provisions of the Emergency Powers Acts of 1920 and 1939 (Stammers 1983). Their function was limited to dispensing summary penalties to those who infringed the voluminous regulations relating to air-raid pre- cautions, rationing and registration. When the Lord Chancellor in May 1939 introduced legislation permitting him to move magistrates around the country at will, *Justice of the Peace* magazine added quiescently: 'It is not difficult to imagine circumstances in which in some areas and for some purposes the military would have to take charge.'[51]

By the end of the war the practice of maintaining rotas of magistrates for riot duties had fallen into desuetude,[52] and the police were proclaiming their full 'responsibility' (under the army) for the exercise of authority in civil disorder.[53] Although the metropolitan commissioner had lost the title of 'justice' in 1839 (Melville Lee 1901, p. 234), he had still retained the powers. In 1962, the current commissioner defended his status as a justice on the grounds that 'it does enable the commissioner or assistant commissioner to read the proclamation under the Riot Act if that should be necessary'.[54]

The powers of the magistracy under the Riot Act 1715 were abolished finally by the Criminal Law Act 1967.[55] Writing in the same year, Williams (1967, p. 30) insisted that 'in periods of very severe disorder the magistrates can be turned to even now'. However, he went on to add: 'It would also seem likely that, in present conditions, the chief officer of police . . . might tend to assume part of the traditional role of the magistrates in co-operating with the military authorities' (1967, p. 35). The statutory authority under which such a role might be assumed was not made clear.

In 1973, shortly after the Saltley Gates encounter, an amendment to Queen's Regulations redefined the 'civil power' (a term which had hitherto referred to the magistracy) as the local chief constable. This amendment was not made public until 11 March 1976 when it was mentioned in a speech by Sir Robert Mark at Leicester. Jo Richardson, in the House of Commons, pointed out that Mark had 'revealed a change of practice under which the use of the military is no longer sanctioned by the magistracy; it is to be sanctioned by the Home Secretary'[56] and demanded to know under what authority such powers would be exercised. No satisfactory answer was forthcoming.

The amendment marked the final demise of the executive power of the magistracy (Whelan 1981, pp. 168–70; Bunyan 1981b, pp. 7–8). Significantly, for Mark (1977, p. 30), it was the professional character and status of the new police which entitled them to move beyond the existing legal position:

> Such assistance was formerly sought by police from the magistracy rather than from the Home Office, but whatever the legal position present practice reflects the emergence of a professional, well-organised police service which has inevitably assumed the primary responsibility for law and order.

This 'inevitable' withdrawal of magistrates from their dominant role in the repression of disorder had been accomplished *de facto* before the

Second World War and thereafter formal relations were adjusted in an entirely extra-statutory manner. The replacement of magisterial by police/military power over street disorder must be seen in the wider context of the growing economic crisis of the local authorities. These developments follow on from the crucial failure of the late Victorian magistracy to develop a professional autonomy in relation to the other agencies. From 1888 magistrates became totally dependent upon the police for a determination of the nature and quantity of their work. Until 1945 they had no bureaucratic infrastructure or central organization, and they also lacked any distinctive political ideology. They had, in short, no institutional presence at the level of the central state and, as we will see, the relation of dependency with other agencies was to have a marked effect in the disorders of the 1980s.

The growth of centre dependency

Since the Second World War, changes in personnel and organization have been dramatic. For the first time the justices had developed a strong national organization, the Magistrates' Association, to enable them to break out, to some extent, from 'the water-tight compartments' of the petty sessional divisions.[57] This association, together with its sister organization, the Howard League, championed the new concept of the magistrates' court as a forum for the skilled application of treatment and rehabilitation strategies rather than as a trial court, and helped frustrate the long campaign to achieve a significant working-class presence on the bench (Vogler 1990). After 1948, the number of working-class magistrates declined, whereas the numbers of professionals increased significantly (Vogler 1990).

These changes were accompanied by a revolution in organizational structure produced by the massive increase in the number of magistrates (Vogler 1990, p. 80). Growth in the size of magistrates' courts bureaucracies after 1949 has been significant. Many metropolitan courts such as Manchester and Liverpool, had staffs in 1981 in excess of 135.[58] The total number of court employees in 1979 was put at 3,500 by Skyrme (1979, p. 181) and in 1989 at 10,000 by Le Vay (1989, para. 2.5). The population of clerks had risen to 1,700 (Le Vay 1989, Annex G). The promotion of the justices' clerks to senior positions within these bureaucracies has been of great importance, especially since their professional society had become a pressure group of considerable influence.

In the period immediately before the Second World War the magistrates' courts had become for the first time a net financial liability to the local authorities (Le Vay 1989, para. 4, Annex B). In 1949[59] the Exchequer took over receipt of all fines and fees but in return the Home Office was to provide support for local authority funding. Under the Criminal Justice

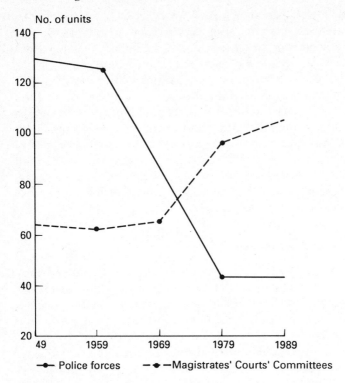

No. of units

—•— Police forces   — • —Magistrates' Courts' Committees

Figure 4.1   Changes in the numbers of organizational units: police and magistracy.
Source: Le Vay (1989)

Act 1972, however, the Home Office assumed responsibility for a fixed 80 per cent of all costs. This was of the greatest possible significance for the magistrates' courts, which were now dependent on the Home Office for a far greater percentage of their funding than were the police (see below). Also, in contrast to the police, the number of territorial divisions was actually *increasing* (Figure 4.1). It was to be only a matter of time before the Home Office would seek an organizational dominance commensurate with its financial responsibilities.

In February 1989 the Home Office announced that it was going to conduct an internal scrutiny.[60] This, not surprisingly, found that 'the structure as a whole is fundamentally unsound' (LeVay 1989, vol. 2, para. 12.1) and proposed a radical 'nationalization' of the service as an 'executive agency' under the general authority of the Home Office (1989, vol. 2, para. 8.13). It pointed to the lack of any cadre of middle-ranking officials (1989, vol. 2, para. 6.12) and the weaknesses of the magistrates' courts committees (1989, vol. 2, para. 3.7). It was, indeed, precisely these features that had made the magistrates' courts vulnerable to a predatory attack by the Home Office.

Despite resistance from the Magistrates' Association[61] and the Justices' Clerks' Society[62] it seems unlikely that the organization has the strength to resist this determined approach from the Home Office. Incorporation into the central state in the case of the magistrates' courts, therefore, must be seen in a completely different light from that achieved by the police. The magistracy, as we have seen, is already a subordinate agency within local systems of authority; and magistrates have been unable to resist the organizational and ideological pressure of the police. Their co-option by the Home Office into a centralized managerial structure will doubtless place the institution in a yet more dependent position.

Briefly, the slide of the magistrates' courts into a relationship of almost total dependency on both the police and the Home Office during the post-war period may be related to a number of factors. First, the magistracy failed to establish any central organization of sufficient authority to negotiate directly with the agencies of the central state. Similarly, the magistracy failed to prevent the fragmentation of jurisdictional boundaries which therefore no longer reflected the economic and political balance of forces. Finally, no ideological identity was developed to replace the discredited treatment strategies of the post-war Magistrates' Association. These organizational and political weaknesses, which occurred at a time of rapid advances by the other agencies involved in the repression of disorder, were to have important implications.

However, before the significance of this more recent loss of authority is examined in the account of the 1981 inner-city riots in Chapter 8, it is important first to review in greater detail some of the earlier shifts in relations. The actions of the magistrates in Bow Street in 1887, in Featherstone in 1893 and in Tonypandy in 1910 provide a striking contrast with those of the 1980s benches.

5 Shifts in the relations of power: Trafalgar Square, Featherstone and Tonypandy

Trafalgar Square 1887

The successful suppression of demonstrations by the unemployed in Trafalgar Square in 1887 marks the high point of co-operation between police and magistracy in London. The whole operation, which lasted from 10 October until early December 1887, bears the hallmark of careful strategic planning.

During the mass laying-off of labour which occurred during the severe depression of the mid-1880s (Cole and Postgate 1961, pp. 441–9), the unemployed and starving had taken to camping out in Trafalgar Square and under the windows of clubs in Pall Mall and the Strand. By 1885 the Socialists and Radicals had realized the potential of these gatherings and working men's orators, such as Oldland, Allmann and George, were organizing regular meetings of what clubland derided as the 'Black guard'.[1] Engels (1959, p. 334), in his private correspondence, described the crowd as 'masses of poor devils of the East End who vegetate in the borderland between working class and lumpenproletariat'.

The Radicals were not the only ones to appreciate the potential of the situation. On 8 February 1885 the London Fair Trade League, a right-wing group with a programme of tariff restriction, public work and agricultural reform (see, for example, Burgess 1911, pp. 45–50; Brown 1977, p. 20), organized a rally in Trafalgar Square. The police deployed only 66 men in the area but kept 563 officers in reserve.[2] When the Social Democratic Federation (SDF) began to attract large numbers to a rival demonstration led by John Burns, the police, heavily outnumbered, were obliged to propose that this group should move off towards Hyde Park. On the way the procession was abused by jeering clubmen along Pall Mall and in response there was considerable damage to property. The low police numbers ensured that there were few arrests although H.M. Hyndman, Burns and two other SDF organizers were unsuccessfully prosecuted for sedition. The whole incident provoked a quite extraordinary revolutionary panic which lasted for several days (Mace 1976, pp. 160–70).

After a Committee of Inquiry had reported, the commissioner, Henderson, resigned and was replaced by Sir Charles Warren. Never a popular commissioner (even with the police: see, for example, Macready 1924, p. 305), he was chosen no doubt on account of his military background and his support for the Liberal ministry. He was appointed, above all, to organize the response of the government to the events of 'Black Monday'. After the change of ministry in 1886 it was only a matter of time before the Tories, represented by Matthews at the Home Office, were ready to deal with the SDF and the unemployed demonstrators. At first D.R. Plunkett at the Ministry of Works denied that he had either the authority or the will to 'banish the unfortunate creatures' sleeping in Trafalgar Square, while Warren adopted the policy of moving them on at night.[3] For *The Times* Trafalgar Square had become 'a sort of Alsatia in which the mob is supreme', and warned that the demonstrators there would be 'firmly dealt with'.[4] For the *Daily Telegraph* it was a 'bear-garden' full of 'desperadoes who flock to the black banners [in order to] engage in indiscriminate pillage'. They too warned that 'the meetings of the so-called unemployed in Trafalgar Square . . . cannot be allowed to continue'.[5] Processions to the Lord Mayor's residence and Bow Street and later to Westminster Abbey, resulted in conflicts between the 'more desperate roughs' and the police and to a handful of arrests.[6]

On 18 October *The Times* demanded that meetings should be confined to Hyde Park,[7] but a gathering there was violently broken up by mounted police. The next day Trafalgar Square was temporarily closed by the police to all traffic. From this point a new clarity and sense of purpose began to emerge from the actions of the authorities. According to the *Pall Mall Gazette*, Sir Charles Warren was 'heading fast and straight for riots'[8] while the *Commonweal* on 29 October took the view that 'the police have, it cannot be doubted, received orders to fall upon any assembly of ill-dressed persons who may have the temerity to assemble together to find out why they are ill-dressed and starved'.[9] Indeed, William Morris and some of the leaders of the Socialist League began to be apprehensive that a trap was being set (Besant 1893, p. 324; Thompson 1977, p. 486). Sir Charles Warren had only to sit 'firmly on the safety valve' and await the explosion.[10]

The 'extensive preparations' made by Sir Charles Warren in the weeks before the riot did not entirely gain the approval of the Home Office, which was distrustful of his assertions of independence and his paramilitary approach to policing (Pellew 1982, pp. 47–8). Nevertheless it felt obliged to support him and, as a first step, on 22 October an order was issued that

> all persons taken into custody by the police concerned in any riotous conduct or assaults in connection with the 'unemployed' demonstrations should be taken to Bow Street court to be dealt with by one of the magistrates there, irrespective of the district in which the arrests were made.[11]

The two magistrates selected to deal with the anticipated riot arrestees, Sir James Ingham and Mr Vaughan, were almost the oldest serving metropolitan magistrates (Sir James was 83) and had a record of loyalty to the police. Early in November, as if in order to emphasize this commitment, they began inviting Sir Charles Warren and the senior prosecuting police officer to sit with them on the bench.[12] The *Pall Mall Gazette* was scandalized:

> By what right, we would like to know, or with what decency, does the prosecuting chief constable take his seat on the magistrates' bench when the charges which he has preferred against citizens for defending the liberty of public meeting are heard at Bow Street?[13]

Pressure on the magistrates did not, however, emanate merely from the police, and on 25 October the Oxford Street traders petitioned the police court bench for vigorous action against rioters.[14]

Warren's policy towards the demonstrators revealed the considerable rifts which had developed between the metropolitan police and the Home Office in the past 50 years. He insisted that neither he nor the metropolitan police 'have anything to do with the Home Office' (Pellew 1982, pp. 48–9) whereas on 30 October Lushington, at the Home Office, was maintaining that the London police were merely a 'department of the Home Office'.[15] During the last days of October and early November Lushington was calling for reports on cases heard at Bow Street,[16] and on 12 November orders went out for the Treasury Solicitor to take over conduct of all prosecutions. In spite of this atmosphere of distrust, Warren, who clearly enjoyed the support of the stipendiaries, was now ready to force the issue.

On 8 November, he 'took the bull by the horns'[17] and banned all processions and demonstrations in the vicinity of Trafalgar Square. The constitutional propriety of this step (which was opposed by the Home Office (Pellew 1982, p. 49)) was doubtful, and a test case prosecution against a Member of Parliament, William Saunders, was abandoned. Sir James Ingham conceded that 'the police are not lawyers'.[18]

The arrest of Saunders had shown how close Sir Charles Warren and Sir James Ingham had come to the notion that mere presence in Trafalgar Square constituted a criminal offence. On 21 October, one of the stipendiary magistrates dismissed the case against an alleged rioter who had merely had the misfortune to be caught in a police sweep. The magistrate nevertheless added: 'You had better not go and listen to the speakers again, you see what comes of it.'[19] The *Commonweal* interpreted these remarks as meaning that 'when the police are running a-muck it is the business of peaceable citizens to prove on the spot, when they are under the batons of these philosophers, that they are peaceable citizens.'[20]

This policy gave rise to some unfortunate and embarrassing consequences. On one sweep of Trafalgar Square the police inadvertently arrested several plain-clothes constables,[21] and on another a former French ambassador who had also been prefect of police in Paris was knocked to the ground and assaulted.[22] Shortly afterwards, a group of journalists, including the distinguished *Daily Telegraph* war correspondent Bennett Burleigh, were arrested and charged with being 'idle and disorderly fellows' and offered bind-overs by Sir James Ingham. When this was refused by the indignant Burleigh, the police and magistrates were obliged to withdraw and to admit that 'an unfortunate mistake' had been made.[23] This was too much even for the *Daily Telegraph*, which launched a bitter attack on the police for arresting and abusing their reporter when he was 'merely in the act of complying with a police order'. Vaughan and Ingham were pilloried as 'senile and used-up magistrates . . . perfunctory and ill-informed' and capable of 'senseless abuse of magisterial authority'.[24]

The ferocity of the police response to the demonstrations of the unemployed was a measure of the weak position of the Liberal opposition after their defeat on Irish Home Rule. While Gladstone might complain about Irish police atrocities,[25] the same argument could not with safety be applied in London. He astonished the Radicals by throwing his full support behind Warren's police.[26] The *Daily Telegraph* and *The Times* considered that this was a matter of electoral politics. The Liberal leaders, it was pointed out,

> rage furiously because Irish anarchists are interrupted by the police but they are silent when the London roughs are dispersed and ridden down. The explanation is quite simple. The Irish have eighty-six votes in the House of Commons, the Socialists, none.[27]

Engels (1960, p. 71) pointed out that, with the Liberal press behind the police and no general election in prospect, it was very probable that Matthews and the Tory government would 'show fight'. The Radicals denounced 'the age of Janus'[28] and found themselves isolated and ill-prepared to face the challenge when it came on 13 November. The defection of Gladstone from their cause delivered the London unemployed demonstrators up to Warren's police.

A meeting planned by the Metropolitan Radical Association as a protest against the imprisonment of O'Brien in Ireland was to be held on 13 November as the culmination of processions from several parts of London. In anticipation, Warren issued a further proclamation on 12 November, forbidding processions, and the next day occupied Trafalgar Square with 2,000 police:

> Upon the three sides where the stone balustrade extends, the police were ranged two deep; on the fourth side . . . the constables stood four deep. Not a break of a single yard presented itself. The thick black line encircled the Square completely.[29]

Additional police were positioned on the London bridges to cut off the major processions from the south of London (Burgess 1911, p. 100) and there were further officers covering all the roads into the Square (Mace 1976, p. 187). The entire force totalled 4,000 officers, including 300 mounted constables, with 300 Grenadier Guards and 300 Life Guards in reserve.[30]

By noon a crowd of sightseers and demonstrators had congregated, only to be broken up and moved along by constant charges of the mounted police. At St Martin's Lane the Clerkenwell procession, headed by William Morris, Annie Besant and George Bernard Shaw, was attacked and dispersed. Even *The Times* was surprised by the violence of the police charge:

> So far the people had gone quietly and rather exultantly on their way towards Trafalgar Square; but at this point matters took a serious turn. The police, mounted and on foot, charged in among the people, striking indiscriminately in all directions . . . The blood in most instances was flowing freely . . . and the spectacle was indeed a sickening one.[31]

The south London contingent was similarly demolished after fierce fighting at Westminster Bridge and a further procession from Notting Hill and Paddington met the same fate on Haymarket. At 4.00 p.m. a group of about 200, headed by Robert Cunninghame-Graham MP and John Burns, made a determined attempt to penetrate the Square at the Strand entrance. With linked arms they marched towards the police ranks where they were assaulted and arrested.[32] Shortly afterwards, 200 troopers of the Life Guards in the company of a metropolitan magistrate from Greenwich, Mr Marsham, rode into the Square, and the traditional forces of riot control were greeted with cheering while the police were subjected to hoots and boos. A further 150 troopers of the Life Guards were deployed in reserve in Whitehall (Mace 1976, p. 189). At 4.40 p.m. they were reinforced by a detachment of Grenadier Guards, who fixed bayonets[33] and formed up outside the National Gallery while the mounted police cleared the remnants of the demonstration from Trafalgar Square in repeated charges. This operation appears to have been one of the first occasions on which the military submitted to the operational control of the police.

By the end of the day some 200 civilians were undergoing treatment at London hospitals for injuries occasioned by the 'vigour with which the police indiscriminately plied their truncheons on the heads of rioters and peaceful citizens'.[34] Three civilians subsequently died from their injuries. The number of arrests was described by the *Daily News* as 'wholesale'.[35] Police instructions were clearly to refrain from arrest whenever possible and the *Daily Telegraph* reported the use of summary chastisement:

> Throughout the afternoon the police instructions appeared to be not to make any more arrests than they could help, for numbers of people who might fairly have been charged were merely beaten and, in a sea phrase, turned adrift.[36]

Of those actually arrested, amounting, according to the *Daily Chronicle*, to 400,[37] a great number were speedily released[38] and by late evening there remained only 52 in custody.[39] As Burleigh had found, those detailed were subjected to abuse and jeering as well as choruses of 'Rule, Britannia!' from Scotland Yard police reserves,[40] and anyone not dressed respectably was kicked and derided as a 'bloody socialist' or a 'bloody German' while passing through the police yards. All were kept without food until 7.30 p.m. when they were dispersed under heavy guard to neighbouring police stations.[41] On instructions from the commissioner, all those charged were retained in custody and an elderly Tory relative of Cunninghame-Graham, Colonel W. Hope VC, complained: 'privates and the police force took upon themselves to inflict upon [Cunninghame-Graham] corporal punishment after which the Commissioner sentenced him without trial to twenty four hours imprisonment. This, Sir, is not the freedom which I fought and bled for'.[42]

A *Times* correspondent, on the other hand, wrote from the Reform Club: 'Let us confess it with that candour which is good for the soul. A little firmness of purpose has saved the state, and how easy it seems.'[43] In an energetic leader the next day, *The Times* demanded swift action:

> It may be hoped that the magistrates will not fail to pass exemplary sentences upon those in custody and more particularly upon their ring-leaders . . . For that despicable breed there ought to be some short, sharp and summary process of punishment affording no room for their coveted self-advertisement.[44]

The Times was not disappointed. Although it had claimed that many of the cases were of simple footpad crime, 'showing that these gatherings encourage the assemblage of robbers of the worst description',[45] in fact nearly all the offences charged were of assault on the police or riotous conduct (Table 5.1) and none of robbery. Bow Street on the morning of 14 November was filled with the results of the police action:

> In the corridors leading from the cells to the courts a large number of wounded men, some with their heads enveloped in surgical bandages, some with their heads strapped up and others with their arms in slings were seen . . . Except for the large numbers of men in uniform, the passage to and from the gaolers' room looked very much like the approaches to a surgical ward of a large hospital after a serious explosion or other accident.[46]

Annie Besant attended at what she described as 'a regular court-martial in Bow Street police court'. She saw 'witnesses kept out by the police, men dazed by their wounds, decent workmen of unblemished character who

Table 5.1 Defendants arrested in London unemployed riots, October–November 1887

	Before 13 November	13 November	After 13 November	Total
Offences				
Riot	–	2	–	2
Seditious words	1	–	3	4
Assault PC	5	26	2	33
Riotous conduct	21	14	–	35
Obstruction PC	1	–	1	2
Idle and disorderly	5	–	1	6
Breach of the peace	1	1	–	2
Other	–	2	1	3
Total	34	45	8	87
Sentences				
Imprisoned:				
3 months or more	4	10	–	14
less than 3 months	10	20	1	31
Committed	–	4	–	4
Fined	–	1	–	1
Discharged	5	3	2	10
Bound over	10	3	5	18
Remanded	5	4	–	9
Total	34	45	8	87

Source: Newspaper reports (various titles).

had never been charged in court before, sentenced to imprisonment without chance of defence' (Besant, 1893, p. 326).[47] Later in the proceedings, the bench was to adopt the expedient of refusing to admit evidence of police attacks on processions, thereby neatly circumventing any attempt to raise a plea of self-defence:

> We confess we are literally aghast at the ruling . . . for the whole case for the defence rests upon the fact that the prisoners were chased out of High Holborn into Southampton Row by an unprovoked attack by the police.[48]

Members of counsel found their services unwelcome in court[49] and Mr Vaughan made it quite explicit that the onus of proof in riot cases lay with the defendants.[50] Sir James Ingham had added that in cases brought in connection with the riots 'he looked at the substance of the police case and not at the wording of a particular Act'.[51] Writing in the *Pall Mall Gazette*, Stead objected strongly to these proceedings: 'Sir James Ingham's conduct at Bow Street ought to be brought before the Lord Chancellor . . . It is time a grave and emphatic protest was raised against so grave a scandal.'[52]

In the meantime, Sir James worked his way through his list with a ferocity which not even Mr Vaughan could match (see Table 5.2). Only one defendant emerged from his court without a custodial sentence or remand. As the *Daily News* put it:

> There is very little doubt that those who were only fined by Mr. Vaughan will, on reading the result of some of the cases before Sir James Ingham be very glad that their number on the list of accused was below and not above forty.[53]

In short, the evidence from all sources is overwhelming that the Bow Street bench operated a comprehensive policy of supporting the police in relation to the riot defendants. William Morris, who sat through many of the cases, found the magistrates 'practically under orders',[54] while Annie Besant wrote letters unwearyingly to complain about the 'shameful travesty of justice which has been going on at Bow Street'.[55] Certainly these were partisan witnesses. However, even the right-wing press, which had urged retribution, noted that Sir James and Mr Vaughan 'showed no inclination to take a lenient view'[56] and adopted 'every official account for gospel, never giving themselves the trouble to listen to the other side'.[57]

If there was no complicity between police and magistracy in these cases, it was clear that the Bow Street bench felt obliged to accept police priorities. Many on the right believed equally that a revolution had only narrowly been averted by the actions of Warren and Ingham. According to George Bernard Shaw, Warren was preoccupied by the idea of revolution.[58] In one speech the commissioner announced:

Table 5.2 'Bloody Sunday' defendants: Bow Street police court, 14 November 1887

	Chief Court Mr Vaughan	'Extradition Court' Sir James Ingham	Total
Offences			
Riot	2	–	2
Seditious words	–	–	–
Assault PC	13	13	26
Riotous conduct	9	5	14
Obstruction PC	–	–	–
Idle and disorderly	–	–	–
Breach of the peace	–	1	1
Other	2	–	2
Total	26	19	45
Sentences			
Imprisoned:			
3 months or more	2[a]	8	10[b]
less than 3 months	13	7	20[c]
Committed	4	–	4
Fined	1	–	1
Discharged	3	–	3
Bound over	3	–	3
Remanded	–	4[d]	4
Total	26	19	45

[a]   Includes 2 sentences of hard labour.
[b/c] Includes 5 sentences of hard labour.
[d]   Includes 1 on bail.

sons and in London they had about 50,000 criminals and loafers of the worst class. With that fact staring them in the face they could not afford to stand idle or the consequences might be something awful.[59]

The *Saturday Review*, for itself, opined that 'the defeat of the police and the troops would have been the beginning of a revolution'.[60] Despite the massive concentration and co-ordination of the police and military on 13 November it was still felt that numbers were insufficient. It is a measure of Warren's fears that he immediately instituted a mass enrolment of special constables and on 20 November invested Trafalgar Square with 20,000 of them, supported by 5,000 regular constables (Burgess 1911, p. 55; Mace 1976, p. 190).[61] Warren's handling of the disorders shows the London police, for the first time, able to resist domination by the central state and to exercise independent authority over both the magistracy and the military. The situation for the provincial police, however, was still very different, as the disturbances at Featherstone, six years later, were to demonstrate.

Featherstone 1893

The 1893 lock-out of coalminers was the largest trade dispute in the history of the Mine Workers' Federation of Great Britain, and paralysed the Federated areas between July and November 1893. Over 80,000 men and 250 pits were involved and the subsequent disorders were thus of a character completely different to those of the earlier part of the century. A drop in coal prices had induced the mine owners to demand wage-cuts of 25 per cent in the expectation that the resulting strike would not only weaken the Federation but also force prices up again (Burgess 1975, p. 206). After six weeks' lock-out the effects of hunger made themselves felt and there were disturbances in Yorkshire. However, the police in the West Riding were not well prepared. A quarter of the force (259 officers) had been sent for racecourse duty and the chief constable, Captain Russell, was on holiday in Scotland (Geary 1985, pp. 7–8). Only three officers, for example, were posted at Featherstone colliery.

The Barnsley magistrates met on 4 September and resolved to contact the military commander at York. Troops had already been moved into South Wales, and the Tory press were anxious for more vigorous action. On 7 September the *Daily Graphic* wrote:

> How much longer is this sort of thing to last? . . . Inasmuch as there is always a railway wherever there is a colliery there can be no difficulty as to the rapid transport of troops to the scenes of disorder. It is about time for the local authorities to wake up . . .[62]

On the same day, surface workers at the Ackton Hall Colliery in Featherstone were ordered to load 'smudge' (a low-quality coal, then fetching high prices) for transportation and sale in apparent breach of the Union agreement with the colliery agent, Mr Holliday. When 200 miners marched to the colliery to complain and to overturn the smudge wagons, the agent panicked and prevailed upon an adjoining mill-owner, Lord St Oswald, to exert his influence as a magistrate in order to obtain assistance from the military. In response to his requisition, channelled through the deputy chief constable, a small contingent of 50 men of the South Staffordshire Regiment was ordered out of barracks in Bradford. When this party arrived by train at Wakefield, the deputy chief constable insisted, contrary to the judgement of the commanding officer, Captain Barker, that it be divided, and a small troop of 28 soldiers eventually appeared at Ackton Hall. Due to a further misunderstanding, no magistrate was there to meet them and their arrival initiated an outbreak of stone-throwing and violence from the crowd.

Since Captain Barker had been obliged to accept the orders of the police, acting with the authority of the magistrates, his military priorities had been overruled by policing ones. He now found himself with a totally inadequate force, isolated from any civil authority and besieged in the engine-house by an angry crowd. Attempts to set fire to the engine-house persuaded Captain Barker to withdraw on the somewhat unrealistic condition that there be no further damage to property. He marched his troop back to the railway station from where he was able to see flames rising from the colliery.

As darkness fell, a larger crowd had assembled in the light of a burning timber stack and, when a magistrate appeared finally at 8.00 p.m., he judged that the situation was by now completely out of hand and that the colliery had to be cleared. An hour after reading the Riot Act, the magistrate, Mr Hartley, ordered the troops to fire on the crowd. Two bystanders, one of whom was a Sunday school teacher, were killed and 16 more were injured.[63] The next day the Ackton Hall colliery had the appearance of a military camp.

With only a small police presence, few arrests were made at Featherstone, but 127 people were apprehended in the West Riding during the disturbances of the first week of September. The central position of the magistrates, some of whom were colliery owners, at all stages in the disorders was in marked contrast to the practice in the metropolis. From the start they were called upon, via the joint committee, to superintend the deployment of the remaining constables and military. The chief constable complained: 'I had exhausted every means of obtaining men and I had telegrams coming in every quarter of an hour urgently demanding the military and extra police . . . I understand I am looked upon as a constable manufacturer.'[64]

When the troops arrived they could act only on the instructions of the magistrate. Indeed, the absence of any justices with local knowledge to give orders at an early stage in the Featherstone colliery was, according to the Committee of Inquiry, one of the major causes of the disaster.[65] There was much criticism of the fact that, among 500 justices in the Riding, not one could be found before 8.00 p.m. It seemed to B. Coleridge in the Commons on 10 January 1894 that 'the Magistrate was the man who should be held responsible' and that the military should not be blamed.[66]

The major single issue, however, omitted from the Report of the Featherstone Inquiry was the extent to which the magistrates, in suppressing the disorders, were acting at the behest of the mine-owners. Throughout August, before the disturbances began, the South Wales bench had been demanding troops in the hope of intimidating the miners. Despite the complete absence of any disorder, 1,100 soldiers were dispatched and their officers then proceeded to consult directly with the Mineowners' Emergency Committee and to allow the President of the Coalowners' Association, James Williams, to accompany the commanding officer on his rounds of inspection.[67] Keir Hardie demanded to know:

> Why a civilian is allowed to accompany the staff on a visit of inspection . . . What benches of magistrates in South Wales have applied for military assistance . . . how many of these were directly or pecuniarily interested in the mines?[68]

However, not only had many requisitions gone directly to the War Office without the Home Secretary's knowledge, but also some of the coalowners had taken it upon themselves to send requisitions without even consulting with the local bench.[69] As the Mine Workers' Federation put it: 'We cannot help believing that the pressure of imported police and military in such large numbers acts as a forcible incentive to rioting and disorder.'[70]

Troops were called to the Frome Division of Somerset in mid-September 1893 without Home Office approval (Arnot 1949, p. 240), and also to East Denbighshire in October.[71] According to Arnot, 'the picture given almost resembles an armed occupation'. John Burns gave the following description:

> Under the present Magisterial system the administration of the law was practically in the hands of a body of men who, when a dispute took place and a riot was threatened, thought less of the interests of the community and the maintenance of law and order, than of using the soldiers and police for morally intimidating men who they, as masters, were fighting. (Cries of Oh! Oh!)[72]

The readiness of the justices to act in the interests of the mine-owners is well evidenced by a 'singular proclamation' made a few days after Featherstone and signed by Francis Darwin, the chairman of the West Riding Quarter Sessions, and calling on 'the peaceful inhabitants of the West Riding . . . to take no part whatever in any riotous assembly'.[73] The document then went on to recommend the mine-owners' negotiating position in terms identical to those used in a bulletin published on the same day by the joint secretaries of the Coalowners' Federation in Derby![74] Clearly the local benches were quite beyond the control of the Liberal government which nevertheless found itself taking the blame for their excesses. Cunninghame-Graham announced at an open air meeting in Bradford: 'The people should hurl from power any government . . . who dared to spill the blood of English citizens.'[75] An effigy of Asquith was carried to Trafalgar Square (Arnot 1949, p. 238) and the unfortunate Home Secretary complained that MPs had gone about denouncing him in a 'ridiculous fashion':

It would seem difficult and almost impossible to get the people of this country to understand what are the functions and responsibilities of the Executive Government with reference to local disturbances . . . the responsibility for the prevention and the suppression of local disorder lies where it has always lain from the earliest period of our history, with the Local Authority . . . I entirely disclaim . . . any authority . . .[76]

Although *The Times* scorned Asquith's attempt to dissociate himself,[77] the *Daily Chronicle* was more sympathetic:

Knowing as we do the composition of the magisterial benches of the country we recognise the difficulties which beset the Home Office in times like these. The shameless manner in which the South Wales coal-owners manipulated the forces of the Crown to suit their own convenience will be fresh in the recollection of many of our readers.[78]

On 13 September a Coroner's jury deliberating on the two victims of Featherstone produced what a Tory described as one of their typically 'erratic and chaotic and frequently ridiculous verdicts'[79] which implicated the magistrates, barely shrinking, as Asquith put it, from recording a verdict of wilful murder against them and the troops.[80] Within a week, an Inquiry had been announced. This, however, did little to deflect criticisms of the Conservative domination of the benches[81] and calls for an elective magistracy.[82]

When the magistrates themselves came to deal with those arrested in the disorders, little mercy could be expected. The Barnsley (Staincross) bench, for example, committed 19 men for trial for riot and one for assault on police, imprisoned six more and fined two. Only three cases were dismissed out of the 31, and only eight of the men committed were bailed. The whole process was completed with great rapidity[83] and with scant attention being paid to the alibi evidence tendered by the defence. When halting the trials at the assizes, Mr Justice Williams reprimanded the magistrates for refusing to hear defence evidence:

He did not know the whole of the circumstances and would not therefore criticise the actions of the magistrates but he would remark that generally speaking it was very desirable that witnesses for the defence should be heard when the case was before the police court.[84]

The magistrates also attracted the attention of the Home Secretary for refusing to bind over defence witnesses in order to deny them their costs of attendance at the assizes.[85] The Dewsbury bench imprisoned 19 out of 24 appearing before them, but the firmest line was taken by the Rotherham bench, which committed 21 out of 23 defendants charged with riot. At the West Yorkshire assizes, most of the cases collapsed or were withdrawn, and only six were convicted of riot or unlawful assembly (Table 5.3).

Table 5.3 Defendants arrested in West Riding miners' strike riots, July–September 1893

(a) Magistrates' courts proceedings

Offence	Prison	Fines	Discharged	Withdrawn	Committed	Total
Begging	–	–	–	6	–	6
Obstructing footpath	–	–	–	6	–	6
Throwing stones	–	1	–	–	–	1
Wilful damage	1	–	–	–	–	1
Assault	–	1	–	–	–	1
Assault PC	31	5	4	–	2	42
Conspiracy	–	–	–	15	–	15
Rioting	–	–	4	–	39	43
Total	32	7	8	27	41	115

(b) West Yorkshire assizes: 11–15 December 1893

	Total	Acquitted	No evidence offered	Plea to unlawful assembly	Convicted of riot	Total imprisoned
Hoyland Nether riot	20	3	8	9	–	–
Wathmain riot	21	6	6	3	6	9
Total	41	9	14	12	6	9

Source: PP 1893, xvii, Appendix 1.

The policy of high charging by the police and automatic committal by the bench caused severe problems at assize. Well over half the cases were abandoned or thrown out. By this time, however, a 'truce' had been concluded between the mine-owners and the pitmen, and, according to the judge, 'excitement had a good deal abated' and it was hoped that the proceedings would 'tend to peace between master and man'.[86]

The Liberal government had clearly been shocked at the extent to which the Tory benches could act independently and dictate to the War Office. The magistrates had a natural preference for the cheaper expedient in disorder of calling in the troops,[87] and the Featherstone Inquiry took the revolutionary line that the only way to bring the magistrates under control would be to integrate them further with the military agencies of the central state. Individual capitalists could no longer be permitted direct authority over the forces of the Crown and some radical change was needed: 'Indeed when matters are so grave as to render military intervention probably necessary there should be the most complete organisation of justices and the [military][88] power.'[89] Although the magistrates lost their right of direct requisition after Featherstone, more radical changes had to await the outbreak of the serious disorders of the Edwardian period.

Tonypandy 1910

The connection between these developments and the new forms of capital accumulation which were being created at the time, is nowhere more evident than at Tonypandy. The so-called 'Klondyke era' (Thomas 1930; Boynes and Baber 1980, pp. 342–3) in South Wales had seen a massive expansion of coalmining, particularly in the steam-coal areas of Mid and South Glamorgan. Under the pressures of maritime imperial expansion the region's coal output trebled from 11.7 million tons in 1876 to 38 million tons in 1913 (Williams 1980, p. 182). Glamorgan coal was unsuitable for domestic use and the major part of the production went to the naval and merchant fleets and for export. 'Supply me with Welsh steam coal or I cannot be answerable for the safety of the fleet', demanded Admiral Napier (Morgan 1918, p. 136) and in 1880 the Admiralty ruled that only Welsh steam-coal should go into naval bunkers (Williams 1980, p. 183). As Smith (1980, pp. 160–1) points out, the hyper-expansion of Glamorgan mining was a product of imperialism and therefore acutely vulnerable to fluctuations in imperial development. Moreover, the steam-coal beds were deep and difficult to mine. Falling profits, coupled with the restriction of working hours achieved under the Eight Hours Act 1908 and growing union solidarity (Arnot 1967; Morgan 1973; McLean 1975; Holton 1976) produced a series of crises in the Edwardian period. The response of the South Wales coal-owners was the creation of 'super-combines' by the amalgamation of capitals from various mining interests around the UK into units of nationally centred capital.

This new breed of capital enterprise is well exemplified by the Cambrian Colliery, 'the most outstanding example of the concentration of the coal industry at this time' (Williams 1980, p. 193). Cambrian Collieries was formed in 1895 with a share capital of £600,000 by the industrialist D.A. Thomas (Morgan 1918, p. 137). Frustrated in his efforts to obtain office in the 1906 Liberal ministry, Thomas set about assembling a massive collection of colliery interests. He acquired the Glamorgan Colliery in 1907, the Naval Colliery in 1908 and the Britannic Merthyr Company in 1910 (Arnot 1967, p. 223). Even before Thomas's intervention, 80 per cent of the output of steam-coal was produced by only 20 companies (Williams 1980, p. 194), but his own combine in 1913 was capitalized at

£18 million, produced 18 million tons of coal annually and employed between 50,000 and 60,000 men.

The levels of exploitation and the safety record of the deep steam-coal pits were appalling. Secondary exploitation by the shopkeepers and traders of the Rhondda valley was also to play a part in the disturbances.

The events of November 1910 arose out of a long-standing dispute over piece-rates for the 'Five Foot' or 'Bute' seam at the Naval Colliery Penygraig. On 1 August 1910, 900 men (most of whom were not involved in the dispute) were locked out of the Ely pit (Arnot 1967, pp. 174–231; Morgan 1981, pp. 146–8; Geary 1985, pp. 25–6). It was widely felt that this move was to be a prelude to the establishment of similarly reduced piece-rates throughout the Cambrian Combine and the Committee of the Naval Lodge argued: 'it is a fact of infinite moment that the Ely pit should at this moment be made the cock-pit – the centre of this despotic attempt to force upon us a starvation price list' (quoted in Arnot 1967, p. 177). After a number of inconclusive ballots and against the wishes of the union executive, a strike broke out throughout the Cambrian Combine area and spread to the Aberdare valley. Eventually at least 30,000 miners had withdrawn their labour (Arnot 1967, pp. 174–83; Morgan 1981, pp. 146–7).

The miners formed a Cambrian Combine Committee (CCC) which was influenced by the radical syndicalism which was to provide the basis for *The Miners' Next Step* (Holton 1976). The owners had clearly been expecting a showdown and Thomas enjoyed the support of the Monmouthshire and South Wales Coal Owners' Association (MSWCOA) which adopted a scheme to provide collective indemnity to those members involved in the strikes (Arnot 1967, pp. 180). Blackleg labour was imported and the colliery managers and those outside the Mine Workers' Federation were used to keep pumping machines working. Trains carrying the blackleg labour were intercepted (Holton 1976, p. 81) and the stoppage was to extend to the pumping and ventilating machinery in the pits.

It is important that the nature of the relationship between the coal-owners and the 'civil authority' is made clear. Thomas and his manager, Leonard Llewellyn, for example, were not themselves magistrates but often attended meetings.[90] The MSWCOA met on 4 November in Cardiff and resolved to call on the chief constable of Glamorgan, Captain Lindsay, for efficient police protection. Throughout the disturbances both the MSWCOA and individual managers and owners saw fit to communicate directly with the chief constable, the military authorities and the Home Office without the mediation of a magistrate.

On 2 November the clerk to the Merthyr justices wrote to the War Office asking to know the cost of military assistance.[91] A good proportion of the local county police force of 1,400 had been drafted into the Aberdare and Rhondda valleys by the night of Sunday 6 November, together with 143 officers from neighbouring forces (Arnot 1967, p. 183).

The course of the disturbances is well documented (see for example, Evans 1911; Arnot 1967, pp. 190–4; Fox 1973; Geary 1985, pp. 25–8; Morgan 1987, pp. 44–8, 154–64) and has achieved the quality of myth. By 7 November picketing of most of the pits in the Cambrian Combine had been successful in stopping pumping work, but the police and mine-owners were clearly determined to stage a confrontation at the Llwynypia pit of the Glamorgan Colliery outside Tonypandy. Here Lindsay concentrated his force of 120 police, including 18 mounted men from Bristol, and set up his headquarters with Llewellyn, the manager. It was, as Arnot (1967, p. 185) puts it, 'a fortress against trade union action'.

Throughout the evening of Monday 7 November the Llwynypia pit was surrounded and stoned by a large crowd which was driven back by police baton charges. Sporadic fighting continued overnight until 2.00 a.m. However, in the early hours, Lindsay decided that the situation had deteriorated sufficiently to justify him seeking the assistance already authorized by the magistrates. At 1.00 a.m., and without informing the Home Office, he cabled directly to Salisbury for troops (Arnot 1967, pp. 186–90; Fox 1973, p. 72). The first direct intimation which the Home Secretary, Winston Churchill, had of this crucial development was an alarming wire received from Lindsay at 10.00 a.m. informing him that the position was grave and that he was expecting two companies of infantry and 200 cavalry.[92]

Churchill, doubtless annoyed at being sidelined in this manner, hur-riedly convened a conference with the Secretary of War, Lord Haldane, and the Adjutant-General at the Home Office. His position was clear. There was to be no repeat of Featherstone. Similar bloodshed in the Liberal stronghold of South Wales in the approach to a general election could have disastrous consequences. Within an hour of receiving Lindsay's telegram, Churchill had taken the decision to intercept the troops *en route* for the Rhondda (Churchill 1967, p. 1206; Fox 1973). By noon, Major-General Neville Macready, a staff officer from the War Office, had been summoned to the Home Office:

> It appeared that Mr. Churchill was anxious to send at once a special officer, to whom he could give personal directions, to command the troops which were being despatched. The first intention was to send an officer from Salisbury, but as Mr. Churchill wished to see him there would necessarily be delay.
>
> (Macready 1924, p. 137)

Churchill cabled Lindsay at 1.30 p.m.:

> Your request for military. Infantry should not be used until all other means have failed.[93]

He arranged for the troop movements to be halted and the forces to be held in reserve outside the disturbed areas. He then authorized 300 officers of the metropolitan police (100 of them mounted) to proceed by special train to Pontypridd, to arrive (it was hoped) at 8.00 p.m. (Macready 1924, pp. 138–9; Churchill 1967, p. 1206). Macready was to leave for Pontypridd right away.

By interrupting relations between the civil authority and the military, Churchill was flouting both law and convention and asserting the right of the central state to intervene to break up local circuits of power in a manner which was not contemplated in the careful consideration of the problem by the Select Committee two years earlier.[94]

That afternoon a large crowd assembled on the athletic ground and heard Churchill's appeal read by the stipendiary magistrate. 'Trusting in their good sense', he demanded that 'rioting must cease at once . . . We are holding back the soldiers for the present.'[95] After hearing the appeal, a body of between 7,000 and 9,000 strikers marched in an orderly procession to Llwynypia where the power-house was again stoned.

Before serious fighting began, however, Lindsay held a hurried conference with two strike leaders. He then ordered his 18 mounted officers to charge the crowd and shortly a pitched battle developed between police armed with batons and strikers armed with stones and staves (Arnot 1967, p. 193). Serious fighting lasted for two hours from 5.00 p.m., while Llewellyn and his managers worked the pumps.

There was no attempt to enter the colliery, which could easily have been overwhelmed,[96] and the 'attack' seems to have been confined to throwing stones and the tearing down of a fence. Claims by Evans (1911) and Churchill (1967, p. 1207) that the strikers were driven back by the heroic band from the colliery and then sacked the town by way of vengeance are contested by Arnot (1967, pp. 191–3). What is clear is that the concentration of police resources by Lindsay at the colliery left the town totally unpoliced. Rumours of the imminent arrival of troops at 8.00 p.m. sent parts of the crowd surging back through the streets to the railway station. There seems to have been some more systematic looting in Dunraven Street and Tonypandy Square, and the drapers shop of the senior magistrate T.P. Jenkins, who had already been involved in legal action against the strikers, was the first to be attacked (Holton 1976, p. 82). Shopkeepers boarded up their premises but these defences were torn down and between 8.00 and 10.00 p.m., when the disorder ceased, many small businesses were ransacked (Smith 1980, pp. 164–7). Only five constables were available to patrol the streets and not until later did Lindsay send help: 'Less than a dozen additional police were sent down by the Chief Constable from his fortress in Llwynypia Colliery and these made various charges and cleared the streets' (Arnot 1967, p. 193).

As the situation deteriorated yet further on Tuesday evening and following consultation by telephone with Macready and Lindsay, Churchill sent an additional 200 officers of the metropolitan police[97] on the train leaving London later that night at 3.00 a.m. A further contingent of 300 metropolitans were sent at about 4.25 p.m. on the same day,[98] bringing the total force of police in the Rhondda area up to 1,400, of whom 120 were mounted. None of the metropolitans arrived in time to assist Lindsay on Tuesday night.

Whereas the metropolitan police officers were sent directly into the disturbed areas, the movement of military reinforcements was a catalogue of indecision. Two companies of the 18th Hussars, 100 men of the Loyal North Lancashire Regiment and 100 Lancashire Fusiliers left Tidworth at 7.00 a.m. on Tuesday, having already been delayed by the War Office from their original departure time of 3.00 a.m. They were halted soon afterwards at Marlborough and orders were received for them to detrain at Swindon. However, at noon, while Churchill was meeting Macready, the cavalry were ordered back on the train for Pontypridd. Following a further conversation with Lindsay, and while Macready was himself *en route* for South Wales, Churchill decided once again to halt the cavalry, this time at Cardiff.[99]

Macready (1924, p. 138) was clearly angered by this further change of plan which effectively deprived him of any command in the disturbed areas: 'while I was in the train, Mr. Churchill, misled apparently by some information that had reached him, sent instructions that the cavalry should detrain at Cardiff, an unfortunate decision under the circumstances'. The cavalry was to remain in Cardiff pending 'further developments' (Churchill 1967, p. 1206) and a further requisition from Lindsay.[100]

In the meantime, as we have seen, rumours of the imminent arrival of the military in the Rhondda had provoked fresh disorders. Without waiting for instructions from the police, 'who struck me as being unduly perturbed by the reports that were coming in from Tonypandy' (Macready 1924, p. 138), Macready ordered one company (50 men) of the unfortunate 18th Hussars back onto the train and up to Pontypridd where they arrived in the pouring rain shortly before midnight (1924, p. 139). The first detachments of metropolitans, delayed by the train schedules, had arrived there some three hours earlier, likewise too late to participate in the disturbances in Tonypandy. Churchill's intervention had merely served to postpone the arrival of the Hussars by 12 hours and the substituted metropolitans were unable to provide any assistance whatsoever in the interim.

The MSWCOA was furious and the Secretary wrote to Churchill:

I have been instructed by the members of the Association to very strongly protest against the delay which occurred in the sending of the troops into the district in the first instance and to say that the owners attribute the serious rioting which has occurred both in the Rhondda and Aberdare valleys to the lack of a sufficiently protective force.[101]

Lindsay, whose original dispositions were regarded by *The Times* as 'amply vindicated',[102] more tactfully reminded the Home Secretary of 'our bad luck' on Tuesday night.[103]

What, then, was the outcome of this débâcle in terms of the relations between the police and the army? Lindsay, with considerable support from the local magistracy, the MSWCOA and the Tory press, seems nevertheless to have suffered an almost complete eclipse of authority.

Despite the radical nature of his intervention, Churchill was at first loath to remove Lindsay entirely from his central position. On the night of 8 November he cautioned Macready continuously to act only 'if the chief constable or local authority desires it'.[104] However, after the disaster on Tuesday night, Churchill cabled Macready telling him that he might assume 'general control' if his assistance was sought by the civil authorities.[105] Macready (1924, p. 139) was delighted:

> although Mr Churchill could not refrain from telling me where I ought to sleep on the night of the 9th, he gave me authority to exercise control over both police and military in the event of the military being called upon to participate actively in quelling disorder. The position during the previous forty-eight hours had been difficult and unsatisfactory, as must always be the case when operations of whatever kind are directed by a dual control.

This was a momentous shift in power relations (Evelegh 1978, p. 16; Morgan 1987, p. 164). Whereas the troops and police had originally been sent 'to carry out the instructions of the chief constable',[106] the entire force now fell under the command of a military officer. Macready (1924, p. 138) clearly had little regard for Lindsay whom he found 'to be too much under the influence of the mineowners'.

Macready and the military were in complete control,[107] sending in daily reports to the Home Office and channelling instructions to the police.[108] As Fox (1973, p. 76) put it, this was 'an unprecedented unity of command under a professional soldier with experience of martial law in Egypt and South Africa'.

The Home Office itself, according to Macready (1924, p. 139), was being 'bombarded by every sort of civil authority and employer in South Wales'. Moylan, the Home Office's confidential agent, complained that: 'The presence of such a large force of police and military here has undoubtably given Colliery Managers the impression that they can obtain unlimited supplies of men on any pretext.'[109] Percy Jacob, the manager of the Cynon colliery, complained of insubordination by the metropolitan police, adding: 'these men were now sworn constables for Glamorganshire and that I had made a special requisition for their services and that they were employees of mine as long as I wished'.[110] The view that the police were the servants and employees of the mineowners (whether or not they were magistrates) was common in the MSWCOA. Macready noted that police were drafted from one pit to another 'by kind permission' of the mine manager and the local police deferred to the mineowners in all matters: 'This curious misconception of duty probably originates from the fact that the mineowners pay for the extra police who are employed on the collieries and in normal times are at their beck and call.'[111] He had been at pains to interrupt this circuit of local class deference, pointing out repeatedly that the 'decision and responsibility for the distribution both of police and military rested with him' and not with the mine-owners (Macready 1924, p. 144).

The Home Office responded to Percy's complaint by asserting that 'the Secretary of State will support the Officers in command in refusing to be influenced by managers or owners who may share the manager's misapprehension as to his position and powers'.[112]

Powell Duffryn Collieries, through their solicitors, not unreasonably demanded to know why the collieries were paying for the upkeep of the metropolitan police officers when the magistrates and chief constable had requisitioned troops only, which would, of course, have been provided free by the War Office. They complained:

> and inasmuch as no provision for the housing and feeding of the men and their mounts had been made, our clients, the Powell Duffryn Steam Coal Company Ltd., undertook the housing and feeding of them at great expense to themselves.[113]

Who was to pay for Churchill's radical intervention? In his first cable to Lindsay he had said that 'The County will bear the cost'[114] but admitted later that this was only an 'assumption'.[115] Despite an abortive attempt to introduce legislation to permit the Home Secretary to send police around the country at the expense of the receiving local authorities but without their consent or requisition, the Home Office was obliged to foot the bill (Morgan 1987, pp. 48–9).

By this period, after two weeks of disturbances, three pitched battles, numerous casualties and extensive damage to property, no arrests had been made whatsoever. This clearly testifies to the military rather than policing priorities adopted by Macready.

In the disorders of 21 November three arrests were made, but the police concluded that it was 'quite unsafe to make any more'[116] for fear of rescue.[117] No proceedings were successful against any of them and the Tory press were incensed.

The next day Churchill telegraphed to Macready:

> Arrest and prosecution should follow in all cases where evidence is forthcoming against law-breakers . . . there must be a regular process

of bringing offenders, particularly rioters and thieves, to justice. Please impart this to the Chief Constable.[118]

It is difficult to escape the conclusion that the subsequent events at the Britannic Colliery at Gilfach on 29 November were a direct response to this directive. Macready agreed to the reopening of the Gilfach pit and troops and police were concentrated on the area.[119] A manager, Mr Gould, was assaulted by a group of strikers and, although he was un-aware (until the next day)[120] of having suffered any injuries whatsoever, he was persuaded by Lindsay to swear out informations against ten strikers he knew by name.[121]

Summonses under the Conspiracy and Protection of Property Act 1875 were eventually issued against 13 men and the cases (which were prose-cuted by the Solicitor for Powell Duffryn Collieries, Mr Kenshole, were heard at Pontypridd police court on 14–20 December 1910.

The defendants, wearing their summonses in their hats, were accom-panied to court by a procession of 10,000 strikers with bands playing.[122] With 'various itineraries', commented *The Times*, 'these processions have continued through each day of the hearing . . . suggestive of lawless intent'.[123] The men would call out ' "Shall our comrades go to chokey?" – "No!" comes the thunder of a hundred voices.'[124]

The Stipendiary, Mr Lleufar Thomas, was due to give judgement and sentence on 20 December. The town was boarded up in preparation and Macready drafted large numbers of extra troops into the area to prevent a rescue (Macready 1924, p. 153).

Summonses were dismissed against most of the accused but two men were convicted and sentenced to six months' imprisonment each. They were spirited away by motor car to Cardiff prison before news was relayed to the crowd. The Home Office disapproved strongly of such leniency (Morgan 1987, p. 161). Although there were a number of further prosecutions (including William John and John Hopla, leading figures in the CCC, who received eight months each) there was no further attempt at mass arrest.

The events of November 1910 provide clear evidence of a considerable shift in the relations both between police and army and between the local and central state. The super-combine of Cambrian Collieries spread itself across a number of petty sessional boundaries[125] and its significance as a national amalgamation of capital and as an imperial pressure point, took responsibility for its security out of the hands of the local authorities. The army, with its national organization, close links with the central state and degree of distance from the local state, was a more appropriate agency than either police or magistracy, and it was the army, in the teeth of bitter local resistance, which assumed overall control.

The 'Macready System' for 'holding the valleys', as the Home Office put it,[126] required the military to act as a *cordon sanitaire*, keeping to the high ground, out of sight, thus avoiding confrontation while at the same time defining the area of conflict (Fox 1973, pp. 76–7). It was the police that attacked the crowd with their batons. Nowhere was the Riot Act read, nowhere was ball cartridge loaded. As the special correspondent of *The Times* put it:

> The troops have in the past been dumped down upon the threatened property, and the officers have become the guests of the owners. In the present case, the troops – and there are not many of them – two squadrons of cavalry and six companies of infantry – are held as a reserve for the police, and it is clearly explained that their presence is not to do police duty but to preserve order and property if the police are unable to cope with any situation that might arise.[127]

Macready managed his police and military forces like a field commander, calling up reinforcements to meet threats and maintaining a strategic reserve of fresh troops and police. A magistrate was in continual attendance at the Glamorgan Colliery.[128]

It is interesting to note that the suppression of the disorders was essentially a policing operation but was carried out under military direction and with military objectives. It was as if the local police structures were being co-opted and reorganized to permit a temporary flow of authority from the central state via the army.

The radically different systems of repression evident in the three incidents examined in this chapter, separated by only 23 years, demonstrates again the extent to which variations in the relations between the agencies can occur over a comparatively short period and across a fairly narrow geographical territory. Clearly the regional context is important in power relations, but in order to comprehend more fully the shifts in emphasis evident in these studies we must return to a consideration of the individual perspectives adopted by the two remaining agencies.

6   The army

Domination by the justices

The incidents described in the foregoing chapters demonstrate the extent to which the magistracy had come to depend for its authority upon the material forces deployed by the army and the police. The justices' longest-standing relationship was that with the military, an agency which, in contrast to the others, has always enjoyed a national organization and structure. Hayter (1978, p. 57) has argued that the crucial role of the army in suppressing disorder had, by the eighteenth century, established the Secretary at War as 'a sort of police chief or minister of the interior', but this picture is too simply drawn. Several factors served to link the military to local centres of power in a way which effectively neutralized its action and independence.

There was, for example (in mainland Britain at least) no notion of *Notrecht* or military rule until at least the early part of the twentieth century (Clode 1869, pp. 163–7; Brewer 1989, p. 48). 'There is no such Thing', insisted Gould J. at the trial of the magistrate Gillam in 1768 (quoted in Clode 1869, p. 630). Thus while the proclamation of martial law was a regular feature of colonial practice throughout the nineteenth century (see Townsend 1982, pp. 167–8), the solid resistance of both the Lockian Whigs and the Tory squirearchy to the cost and imposition of a standing army (Howard 1957, p. 14; Thompson 1963, p. 88) ensured that such concepts were for export only.

Accordingly, the military were unable to operate within England and

Wales unless accompanied by a representative of the civil power – in effect, a magistrate. Reith (1943, p. 9) has maintained that the military in civil disorder 'are no longer soldiers but instruments of law functioning in accordance with police principles'. However, the ideology of law has never been strong in the army. The military code, according to Sir Charles Napier (1837, p. 38) 'ought to be wholly unconnected with the ordinary courts of justice . . . The more we become lawyers, the less we are soldiers.' Arrest procedures and offence categories are clearly irrelevant to a force which represents the immediate deterrent violence of the state. Thus, in periods when the army has been involved in the repression of disorder, there has been relatively little work for the courts.

What, exactly, were the relations of the army with the justices of the peace? The direct, personal authority of the magistracy over the troops appears to have been established shortly after the passage of the Riot Act (Clode 1869, pp. 131–3). Clode (1869, p. 151) insists that 'if the Magistrate be present, the Military Officer must act under his orders'. In April 1768 Lord Weymouth wrote that a military force could never be employed 'to a more constitutional purpose than in support of the authority and dignity of Magistracy'.[1] Standing orders to this effect had been issued in 1766 (Clode 1869, p. 134) and this restoration of local magisterial authority in the eighteenth century seems to have been based on Lord Mansfield's doctrine of the soldier as citizen (Whelan 1985, p. 268). The authority of the magistrates was twofold: first they could requisition troops to put down disorder; and second, they had personal command of the troops when they arrived.

The conflict of authority over requisitions was to prove disastrous for the army. Until 1855, the sanction of a central state official was required for all domestic troop movements. The elaborate 'quadrilateral' chain of command which apportioned strategic control between local and central states therefore acted as a severe inhibition upon the use of the military as a conduit of state power. According to procedures current before 1855, a request for troops by the local justices was transmitted to the Secretary at War, who would then issue troop movement orders to the nearest available units.[2] Needless to say, this process was slow and the size of contingents was therefore rarely appropriate to the disorders in question.

The local interests of the justices constantly frustrated efforts by the military to concert their forces. As General Sir Charles Napier put it: 'The Bradford Justice of the Peace would willingly see Manchester, Leeds and Newcastle given to the flames provided his own city had a soldier billeted in every attic' (Butler 1894, p. 89). Despite his wider, regional responsibilities, he did not 'dare' to refuse their requests (Napier 1857, p. 53). Fifty years later the position was still the same and General Wilkinson was reprimanded by the War Office: 'It must distinctly understood that the Mayor is responsible for the maintenance of order in the Borough, and his demands therefore must be complied with, notwithstanding any contrary opinions held by you.'[3]

In many ways, Wilkinson was in a worse position than Napier, since after 1855 requisitions had become largely a local matter between magistrate and the District General Officer Commanding without any central state intervention. In 1898, the Home Secretary insisted: 'the sanction of the Home Office is not required in these cases. I do not say we do not hear of it, but the application is not made to the Home Office.'[4] This point was reinforced by the fact that the authority of the justices of the peace was strictly personal. Until the close of the nineteenth century, the magistrate had operational command (subject to military law) as if he were a military officer himself. In his absence, the troops were sometimes unable to act. During the Gordon riots in 1780, requisitioned military units were abandoned by the fleeing magistrates and 'exposed to the fury of the populace' (Clode 1869, p. 636) without being able to respond. Napier (1837, p. 46) recalled a conversation at Burdett's riots in which an officer asked how he was to disperse the rioters when the magistrate had forbidden him to fire or to charge. The magistrate replied: 'Oh, that is your business not mine. Do it as you like, only you must not fire or use your bayonets.'

The precise relationship between the commanding officer and the justices, despite frequent appeals for advice from the law officers (Radzinowicz 1968, pp. 178ff.) was imprecise in the extreme. Criminal liability for murder could arise in respect of lethal military actions against crowds and Carlyle (1888, p. 209) complained that 'any governor, commanded soldier or official person, putting down the frightfullest Mob insurrection . . . shall do it with the rope around *his* neck by way of encouragement to him'. Thus the quasi-dependent relations of the military with the magistrates as representatives of local capital fatally injured its ability to take energetic action. Major Beckwith in 1832 recounted a typical incident:

> I requested that one or two of the magistrates would accompany me on horseback and I promised presently to restore order. They all refused; one stated that it would make him unpopular – another that it would cause his shipping to be disrupted – another his property; in short they all refused, they also informed me that none of them knew how to ride on horseback except one gentleman, and they pointed to H . . . H . . . said that he had not been on horseback for 18 years and he remarked that he would hold anybody responsible who said a second time that he could ride.[5]
>
> (Anon. 1833, p. 185)

In these circumstances it is scarcely surprising that relations between the military establishment and the justices, despite the congruity of class interests (see below) were at best strained and at worst openly hostile

(Hayter 1978, pp. 16, 58 and 129). General Sir Charles Napier, in his correspondence of the Chartist period, gave vent to considerable anger against 'our little master-generals called magistrates' (Napier 1857, p. 45). He went on: 'I shall be defeated by the magistrates, they are so powerful, but the safety of the country is at stake and I will do my utmost' (1857, p. 63).

In many senses then, the military, in suspension between the magistracy and central state, and neutralized by impossible rules of engagement and weaponry, was caught in a vacuum of power. When their aid was sought, therefore, they showed themselves to be mishandled and undertrained and they complained frequently of their 'extreme dislike of the obligation to discharge this most disagreeable and painful duty'.[6]

Their difficulties were compounded by the lack of an independent command structure. From 1660 to 1855 the British army (that is, the Guards and the Horse and Foot Regiments) was administered by a largely civilian establishment known as the Horse Guards, which comprised the Secretary at War, the Adjutant-General, the Quartermaster-General and a civilian staff. It was only after the Crimea that the War Office was established (Hamer 1970, p. 5) but this was still under the domination of civilians. Therefore, the military, after the eighteenth century, had little autonomous existence (Brewer 1989, p. 45). Indeed, its subordination to the justices while on active service in Britain represented a crucial political principle. Even within the organization itself there was little continuity. According to Hamer (1970, p. 21), different regiments 'were as far removed from one another as Swift's Lilliput and Brobdingnag'.

Harries-Jenkins (1977, p. 3), discussing the social composition of the home military establishment, has stressed the critical failure of the Victorian army to construct an officer cadre on the continental model:

> On the continent, armed forces were already becoming a world in themselves, characterized by a separate profession, closed organization, their own value-system and norms, a special technology and their own system of law. In short, these were the armies of an industrialized society . . . in contrast, the Queen's army was a heterogeneous collection of regiments and corps, each of which sought to maintain its own identity. They were linked not by any universally accepted code of military values, but by the civilian interests of their members. A common acceptance of the standards and norms of the English ruling class . . .

He argues persuasively that the inability to establish in Britain 'a preponderance of the military in the state' (1977, p. 7) resulted from the disorganization occasioned by imperial commitments which dispersed troops around the globe and ensured that the home establishment comprised only a tiny and scattered network of untrained recruits incapable of 'para-military operations'. It was only in the years after the Napoleonic wars (Barnett 1970, p. 278) and the First World War that substantial forces were available in the UK. In 1840, at the height of the Chartist agitation, the army had a total of 103 battalions on strength, of which 59 were stationed in the colonies, 22 in India and only 22 in the British Isles (the great majority in Ireland) (Harries-Jenkins 1977, p. 203).

The fact that senior army officers belonged to the same class of landed gentry which supplied the magistracy ensured permanent influence in the local state, but not through the military connection. Although the lord lieutenancies and chief constableships had become the natural preroga-tives of the officer corps (1977, pp. 252–7) and we find military magis-trates and military chief constables involved at Featherstone, Trafalgar Square and Tonypandy, such powers as they exercised were derived from their civil offices and not from any professional military establish-ment. The year 1895, according to Harries-Jenkins (1977, pp. 258–73), saw the low point of military influence.

Otley (1968) points out that nearly 40 per cent of all generals in this period were the sons of great landowners. The army was 'the last bastion of the old neo-feudal order and . . . it successfully resisted the encroachments of the new business and industrial élite longer than most other institutions' (1968, p. 91). Mosca (1939, p. 233) and Hamer (1970, p. 14) have also noted the interconnection between the military hierarchy and the county elites. It is clear that the class composition of the officer corps remained stable until 1855 (Hamer 1970, pp. 15–22) and it was only after 1870 that the landed interest began to lose its dominance (Otley 1968, p. 91; Van Doorn 1975, p. 36). Indeed the fact that the army, in its civil role, remained until 1910 in a state of dependence with regard to the magistrates, is in sharp contrast to the freedom and authority it had by then established in suppressing disor-der elsewhere in the Empire. The controlling role of the military in colonial administration which necessarily attended its prominence in maintaining social order in the colonies cannot have gone unremarked.

The corporate independence of the army 1902–26

Britain experienced its military revolution much later than other Euro-pean powers. The abolition of the purchase of commissions and the local-ization of regimental structure in the second half of the nineteenth century had opened the way for more sweeping changes but these were not completed until the Edwardian period. The Haldane reforms, which were accomplished by 1909, abolished the figurehead commander-in-chief and created a General Staff which was able to negotiate directly at the level of the central state. Correlli Barnett has described the impact of the post-Haldane reorganization of the period following the Boer War upon a military elite which, until then, had preserved a 'neo-feudalist attitude to senior responsibility' and 'pre-industrial techniques of organisation' (1967, p. 30). Blake has similarly demonstrated the decisive severance of relations between the military and the 'landowning aristocracy which governed the country' (1957, p. 27).

We note in this period the inauguration of officer training schemes, and the drafting of fresh organizational and disciplinary codes. Indeed, the rapidly accomplished professionalization from 1902 provided the platform upon which the massive expansion of 1914–18 took place (Blake 1979, pp. 64–7). The significance of these changes may be observed at two levels.

First, during this period we see the decisive intervention of the military at the level of central state administration and policy. With recent experience of the exercise of extensive powers under the martial law regulations in Egypt and South Africa, it was inevitable that the new military elite – Kitchener, Macready, Wilson, Haig and others – should seek greater influence at home. According to Howard (1957, p. 19), the army in the Edwardian period underwent an enormous lateral expansion

> leaving virtually no aspect of national life in which the military leaders might not be legitimately concerned. No longer was the soldier simply the hero to whom a people turned to lead it in battle; he was now a technical adviser whose views had constantly to be given weight in almost every branch of policy, internal as well as external.

Similarly Blake (1979) has described the military penetration of the central state which took place during the 'Macready Era', 1910–26, under the impact of civil disorder. Both the mutiny at the Curragh in 1914 (Ryan 1956) and the conflict between the service chiefs and Lloyd George (Blake 1957; Taylor 1965, p. 76; Blake 1979, p. 140) had a profound effect upon imperial policy and snapped the relations of dependency between the military and the central state (Hamer 1970, pp. 257–8; Jeffrey 1985, pp. 58–62).[7] The dominance of military officers in the 'super-cabinet'[8] during the First World War was reproduced in a succession of similar bodies[9] which delegated 'local authority' power to regional military commanders during the periods of 'emergency' between 1919 and 1926.

Whelan (1981, p. 173) has described the opaque mass of 'emergency legislation', at its most extensive in the Emergency Powers Act 1920 which operated in tandem with the residual powers of the Royal Prerogative: 'In fact, the nature of this law, through its somewhat tangled web, allows almost total discretion to the government . . . the law enables any government to use troops in any dispute without effective legal or parliamentary controls.' Both the 1920 Act and the wartime legislation are marked by the professional imprint of a powerful state agency capable of shaping juridical forms.

The second feature of this period was the final appropriation of supreme power in civil disorder which had hitherto been wielded by representatives of local capital – the magistrates. It is of great significance that this appropriation was carried out in the first instance not by the police, but by the military.

Churchill's intervention in 1910 at Tonypandy overturned completely the existing structure of riot control and deprived the magistrates of their traditional authority over police and military forces. His actions were clearly illegal (Carver 1983, p. 7) and well beyond the limits of central state action as defined by Asquith in 1893 (see above). Macready (1924, p. 140) explained the reason for the change as follows:

> On previous occasions when troops have been employed in aid of civil power . . . the responsible officer [accepted] without question the construction placed on the situation by employers and magistrates . . . Furthermore on these occasions troops were often housed and entertained by those on whose demand they had been called in, a fact which produced an impression among the workers that the soldiers were merely the blind agents of the employer class.

The year 1910, therefore, marks the beginning of a radical new system of non-magisterial command in provincial disorder. The change was 'far more significant', according to Fox (1974, p. 300), than any other development in riot law and it enabled Macready to develop a 'hitherto untried policy' (Macready 1924, p. 152) of repression based on the co-ordinated action of police and military,[10] strategic deployment of force on a national scale and the use of advanced intelligence and propaganda services (Blake 1979, pp. 130–6). Macready's system was made operational at a national level during the Triple Alliance strike of 1911.

The growing involvement of the military in industrial disputes after 1910 has been well charted by Blake (1979), Whelan (1981), Geary (1985) and Morgan (1987). Troops operating the Macready system and equipped with tanks were used with devastating effect to break the police strike in Liverpool in August 1919, and in 1921 60,000 army reservists were called up to police industrial areas. Despite the obvious distaste of the local authorities (Desmarais 1971, p. 125), who in many cases refused to co-operate, the Territorial Army was reconstituted in an anti-strike role, first under the guise of a 'volunteer defence force' and then as a 'civil constabulary reserve' (Jeffery 1985, pp. 55–7) in 1926. From 1910, therefore, we see the troops employed not as a last resort but as 'an immediate response to disorder' (Geary 1985, p. 47) and in a position of dominance with regard to the police.

Why was it the military rather than the police which should first appropriate the power of the justices? One explanation is that the corporate structure of the army (under relentless pressure from the central state during the imperialist era (Jeffery 1984, pp. 9–10)) had been developed to a far greater extent than that of the police at this time. As Van Doorn (1975, p. 38) points out, the shift from 'hereditary aristocratic continuity' to 'professional continuity' in the army was achieved through the direct intervention of the central state. Another explanation is that the military was the only agency which by 1910 had achieved an organizational structure and jurisdiction serviceable to nationally centred forms of capital. In short, the rapid creation of a professional force sensitive to central authority was as much a response to the deepening crises in nationally centred capital evidenced by the recurrent labour disruption of the period, as it was to any external threat.

The much vaunted 'neutrality' of the army in comparison with the police merely indicated the refusal of the former to accept the instructions of representatives of local capital against nationally centred interests mediated through the central state. A comparison of the attitudes towards local capitalists shown by the military officers called to Featherstone and to Tonypandy is striking. The police had not yet broken free from the domination of local county interests.

For Churchill, the supremacy of 'national' over 'sectional' interests (local capital) dictated the new and elastic terms of reference for the military:

> To use soldiers or sailors kept up at the general expense of the taxpayer, to take sides with the employer in an ordinary trade dispute . . . would be a monstrous invasion of the liberty of the subject . . . But the case is different where vital services affecting the health, life and safety of large cities or great concentrations of people are concerned.[11]

Thus by the time of the First World War we recognize in the British military all the characteristics of a central state agency free from local controls. It had developed a reformed and centralized internal structure; links at all levels (under the Macready system) with other agencies; complete pre-eminence (up to 1926 at least) in the field of public order and a significant role in national policy formation.

The army and police from 1926

'The antagonism between the police and the army in England goes back a long way', wrote Marx (1980, p. 326), having witnessed off-duty troops fighting the metropolitans in Hyde Park in 1855. Napier (1857, pp. 60–1) noticed similar antagonisms between his soldiers and the new police and Reith (1956, p. 149) has maintained that attacks on the police were 'deliberately fostered by military authority'. Such institutional antagonisms were well entrenched and the ascendancy over the police achieved by Macready was short-lived.

Above all, it was the physical constraints on army resources in the late imperialist period which forced a withdrawal of the military from their dominant role in UK civil disorder. Post-war military commitments were colossal. In November 1918, in addition to the vast imperial garrisons, there were British troops in France, Belgium, Germany, Italy, Greece, Austria, Hungary, Serbia, Bulgaria, the Ottoman Empire and Russia (Jeffery 1984, pp. 1–30). Uprisings in Ireland and India stretched military resources beyond breaking point at a time of rapid demobilization and the post-war army of 3.5 million had been reduced by November 1920 to 0.5 million. The 128 infantry battalions available to deal with disorder in the UK in 1919 were by 1920 cut back to 38. The Adjutant-General wrote:

We have not merely greatly strained the military machine but the British Constitution as well. We should insist on the Home Office doing its own work . . . it will be a bad day for the Empire if the Government of this country has to look to the bayonets of its troops for its support.[12]

The 'Constitution' had proved no obstacle to military domination between 1910 and 1926. The supremacy of the military in civil disorder was destroyed quite simply by the crisis in imperial relations. Although Churchill was anxious for a military response to the General Strike in 1926 (Morris 1976, p. 256; Blake 1979, p. 214) this was by now impossible and it was the reconstituted police force that was to take the central role.[13] Accordingly, we see a policy of mass arrest which could never have been undertaken by the military.

However, the period following the retreat from imperial commitments after 1948 witnessed a significant reawakening of military involvement in the UK. Whereas in 1931 the chiefs of staff were predicting the withdrawal of the military from a civil role, Whelan (1981, p. 162) has claimed that the position has, in the 1970s been reversed: 'Since 1945, military intervention has occurred on about 23 occasions . . . Since 1970 the military have intervened in at least seven disputes.' This view is supported by Bunyan (1977, pp. 276–9; 1981b) and Williams (1974, p. 635). Blake (1979, pp. 255–99) has also sought to demonstrate a number of parallels between the 'Macready Era' (1910–26) and the 1970s which he describes as the 'Kitson Era'. Drawing heavily on the theorization of counter-insurgency work undertaken by Brigadier Kitson (1971), Major-General Deane-Drummond (1975), General Sir Walter Walker (Pocock 1973) and Major Clutterbuck (1973a; 1973b; 1974; 1975) and on the joint police/military exercises at Heathrow in 1974, Blake (1979, p. 253) asserts: 'We can thus suggest a valid link . . . in which 1910–1926 and the 1970s are seen as the two principal cycles of military interest and involvement in the civil arena.'

Although Blake is correct to note the reinvolvement of the military, his attempt to assimilate two vastly different periods into two 'cycles' is misguided. Joint planning between police and army has certainly been instituted since the 1970s (Bramall 1985, p. 84), but on a very different relative balance of authority between the two agencies. Sir Robert Mark, once a major figure in the Association of Chief Police Officers (ACPO), has spoken of a unified command structure in civil disorder and the existence of sophisticated joint military–police planning cannot be denied.[14] 'We must always keep in close contact . . . getting to know each other's command and control systems', Sir Edwin Bramall (1985, p. 84) has advised. The military consensus (see, for example, Clutterbuck 1974; Carver 1983, p. 8) appears to be that military intervention would take place in the event of a multiple outburst of disorder across the country: 'a simultaneous rash of rioting in Glasgow, the North, the Midlands, South Wales and London would have made [concentration of forces] impossible . . . Should this occur Britain would have no final bulwark against chaos other than the Army' (Clutterbuck 1974, pp. 24–5). But this is exactly what did occur in 1981 and again in 1984–5, and, with the exception of the presence of liaison officers,[15] there was no military intervention whatsoever. The prophecies of the so-called 'military panic' of the early 1970s[16] were not fulfilled even during the most serious public order crises of the post-war period (Babington 1990, pp. 176–85).

A closer examination of the period of the Heath administration reveals that much of the discussion of the army's 'counter-insurgency' role in mainland Britain formed merely the background to the military–police dispute over the creation and control of the so-called 'third force'. The sudden interest in counter-insurgency shown by the military (deprived in the last decade of its remaining colonial functions) was well exemplified in articles in the *Army Quarterly* by Fox (1974), Clutterbuck (1974) and Lunt (1974), which reflected the contest waged in the 1972 National Security Committee over control of the proposed force.[17] In the event, the argument was won decisively by the police who, at the same time, developed their own 'commando units' for use in preference to the Special Air Services (SAS) (see Manwaring-White 1983, pp. 118–21). The massive investment in police resources between 1979–82 (Bennett 1983, p. 145) and the corresponding increases in status and manpower, contrast unfavourably with the decline of the military establishment in the same period (Table 6.1).

Therefore, although it is demonstrably true that both the police and the military have now broken free from any remaining control by the local state and the magistrates, we should be wary of overemphasizing the power of the military at the expense of the police.[18] When Carver (1983, p. 11) asserts that, despite 'differences of opinion' over control of operations with the police, 'a Lieutenant Colonel commanding the battalion given the task [of suppressing riot] is responsible to nobody but the law as to

Table 6.1 Comparative numerical strengths of police and army, 1900–87

	Police	*Army*
1900	41,900	759,000
1910	49,600	550,000
1920	56,500	596,000
1930	58,000	463,000
1940	57,300	2,273,000
1950	62,600	688,000
1960	72,300	503,000
1970	92,700	373,000
1980	115,900	321,000
1987	122,265	326,000

Source: Butler, D. and Butler, G. (1985). *British Political Facts 1900–1985*. London, Macmillan.

what he does and how he does it', he is assuming an army bias. Equally, Bramall (1985, p. 74) has argued that, although the police might have charge initially, once the military are called in, 'command would then devolve to the military commanding officer'. In this view, the police would effectively be co-opted into a national military command structure (Evelegh 1978, p. 19). The police, as Mark (1977, p. 30) has indicated, may not necessarily agree:

> There is no question of one service coming under the command of the other. The army commander would act in accordance with the joint police/army plan. He would not be under the command of the police commander but would act in conjunction with him under his duty at common law to come to the aid of the civil power.

It is difficult to understand the legal basis under which the police might have 'overall control' of the military.[19] This lack of clarity clearly indicates that the matter is not yet resolved (Whelan 1985, pp. 122–3) and the question of whether or not a military commander would be justified, even now, in disobeying a direct order by a magistrate is equally unclear (Bennett and Ryan 1985, p. 192). Quite simply, the law has failed to keep pace with the speed of developments in the power relations between these agencies.

7 The police

The powers in civil disorder lost by the magistracy were taken up ultimately, not by the army but by the police. Such powers were assimilated in a continuous process of engagement and conflict with the other agencies, including the joint standing committees and the police authorities on which the justices were represented. The police perspective on these changes, and the development of their authority within the state, must therefore be considered in detail.

Looking over the vast body of work available, it is hard to avoid the conclusion that police historians have become preoccupied with the evolution from a local to a national force and the progressive enlargement of the model established in London in 1829 until it encompassed the whole country. Even authors such as Silver (1967), Bowden (1978) and Scraton (1985), who have sought to locate the process within a class context, have not presented any analysis of the shifting locations of power during these developments. They have tacitly acceded to the Reithian view that the standardization of police practice and authority indicated – for better or for worse – the linear advance of the central state: 'The police penetration of civil society, however, lay not only in its narrow application to crime and violence. In a broader sense it represented the penetration and continual presence of central political authority throughout daily life' (Silver 1967, pp. 12–13). We see similar views expressed by Reith (1956, pp. 264–86), Radzinowicz (1956a, pp. 405–27; 1968, pp. 252–302), Williams (1967), Critchley (1978), Stead (1985) and Palmer (1988) as we do by more radical theorists such as Hall (1980b), Rosenhead (1982, pp. 8–9) and Manwaring-

White (1983, p. 18). While it is certainly true that recent work has displayed a greater sensitivity to the complexity of class interests in the political struggles over the growth of police forces, there is still little understanding of the organizational implications. For example, developments since 1964 are seen merely as a quickening of the pace of the inexorable drive towards central state control demanded by capital or system logic: 'At the same time as the number of forces has diminished drastically, governmental control, control exerted through the power of the purse and the Police Inspectorate of the Home Office, has increased very considerably' (Bowden 1978, p. 213).

Brogden (1982, p. 98) has offered one challenge to this orthodoxy, asserting that 'the appearance of a movement towards central direction has all the qualities of a chimera'. By extracting for examination the growing independence of the chief constables, he has been able to argue that their organization, the Association of Chief Police Officers (ACPO), now exerts a collective (perhaps even 'feudal') power which is *outside* the central state. There are, however, difficulties with this approach.

Brogden (1982, p. 2) begins his account with the highly relevant observation that: 'The lack of any precise statement of the nature and form of the state under advanced capitalism has handicapped . . . studies of policing.' Having then reviewed and rejected four theoretical models of the state, he borrows from the chief constables themselves a modified managerialist conception as an alternative theorization. It is difficult to see how this notion (so sharply criticized in earlier pages (Brogden 1982, p. 5)) can be supposed to stand in place of a precise statement of the nature and form of the state.

This theoretical lacuna has serious implications for Brogden's otherwise incisive study. The concern of Bowden and others with the growth of central facilities since 1964 is perhaps too lightly dismissed. The views of Hall *et al.* (1978) and Bunyan (1981a) that the new organs of a centralized police force represent the agencies of the central state acting in the interests of international capital cannot, however, be so easily discarded. Citing the weakness of formal sanctions and controls available to the Home Office, Brogden (1982, p. 107) concludes that 'the police chiefs were increasingly independent of all controls by fractions of the capitalist class. In particular the control of the central state over local costs did not increase.' This position is tenable, however, only when the police complex is regarded as an autonomous agency *outside* the central state, but Brogden has not made it clear why this should be so. He has not defined the limits of the local or central states and, having conceded that the ACPO in many cases exercises corporate authority over the Home Office and takes political initiative in legislation (Brogden 1982, p. 158), there seems no good reason why it should not *itself* be deemed an organ of the central state. If this point is conceded, the modern autonomy and independence of the police chiefs takes on a very different character. It then follows that, over the course of the lifetime of the British police, the chief officers have moved over from a subordinate position inside the local state to full engagement with the central state. A fuller examination of this process is necessary.

Adopting the analysis which we have used in relation to the magistracy and bearing in mind the joint institutional history of police and magistracy up to 1829, we would expect to see a progression of three stages in the development of police power relations. First, we might anticipate the capture by the central state of previously autonomous local magisterial forces in London. Next, we might expect that changes in the balance of authority between the provincial police and magistracy might in some way reflect shifts in productive relations during the nineteenth century. Finally, bearing in mind the work already discussed, a more or less successful move towards institutional corporate independence might be predicted.

Centre dependency in the metropolis

The history of the first stage in London is well documented (by, among others, Radzinowicz 1956a; 1968; Reith 1956; Critchley 1978; Ascoli 1979; Emsley 1983). As we have seen, in 1829 a quasi-military corps of 1,000 officers, trained to operate together in formation and under the sole authority of the Home Office, was created in London to operate in tandem with the forces subordinate to magisterial control (Radzinowicz (1956b, pp. 188–201). At a stroke, the government thereby shortened the chain of command between itself and the material forces of coercion in the metropolis. The two new 'non-judicial' magistrates, Mayne and Rowan, were very much outside the cabals of Union Hall and the Middlesex Quarter Sessions. From the outset, this force was seen as a kind of praetorian guard for the central state, 'an imperial rather than a local force' (Melville Lee 1901, p. 395).

Although the new police made their first essay in crowd control in 1830, the double-barrelled relationship of dependency (of both judicial and non-judicial magistrates) on the Home Office was not fully operational, even in November 1831 when the London Union of the Working Classes called a mass meeting in White Conduit Fields, shortly after the Bristol riot. On this occasion 2,000 police were mobilized and lateral communications were established between police and military barracks (see Reith 1956, pp. 168–94; Hamburger 1963, p. 241; Stevenson 1979, pp. 223–4).

However, in the Clerkenwell riot of 1833 (Thurston 1967) we see the first example of Home Office anti-riot strategic planning extending independently towards both police and stipendiaries. This process, which we may characterize as *centre dependency* and which enabled the Home Office to monitor and control the repression of crowd activity in London from the first issue of prohibitory notices to the final conviction or release of prisoners, was well established by the time of the Hyde Park demonstration of 1855.

The London police came to be deployed outside London in very much the manner adopted by the Horse Guards in respect of the army. Between 1830 and 1838 a total of 2,246 London police were sent to the provinces to quell rioting and in 1839 a detachment of 60 London officers fought alongside the troops against the Birmingham Chartists (Mather 1959, pp. 105–6; Critchley 1978, pp. 80–8; Emsley 1983, p. 69). This tendency was, of course, reinforced by the London focus of the developing rail system, but it antedates 'mutual aid' by 50 years and demonstrates for the first time the ability of the Home Office to project its coercive power outside London without the aid of local forces.[1] However, after the exclusion of the London stipendiaries from a role in civil disorder (see Chapter 3) the chief commissioners waged a lengthy struggle against both the Metropolitan Board of Works and the Home Office (Keller 1976, pp. 301–93) in order to achieve the kind of freedom of action which was evident in Sir Charles Warren's approach to the Trafalgar Square riot in 1887. As Childers, the Home Secretary, admitted, the relations between the Home Office and the metropolitan police had come to resemble those between the Secretary for War and the army – administrative rather than operational.

Under a succession of military chief commissioners, the metropolitan police developed a system of command which was not dissimilar to that of the army. The militarization undertaken by Sir Charles Warren in the 1880s (Melville Lee 1901, pp. 378–87) laid the foundations for that of Sir Neville Macready who, it is reported, aimed 'to bring the discipline of the Metropolitan Police up to the standard of a Guards Regiment'.[2] Lord Trenchard, in the 1930s, consolidated the process.

The metropolitan police was brought into existence by the legislative action of the central state. It was an example of a centrally dependent institution with almost no local links or loyalties. It is wholly wrong, therefore, to see this force as a natural paradigm for the development of policing elsewhere in England and Wales. Such relations as the local forces were able to establish with the central state in the twentieth century were informal and based upon local sources of authority; they were not the outcome of legislative fiat by the central state in the creation of a dependent agency.

Breaking the power of the provincial justices and police authorities

In the second stage we see again close parallels between the development of provincial police forces and magistracy. A permissive Constabulary

Act of 1839[3] initiated a patchwork of forces (Midwinter 1968) in accordance with the composition of local class interests, and, in particular, with the incidence of disorder (Parris 1961, pp. 24–7; Critchley 1978, pp. 76–80). Some imitated the command structure of the London force, whereas others retained pre-capitalist forms of watch until a further Constabulary Act[4] made standardization compulsory in 1856 (Melville Lee 1901, pp. 305–8; Critchley 1978, pp. 101–23). Thus, at exactly the same period when the magistracy were becoming entrenched at a local level (see Chapter 4) in a form of shared power between the 'mongrel aristocracy' of the old corporations and shires (Webb and Webb 1963, p. 700) and the industrialists and non-conformists, the police had become established on a similar basis.

As with the provincial magistracy there was little centre dependency (Midwinter 1968, p. 20). Indeed, Parris (1961, p. 251), Storch (1976, p. 490), Bailey (1977, pp. 231–49) have shown how closely local police and magistrates worked together in the conduct of campaigns of moral or economic regulation. We can see in the approach to disorder in Bristol in 1831 and Featherstone in 1893 the extent to which the short-term interests of local capital prevailed over the long-term interests of the central state. In contrast to the metropolitan police, provincial forces were always the servants of the local elites. It is important to consider how this relation was to develop.

According to Bacon in 1608, the traditional role of the constable (including the chief constable) was that of personal outdoor servant to the justices, 'receiving the commandments and prescripts from the justices of the peace and distributing them to the petty constables' (Spedding *et al.*, 1861, p. 749). This notion of service survived the constabulary reforms of 1839–56 and was reiterated in a succession of justices' manuals down to the end of the nineteenth century. Throughout the period 1880–1930, however, we see this relation of deference first challenged and then broken, as a prelude to its complete reversal after 1945.

It was the sharpness of the economic catastrophes (for provincial small-scale industry and agriculture in England at least: see Mingay 1976, pp. 77–9, 169–70, 308–20) of the 1880s and 1890s which first began to erode this relation. To the Tories it seemed self-evident that, in the collapse of provincial economic power, the government should intervene to appropriate control over the police as it had done in London in 1829. If the police were not to be directed by the representatives of local industrial and landed capital in person, then authority must be exercised by some central custodian of their interests. In no event should power fall into the hands of an elective body composed of 'a very inferior class of persons, who paid little or no rates themselves'.[5]

If this were to happen, and relations between magistracy and police were broken to the extent that the bench could not act freely and independently in the last instance of insurrection, the dangers for local capital were obvious. As Lord Lymington put it in the debates on the 1888 Local Government Act:

Surely it is better that the magistrates should have [the police] under their charge because there might be cases of popular riot . . . where there would be difficulties placed in the way of the chief constable [by a popular assembly] in obtaining his expenses or carrying out his views in the matter of putting down these *émeutes* . . .[6]

Whereas Tory ideologues such as Sir Walter Barttelot insisted that, whatever happened to the other administrative powers of quarter sessions, their control over the police must be retained, more perceptive 'Tory Democrats' and Liberal Unionists sensed that the days of direct linkage to local capitals were passing. The problem was, quite bluntly, that the police budget consumed up to a third of county rates (Dunbabin 1963, pp. 227) and further sums could not be raised by an oligarchical, unrepresentative body. *The Times* therefore concluded as follows:

There is much to be said for Sir Walter Barttlelot's contention that the control of the police should be retained, as at present, in the hands of the magistrates. There is, in our opinion, still more to be said in favour of the view that the police, like the Army and the Navy, should everywhere be controlled by the central government subject to the supervision of the Imperial Parliament.[7]

The Marquess of Salisbury, the Tory Prime Minister, who was much preoccupied with the need for national defence against insurrection, had considered the idea of 'substituting the power of the Secretary of State over the Chief Constable in cases of riot and disorder'.[8] With patrician arrogance he asserted that 'the civilisation of many English counties is sufficiently backward to make it hazardous for the Crown to part with power over the police',[9] but he rejected the idea, fearing, as he said, 'local feeling'.

While Featherstone in 1893 was to show the dangers to government of the traditional model of control based upon the unrestrained interests of local capital, Trafalgar Square in 1887 had already indicated the contrary problem; that the actions of a state-controlled police could be damaging in an equally profound way. Stead at the *Pall Mall Gazette* put this argument forcefully:

many Conservatives have not yet discovered the extent to which the conditions of the problem have been changed by Trafalgar Square. Up to last November it was on the cards that even a Liberal administration might repeat Sir William Harcourt's blunder of 1884 and leave the Metropolitan Police in the hands of the Home Office. Since November the whole Liberal Party and a large section of the

Conservatives have mastered the lesson that unless the police force is in the hands of the local authorities, local self-government cannot be said to exist. The poor fellows who went to the treadmill and the plank bed . . . last November . . . sacrificed themselves . . . but their constancy decided the future of the great battle between a local and a centralised police . . .[10]

Lord Herschell reiterated the point to the government:

The more they brought the police under Executive control, the more they weakened their power and instead of strengthening the Government, they enormously weakened it. The farther they removed the control of the police from the Central Authority the more certain they were of safety . . .[11]

The compromise of 1888 which was intended to distance the provincial county police from both central state and local capital by placing them under a joint committee composed equally of councillors and magistrates, effectively liberated the chief constables. Although much of the existing magisterial personnel was represented on the new joint standing committees, a cleavage of interest was inevitable, especially in view of the Conservative and Unionist stranglehold on the Commission of the Peace (Vogler 1990, pp. 65–70).

Barttelot and Sir Arthur Rollit had warned that a committee so constituted would inevitably be paralysed by a 'division of opinion with reference to the employment of the police'[12] and the *Daily News* pictured an 'ugly crop of difficulties' arising from 'the evils of divided authority'.[13] Events proved them correct.

Even as late as 1901, however, it was still possible for the police historian, Melville Lee (1901, p. 43), to assert that magistracy and police were 'closely allied in their mutual relation of master and servant'. However, the final blow to such oligarchical assumptions was dealt by the landmark decision of *Fisher v Oldham Corporation*[14] in 1930. Relying on *obiter dicta* of dubious relevance,[15] and a number of colonial decisions, McCardie J. promulgated the revolutionary doctrine that the police did not act as servants or agents of the police authority.[16] This decision overturned a line of cases which designated the railway police unequivocally as 'servants of the company'[17] and the municipal police as 'employees' under contracts of service to the police authorities.[18] The master–servant analogy foundered on vicarious liability for the payment of damages in tort, especially where the police were acting in the national interest rather than in the interest of local capital. Therefore, notwithstanding the residual powers for the authorities to appoint and to discipline chief constables, the crucial loss of control must be located in the inter-war period (Marshall 1965, pp. 33–45; Keith-Lucas 1960; Spencer 1985a, pp. 38–41).

By 1929, Sir John Anderson (1929, p. 192) could assert with confidence: 'The policeman is nobody's servant'. Although as late as 1936 some observers still clung to the idea of the 'absolute control' of the police authorities over the police,[19] the old notion was finally laid to rest in the 1959 Popkess affair (Critchley 1978, pp. 270–1) in which, with the aid of the Home Office, the Nottingham chief constable was able to humiliate his watch committee. This incident was of particular significance since the borough chief constables had never enjoyed the relative freedom of action of their county colleagues. By 1960, as Keith-Lucas (1960, p. 10) put it: 'this duty of the constables to obey the magistrates [was] little more than a historical survival'.

It was in this context that the 1962 Royal Commission on the Police[20] was able to persuade the government that magistrates should be introduced onto all police authorities, including those in the boroughs. The municipalities vigorously resisted this threat to their independence (Critchley 1978, pp. 290–1). Not only did the one-third composition of magistrates destroy the democratic credibility of the old watch committees but, as we shall see, it diluted the voting power of the majority party and ensured that the police authorities would never again be able successfully to challenge the authority of the police.

No legal-structural changes of any real significance therefore were needed in the tripartite relation between Home Office, police authorities and chief constables from 1888 (Marshall 1965, p. 30). Indeed, proposals to reorganize the legal basis of relations put forward by the Willink Royal Commission in 1964[21] were decisively rejected by the government (Marshall 1965, pp. 73–92). It was argued as late as 1978 that the tripartite relationship was still intact and that, outside the operational area, no one party could dominate any other (Spencer 1985a, p. 33). The profound alteration in the relations of authority between them therefore was accomplished without recourse to legislation.

It was through more subtle means, such as the power to control agendas (Brogden 1977, p. 331) and the supply of information, as well as the overriding obligations of mutual aid, that the chief constables were able to establish their domination of the police authorities. This was not achieved without resistance. Until the local government reorganization of the early 1970s, no borough area was strong enough to challenge the authority of the revitalized, post-1964 police forces. However, the creation of the six metropolitan authorities gave these larger committees a wider territorial jurisdiction and the political weight to assert themselves. The conflict was given fresh impetus by the election of massive Labour majorities in many of these areas in May 1981 (see Table 7.1) in a period in which the inter-party consensus on policing had been broken (Brewer *et al.* 1988, pp. 42–3). For five years, until their abolition in 1986, the police committees of the six 'big mets' were in the vanguard of a series of bitter

Table 7.1   Political composition of local authorities

	Metropolitan authorities				District/borough councils			
	Lab.	Con.	Lib/ Alliance	Other	Lab.	Con.	Lib/ Alliance	Other
	Merseyside				*Liverpool DC*			
Pre-1981	25	67	7	–	40	21	38	–
Post-1981	55	27	15	2	–	–	–	–
	Greater Manchester				*Manchester DC*			
Pre-1981	24	80	–	–	71	23	4	–
Post-1981	78	19	9	–	–	–	–	–
	Greater London Council				*London Borough of Ealing*			
Pre-1981	29	63	–	–	29	39	–	–
Post-1981	50	41	1	–	–	–	–	–
					London Borough of Lambeth			
					42	22	–	–

Source: The Municipal Yearbook 1980; 1981; 1982.

confrontations with their chief constables (Brogden 1982; Jefferson and Grimshaw 1982; Reiner 1985, pp. 193–5; Spencer 1985a, pp. 62–70; 1985b, p. 5). As the Manchester chief constable put it in 1981: 'The most trying situation for the police is the changing behaviour of some police author-ities since the local government elections last May' (Prince 1988, p. 94). The chair of his authority admitted that it 'developed into a fight for power' (1988, p. 153).

Attempts to assert collective authority by the use of comparative statis-tical data provided by the Association of Metropolitan Authorities (AMA) and other local government associations (Simey 1988, p. 79), and by the joint lobbying of the Home Office (1988, pp. 102–4) achieved some limited success, but ultimately the collective structure was no real counterweight to the ACPO:

> the Chief [Constable] was subject to the requirements of membership of a powerful professional body, ACPO, with strong links with the Home Office. Whereas we had . . . little effective contact with the national movement. The Authority's links with the County Council were threadlike, our contacts with the Home Office unreal and dis-tant. We operated in isolation . . .
>
> (Simey 1988, p. 101)

Put more simply, the national organization of the ACPO was more de-veloped and sophisticated than anything the AMA could provide. The final confrontation during the miners' strike of 1984–5 registered a decisive victory for the chief constables which was to anticipate the abolition of these troublesome metropolitan authorities in 1986. In collusion with the ACPO, the Home Secretary in March 1984 authorized chief officers to spend any funds necessary to support the mutual aid operation. This decision was not communicated to the police committees until considerably later and, as a result, they were deprived of any effective control over their budgets, the only remaining weapon of authority (Spencer 1985b). Attempts to reassert control by refusing to pay mutual aid bills or by cutting the budget[22] were stifled by the courts or by the threat of legal action (Reiner 1984, p. 52; 1985, p. 194; Spencer 1985b, pp. 13–14). The local police authorities, in this national confrontation, were put in the impossible position of being answerable for centrally authorized expenditure over which they had no possible control. Their resulting defeat, and the loss of the right to veto the purchase of particular types of riot control weaponry in 1987 (Scraton 1985, pp. 152–63; Oliver 1987, pp. 210–21; Brewer *et al.* 1988, pp. 20–1; Northam 1988, pp. 148–51) finally destroyed the post-1981 initiatives and effectively reduced the role of the authorities to that of provision only.

Crucial to this loss of authority was the numerical strength of the magisterial groups on the authorities. It is interesting to note, for example, that the substitution of a joint board for the old West Midlands metropolitan police authority in early 1986 diluted the opposition to the purchase of plastic bullets by the chief constable to the extent that the voting power of the magistrates was once more sufficient to ensure the lifting of a previous veto (Brewer *et al.* 1988, p. 21). Simey (1982, p. 56), writing in the context of the 1981 riots, pointed again to the paralysing effects of the joint representation first created in 1888:

> The magistrates have, on occasion, been party to defeating a decision of the majority party, a danger which can only be avoided by the party in power taking a disproportionate number of places and so stultifying the normal political process.

Significantly, the chief constables of both Kent[23] and Greater Manchester (Prince 1988, pp. 94–5) have called for an increase in the proportion of justices on police authorities to 50 per cent. The magistrates sitting on the police authorities had become, in a very significant sense, the servants of local police interests. Not only were they able to undermine democratic resistance to policing strategies in the police authorities but, as we shall see in the 1981 disorders, they could give their crucial support to these strategies in the courtrooms.

As a result of these shifts in emphasis, the organization of the control of disorder after the 1981–6 period must be seen as strictly a bipartisan arrangement between the ACPO and the Home Office, with the police authorities and justices reduced to a strictly subordinate, supporting role.

Corporate authority

The most recent, and possibly most important, development in the relations of the police with other organizations in the central and local state has been the establishment of a national/corporate police identity. The dominant role of the military throughout the disorders of 1893–1919 has been attributed variously to the lack of resources of individual police forces (Geary 1985, p. 101) and the restrictions imposed by their local connections. A military presence was often resented by the police who felt themselves reduced to a supporting role and excluded from the operational relationship between magistracy and army.

The severe army manpower shortage after the First World War (see Chapter 6), the crushing of police unionism in 1919 and the creation of an embryonic conference of chief officers in 1920, all contributed to the reassertion of the position of the police in the control of civil unrest. From 1919 onwards the troops were restricted to a supporting role under the police (Morgan 1987, p. 190). Geary (1985, p. 124) adds that 'from 1919 a police service began to emerge that was conscious of itself as an independent organisation with aims and objectives that did not necessarily coincide with those of the local property owning classes. Moreover the new service . . . regarded the Home Office not the local justices as the natural leader.' As Sir John Anderson (1929, p. 201) put it, the police forces were now able to 'co-operate with one another and with the Home Office as units in one great national service'.

This is not, however, merely to suggest that after 1919 there occurred a 'state take-over' of responsibility (Geary 1985, p. 48) or that the police had become 'an arm of the central state' (Morgan 1987, p. 147). The nature of the 'state' to which these authors refer is left undefined. What is more, police priorities did not necessarily reflect those of the Home Office. It is more helpful to examine the growth of the police service to national/corporate status in this period and to consider the material difficulties which had to be surmounted in this process.

Until the post-war period, the operation of the police on a national level had been inhibited by a number of factors. Notable among these were the lack of an internal professional structure of promotion, the absence of a nationally centred locus of authority and the inability to develop an exclusive role in the preservation of public order. These issues will be considered separately.

The tendency to recruit senior personnel from *outside* the force, and particularly from the army, had serious implications for the structural autonomy of the police. The original 1829 Peelite conception of a civil force commanded by a cadre of military officers (Reith 1943, p. 37; Reiner 1985, p. 53; Stead 1985, p. 36) was reproduced around the country in the mid-Victorian period (see, for example, Midwinter 1968, p. 24; Steedman

1984, pp. 21–5). The system created an impenetrable wall between senior officers and the rest of the service and thwarted the ambitions of policemen who hoped to advance through the ranks. One such 'professional' officer complained:

> In the opinion of all who have had experience of the police force, the government has committed an error in not bringing in greater consolidation and unity in the organisation of the police service . . . The chief and subordinate officers of the police should be transferred from district to district similarly to the collectors of customs and Inland Revenue, Inspectors of Factories etc. . . . The military chief constables have been a most serious impediment to progress in the police force. Their great and only claim has been to keep the superior appointments for nominees of their own caste, and in this, I must admit they have been very successful for they have been quite indifferent to criticism and the legitimate claims of the service.[24]

This deep division between the ranks and the cadre of senior officers ensured that command of the force was in the hands of men who owed their first loyalties elsewhere–notably to the army and to the county and municipal elites. They shared the same interests and social class as these groups and were the means by which their authority was projected into the force. There could be no internal professional ethos nor coherent structure of promotion until the wall was broken down by the appointment of chief constables from within the ranks.

By virtue of a Liberal amendment to the Local Government Act 1888, borough chief constables were thereafter to be appointed by the watch committees (rather than by the justices alone) and this did much to reduce the domination of the army in the towns and cities. By 1908, 86 per cent of borough chief constables had risen from the ranks but in the counties the figure was only 12 per cent.[25] Indeed, the final eclipse of the military chief constable did not occur until the 1960s. As late as 1951 over 51 per cent of all county chief constables had held senior military rank. By 1964 this figure had dropped to 8 per cent, and by 1990 military ranks had ceased to feature in the lists of chief constables.[26] No metropolitan chief commissioner was to be recruited from the ranks until 1959 and two-thirds of all previous commissioners had been soldiers (Stead 1985, p. 68). It was only when the police could lay claim to superior technical skills and professional expertise that they were able to break free from domination by the municipal and county elites and by the army.

A second check upon the development of a corporate structure was the absence of any central point of authority. Until the post-war period, the police had suffered the disorganizing effects of a multiplicity of local power sources and the same jurisdictional constraints which had destroyed the power of the justices. In 1888 Salisbury had advocated that in

cases of disorder: 'If they could combine the police of adjoining counties
. . . and concentrate them on a given spot it would render these abnormal
efforts [the use of troops] unnecessary.'[27] Extra-territorial deployment of
provincial police (without the formality of being sworn in in the receiving
county) was first authorized by s.25 of the Police Act 1890 but, for financial reasons, the provision was little used. In the 1893 miners' lock-out,
Asquith called a meeting of chief constables to encourage them to take
advantage of the section and circularized draft forms of agreement.
However in 1894, according to Charles Troup, the Permanent Under-
Secretary at the Home Office, only 57 out of a total of 192 forces had made
such agreements.[28]

The importance of mutual aid as it developed throughout the twentieth
century was that it formed an operational justification for the establishment of a power bloc around the chief constables. It provided the context
within which the individual local powers of the chief constables could be
concerted. Regular district meetings of chief constables, under the auspices of the Home Office, were first organized in 1918 (Keith-Lucas 1960,
p. 8) and the central conference of chief constables was set up in 1920
(Critchley 1978, pp. 183 and 195–6; Stead 1985, p. 121; Morgan 1987, p.
86). This enabled the chief constables for the first time to make joint
representations to the Home Secretary, and during the General Strike in
1926 the national co-ordination of forces in civil emergency became common (see Critchley 1978, pp. 198–9; Brogden 1982, pp. 154–65).

The freedom from constraint offered by the inter-force arrangements of
this period had a profound impact upon the police. As one legal observer
put it in 1932:

> The extensive powers given to the police during and after the Gen-
> eral Strike had a bad effect upon the Force, from which they have not
> even yet completely recovered. Without actual experience in an in-
> dustrial district during that period, no-one can realise how exceed-
> ingly bumptious and overbearing the rank and file can become.
> Certain officers of higher rank have shared this attitude.
>
> (Solicitor 1932, pp. 113–14)

Yet greater emancipation was offered by the increased responsibilities of
wartime, which were given statutory force by Defence Regulation 39
(Manwaring-White 1983, p. 3; Stammers 1983, pp. 89–91).[29] In 1948, the
foundation of the ACPO ensured that the concerted authority of the chief
constables was effectively organized on a campaigning basis. From that
period, the chief officers were able to make decisive collective interven-
tions at the level of the central state in relation to all issues of enforcement
policy.

The Police Act 1964 placed the primary responsibility for mutual aid on
the chief constables (s.14) and abandoned the last territorial restrictions

on the authority of individual officers (s.19). By the 1960s, the force was in a position to embark upon the massive expansion of national-standard facilities which has so alarmed subsequent commentators (BSSRS 1985; Northam 1988; Uglow 1988, pp. 127–31).

The events of 1981 had a critical effect upon the growth of central facilities. They demonstrated to the ACPO and the Home Office (Whitelaw 1989, pp. 192–5) that mutual aid could not operate without a vastly augmented provision of standard training and equipment. These developments laid fresh emphasis on the National Reporting Centre (NRC), an emergency co-ordinating agency located in New Scotland Yard and activated on the authority of the president of ACPO in consultation with his committee and with the Home Office (Brewer *et al.* 1988, p. 19). Established in 1973, shortly after the Saltley Gates disaster, the system was much improved after the 1980 steel strike and operated extensively during all the major incidents of disorder of the 1980s. To many commentators concerned with accountability, the NRC was the Trojan horse for the centralizing tendencies within the police establishment (Scraton 1985, pp. 154–63; Uglow 1988, pp. 42–4). By contrast, the ACPO saw the NRC as a means actually of avoiding the necessity for more powerful central structures.[30]

It is worth noting that much of the resistance to a centralized national police structure has come from the ACPO itself. Although Macready and other military chief constables had long advocated the creation of a national police force with a single command structure on similar lines to the army (Blake 1979, p. 161), and the issue was extensively canvassed in the 1960–2 Royal Commission,[31] it was resisted by many senior police officers, whose strength, they believed, lay in their regional authority. While some chief constables have argued for a regionally centred force,[32] others have rejected the idea of any boundary changes at all.[33] As Manwaring-White (1983, pp. 39–40) has suggested: 'It is possible that the only reason for not totally amalgamating the police forces in this country has been the need . . . for separate policing arrangements in a state of emergency.' By channelling this local power through their own collective agencies, the police were now able to negotiate policy directly with the central state executive (Mark 1977; Newman 1978). Whereas in the 1930s they could operate only as an *ad hoc* 'pressure group' in the drafting of public order legislation (Blake 1979, p. 238), by the mid-1980s their institutional presence within the central state enabled them to have a determining role in the production of legislation.

The third (and related) crucial development has been the establishment of a sophisticated civil disorder capacity. It has been argued that the massive reorganization of procedures and *matériel* undertaken since 1981 has brought about the most extensive structural change in the police service for 150 years (Northam 1988, p. 41). Reiner (1985, p. 179), however, linking the development of 'militaristic' and 'fire-brigade' policing, has suggested that all these changes were merely the '*unintended consequence of strategies aimed at enhancing professionalism and efficiency*'. Clearly, he is correct to warn against the dangers of conspiracy theorizing but, conversely, the element of conscious corporate decision-making, prompted by an awareness of the crucial police role after 1972 in preserving the existing major forms of state authority, must not be discounted entirely.

The growing authority of the police corporate organization ensured a decisive defeat in the early 1970s for proposals for a paramilitary riot-control force under army direction. Instead, the chief officers themselves would be responsible for this important tactical capability and Special Patrol Groups (SPGs) and support units would be established *within* existing police structures and subject to exclusive police control. By 1985 there were 416 Police Support Units in England and Wales and 130,000 officers had been trained in riot formation tactics (Kettle 1985, p. 30; Babington 1990, pp. 197–201; Jefferson 1990, pp. 1–19). There was, nevertheless, a price to be paid for this institutional ascendancy over the military in the area of civil order. As Northam (1988, p. 36) puts it: 'They decided to equip and train their officers secretly as paramilitary units, prepared to fight like soldiers in the streets and to kill if they had to.'

The creation of an internal third force within the police organization was not achieved (as had previous initiatives been under Warren, Macready and Trenchard) under army guidance. Although the Public Order Manual adopted military terminology and techniques (Northam 1988, p. 17), the source for these was not the army itself. Instead, the police were able to call upon the entirely separate tradition of colonial policing which had developed primarily around the training schools of the Royal Irish Constabulary (RIC) and which were from there disseminated across the empire. Gendarmerie policing, which prescribed an ascendancy of policing over judicial priorities, and which had so disturbed the magistrates in London in 1785 (see above) that it had been designated for export only (first to Dublin and then to the other colonies (Jeffries 1952, pp. 30–2; Palmer 1988)) was now to be repatriated after an absence of two centuries. The dual-model thesis of home and colonial policing (Stead 1985, pp. 61–6 and 83–6), was, to some extent, collapsing. Significantly, the ACPO now had the national status and authority to negotiate directly with officials from foreign and colonial forces. The presence of officers Henry and Quine from the Hong Kong Police at the ACPO meeting at Preston in September 1981 (Northam 1988, p. 39), together with more regular subsequent contacts with Hong Kong and Royal Ulster Constabulary (RUC) officials, allowed the organization direct access to a policing tradition developed during the colonial period in isolation from domestic policing. The resulting 'marriage' of these policing models was first made operational during the 1984–5 miners' strike. Its origins, how-ever, lie in the profound shock administered to the prestige of the police as a 'third force' by the 1981 rioters.

To recapitulate: in assuming a national role and identity, the central organizations of police power have moved into a stage which we may characterize as 'corporate' and which will be seen at its most apparent in the disorders of the 1980s. By this time the police had come to exhibit all the characteristics of an independent national corporate agency. First, they had developed an integrated command structure internally respons-ible for discipline. Second, they now had the ability to establish links at all levels with other similar structures. Third, they enjoyed unique access to the instruments of coercion necessary to ensure the survival of the state in its present form (Bowden 1978, p. 12).

We must now move on to consider briefly the manner in which this corporate agency has developed its relations with the central state over the last decade. In 1981, as we shall see, the mutual aid dispositions were not organized by the Home Office Committee F6[34] but by the ACPO itself, working through the NRC. It is particularly telling that in the after-math of the riot in Brixton on 19 April, the Home Secretary was evidently not informed of the most important operational factor relevant to the riot – the existence of the 'Swamp' offensive in the days before the outbreak.[35] Similarly, when telephoned late at night by a chief constable with a re-quest for authority to use CS gas, the Home Secretary felt able to put the phone down and go back to sleep, comforted by the reflection that here was an operational matter outside his jurisdiction (Whitelaw 1989, p. 189). This was probably the last occasion on which the sleep of a Home Secre-tary could continue uninterrupted in this fashion.

Since 1981, there has been an evident blurring of boundaries between the two agencies. In the immediate aftermath of the 1981 riots, the respon-sibility for the new civil disorder policy and the drafting of the Public Order Manual (Northam 1988) was undertaken by the inelegantly named Community Disorder Tactical Options Inter Force Working Group, a sub-committee of the ACPO. This important committee, by an obscure pro-cess of osmosis, appears in other manifestations as the *Home Office* Public Order Liaison Group (1988, pp. 44–5). Similarly, we find the Home Secre-tary intervening directly to block any threat from local authorities to the independence of action of the ACPO during the 1984–5 miners' strike (Spencer 1985b, pp. 9–13).

Yet the traffic has not all been in one direction. Home Office officials were present at Scotland Yard at the same period to monitor the use of the NRC (Oliver 1987, p. 211; Uglow 1988, p. 43). Indeed, one of the major purposes of the NRC is to act as a means of co-operation and co-ordination with the Home Office (Oliver 1987, p. 211).

The will of the Home Office has been projected into force areas since

1981 by the use of increasingly didactic circulars, and in 1986 Home Office budget subvention to local police authorities was increased to a significant 51 per cent from the 50 per cent level at which it had remained since 1875 (Melville Lee 1901, p. 391). The budgets of the new joint boards which replaced the metropolitan police authorities were placed under direct Home Office control for the first three years (Brewer *et al*. 1988, p. 16). As Weatheritt (1986, p. 104) puts it, the 1981 disorders produced a major revolution in Home Office thinking:

> The dominant ethos within the department – that operational priorities were largely a matter for chief constables to determine without reference to the centre – changed markedly as the Home Office took advantage of a more receptive local climate to extend influence over a wider operational territory.

The possibility that the Home Office may seek to appoint its own nominees directly to police authorities is now very much on the political agenda (Oliver 1987, pp. 226–43).

The institutional interpenetration of the two agencies which, as Brewer *et al*. (1988, p. 19) admit, 'exists in a twilight world of speculation, charge, counter-charge and denial', has increased throughout the last decade, with profound implications for policing. It is not merely, as some commentators suggest, that an unaccountable council of feudal barons (the ACPO) (Uglow 1988, p. 143) has emerged, with the power to dictate orders to their functionaries at the Home Office (Campbell 1987, p. 11), but that the configuration of the central state itself is changing. Although the contribution of the police to the evolving structure of the central state tends to dominate the public debate, it is important to remember that their power base remains firmly in the local areas.

In summary, then, the concept of a nationally co-ordinated structure of power, under the supervision of an internal controlling authority, in negotiation and sometimes in conflict with state agencies at all levels, must be sharply distinguished from the notion of the centrally organized omnipotent state. Brogden and others are right to direct attention to the growth of central power *within* the force, but they have not drawn out its full significance for the form of state in its range of action.

Whereas in nineteenth-century disorders the police stood in relation to the bench in a position of dependency, in 1981 the position was reversed. In July 1981, representatives of local state organizations, notably the police authorities, but also the justices, were treated with indifference (and occasionally contempt) by the police. During the disorders, as Simey (1988, pp. 80 and 102) points out, not only were communications between the relevant police authorities and the Home Office interrupted and mediated by the police, but almost the only contact between the chair of the police authority and the Home Office was achieved by gatecrashing meetings between the police and the Home Secretary. The relation between police authority and central state had been effectively snapped (Brewer *et al.* 1988, p. 19; Uglow 1988, pp. 75–6) and replaced by a relation between the Home Office and the chief constables. The police have become, as Willink puts it, the 'residuary legatees' of the massive locally centred power of the justices.[36]

Unlike the justices, however, they have also been able to create the national structures of authority necessary to establish a presence within the central state. As we shall see in the examination of the 1981 disorders, it was the corporate power of the police at a national level, and not the executive authority of the Home Secretary or Cabinet, which marked out in unequivocal terms the line of conduct to be taken by the magistrates.

8 The 1981 disorders

Threats to the central and local state

We are now in a position to consider the relative position of the magistracy and the police during the violent upheavals which occurred in the inner-city areas in 1981. Despite the absence of any coherent linkage between the incidents and the significant differences between them, it is clear that 'the riots' were perceived as a unity by central state officials. Moreover, they were also seen as a direct threat to their authority. Lord Scarman claimed in the House of Lords: 'There was an occasion in Brixton . . . when a few unreinforced police stood between the inner city of London and the total collapse of law and order.'[1] Similarly, Field (1982, p. 16), at the Home Office, has argued that the rioters challenged assumptions that were 'central to the legitimacy and survival of the state'. Indeed, the evident disarray among central state agencies during the period (McNee 1983, pp. 115–19) testifies to the anxieties with which the events were viewed. Thus, although the material threat posed by the riots was most significant (in terms of damage caused) to the local state, it was the central state which suffered the most severe 'crisis of hegemony'. It would not be surprising, therefore, if pressures on the magistrates and police emanating from the local authorities were concerned with compensation and just retribution for crime and if the central state were to give priority to the re-establishment of order and territorial control.

This was to be the case. While central state officials were calling for a speedy and deterrent response to clear the streets, some local state officers (particularly in the Labour-controlled areas where most of the disorders occurred) stressed the importance of checking the 'provocative' actions of the police in their areas.[2] In Nottingham the council offered financial assistance to enable those alleged rioters convicted by magistrates 'in breach of natural justice' to appeal.[3] Such responses were not universal. In Manchester, for example, criticism of the police and magistrates from within the local state was quite clearly stifled in an attempt (unsuccessful, as it happened) at conciliation.

Before moving on to an examination of the agencies themselves and their conduct during the riots, some attention must be given to the character of the disorders. This will be attempted, first at the level of generality, and then in respect of each individual area in the study.

The context of the 1981 riots

Although the present work is not concerned with the specific character of the riots themselves, some tentative analysis must be attempted in order to define the nature of the challenge which they presented to the courts and to the other agencies of the state.

From the Table below it may be concluded that large proportions of those arrested in 1981 were black, that many were young and that the rate of unemployment was appallingly high. These features, it will be argued, are characteristic of the populations of the inner-city areas in which the riots occurred (Hamnett 1983).

Details of arrests in 1981 Riots

	Numerical total	Black arrestees (%)	Under 20 (%)	Not in paid employment (%)	With CRO record (%)
Brixton	257	67	65	67	62
Southall	61	75	51	51	84
Liverpool ('Toxteth')	244	25[a]	55	85[a]	59[b]
Manchester	216	44[a]	60	74	54

Source: HOSD 20/82 (Metropolitan, Greater Manchester and Merseyside).
[a] Taking into account unrecorded part of sample.
[b] Figure from HOSD 20/82, Summary, Table 1.

In order to provide some explanation for the rioting it is necessary to establish, first of all, why these areas housed such large populations of young black people who had never been involved in wage labour and were unlikely to be so in the foreseeable future. We must return, at this stage, to the broad periodization which has been adopted in respect of the development of productive relations and identify briefly certain characteristics of the current period. The first may be described as the 'international socialization of production'. By this is meant not only the combination, in the form of a single economic ownership, of capital coming from several different countries but also the location of bases for exploitation for a particular capital in different countries around the globe (Poulantzas 1974; Mandel 1975). The second tendency is the continual pressure to raise the rate of exploitation in order to compensate for declining profit levels. In the case of Britain, these features combined to displace large populations of Caribbean and Asian workers from their homelands to the metropolitan areas in the period of post-war expansion between 1950 and 1962 (Rex 1982).

These workers were to comprise a new and docile reserve army of labour (Gorz 1970; Castells 1975; Frobel *et al.* 1980; Cohen 1987), with a precarious tenure of work in the lowest wage sector. In the view of Joshua and Wallace (1983) the arrival of this immigrant population led to the replacement of inter-communal violence directed against isolated black groups by more systematic racist violence at the level of the state. In time, therefore, it was inevitable that the black communities would mobilize in a collective response.

The move towards black collective violence cannot be regarded as merely a factor in generation replacement (Rex 1982). It will be argued here that long-term shifts in the relations of production have had the effect of creating more or less structural unemployment (Cohen 1987, pp. 111–14) concentrated in specific urban areas and groups of workers.

Sivanandan (1980) and Bunyan (1981a) have both given prominence to the revolutionary impact of micro-engineering – what Mandel (1975, pp. 184–222) calls the 'third technological revolution' – in reversing the tendency to move labour to capital. The manufacture of high-technology micro-circuitry could be dispersed to locations outside the metropolitan urban areas and the labour-intensive work of assembly of products could now be undertaken in conditions of intense exploitation in the 'golden' economies of Asia.

Taylorism on a global scale thus presupposes a workforce which is internally sub-divided in terms of class, geographical location and national origin. It establishes the structural inequality in production costs necessary for surplus profit (Mandel 1975). By 1981 British migrant labour, unlike that in the Asian peripheries, had become too well established and organized to provide an attractive prospect to international capital. In sum, these developments have contributed to the permanent deindustrialization of urban areas in the metropolitan countries, particularly Britain (Blackaby 1979; Thirlwall 1982; Hamnett 1983) and to the sequestration of the 1950s *Gastarbeiter* and their families, thousands of miles from the current industrial battlefront.

Consequently, this has meant the isolation of these inner-city populations from traditional forms of social organization associated with the workplace or trade union (Kirsch 1981; Rodrigues 1981). Second, the zones of high unemployment, not being subject to the discipline of the labour market, have suffered the imposition of authoritarian forms of policing targeted on the black populations (see, for example, Kushnick 1981; Rodrigues 1981; Sivanandan 1981; Scraton 1982). Third, politicization in response to these assaults has taken place along the axis of youth culture and not along that of traditional class solidarity (Gilroy 1981; Unsworth 1982).

Brixton (April and July)

The background

The importance of Brixton as a centre for black culture and politics in Britain goes some way to explaining the national significance of events there. West Indian immigration into Lambeth is recent (taking place since the 1950s) and associated with the demand for unskilled labour in the local electronics industry and London mass transport. By 1978 30 per cent of the population in Tulse Hill and Herne Hill wards (rising to 50 per cent among those aged 19–21) was black. The flight of capital during the 1970s was equally dramatic. Philips and Tannoy relocated their factories out of the area and were followed by many smaller firms (Kirsch 1981) with the result that by 1981 nearly 50 per cent of young blacks were without work (Chatwin 1981).

The early political history of the black community was dominated by the Brixton-based Black Panther movement which, without enjoying mass support, was active in campaigning in cases such as that of Joshua Francis (Howe 1982, pp. 62–3). Following police raids on their headquarters in 1971 membership declined, and by the time of the anti-police violence at the Brockwell Park Fair in June 1973, and at the Swan Disco and Stockwell Underground station in autumn 1974, the movement was confined to local schools (Howe 1981, p. 68). The local Labour Party, which lost control of the borough for a short period in the 1960s, was never a real focus of black solidarity (Cockburn 1977, pp. 87–96). Moreover, the Labour government's race-relations strategy, which involved anti-discrimination legislation and the diversion of funds from the urban aid programme into new and existing black community groups, was widely regarded by radical blacks as a (successful) bid to subvert the local black power organizations (Sivanandan 1981; Howe 1982). The co-option of these groups was followed in 1978 by the establishment of a liaison committee between Lambeth Council for Community Relations and the police.

However, within a few days of the creation of this committee, the whole area was cordoned off and a massive SPG operation commenced without consultation. Two months later, after members of the Lambeth Council for Community Relations had themselves been wrongfully arrested, the committee collapsed. New and more aggressive forms of policing (in response, it was alleged, to escalating crime figures)[4] marked a significant worsening of police–community relations (Scarman 1981, paras 4.22–28). In July 1980 a local authority working party produced a final report which described the police in Lambeth as an 'army of occupation' (Turner-Samuels 1981). Quite evidently administrative agencies of the local state (dominated by a substantial Labour majority (see Table 7.1 on p. 102) and the police had by 1980 adopted positions of implacable opposition.

The mid-1970s also saw the formation in Brixton of a new generation of radical organizations, such as the Black Parents and Black Students movements and the *Race Today* collective, which established links with black communities around Britain and internationally. After the New Cross fire, *Race Today* was able to organize a demonstration of 10,000 blacks, signalling plainly the achievement of mass solidarity and mobilization against the police. As Howe (1982, p. 69) put it, they were at this stage 'prepared for operation Swamp '81'.

The disorders

The April 1981 rioting in Brixton has been described in exhaustive detail by Lord Scarman (1981, Part III). He notes the violent reaction of the community to the 'Swamp '81' operation (1981, paras 4.37–42) and recounts a number of set-piece confrontations in which the dominant metaphor used is that of military action. His concern, above all, is to describe the balance of territorial control between the rioters and the police. He records a total of 276 arrests during 10–13 April, and points out that the major incidents of rioting occurred on 11 April and that succeeding days represented a period of 'aftermath' (1981, para. 3.92) during which the police re-established a dominant physical presence. The threat to police control of Brixton had clearly passed by 12 April.

Renewed fighting in Brixton, which is not described by Lord Scarman, broke out at 3.30 p.m. on 10 July 1981 following the arrest of a Rastafarian in Atlantic Road. Lloyd Coxstone, a popular figure in the black community, attempted to intervene but was himself arrested and allegedly assaulted. Within minutes a barricade was erected across Atlantic Road and the police were forced to evacuate the area under a hail of projectiles as a large number of people came out onto the streets. The pavements were crowded for a mile around the centre of Brixton; the focal point was clearly Lambeth Town Hall, in which Lord Scarman had recently concluded Part I of his Inquiry and which was, at the time, being used for an anti-fascist meeting addressed by the then leader of the Greater London Council, Kenneth Livingstone. Although looting took place in Brixton Road, the major preoccupation of the large crowds was clearly with the symbolic occupation of the area. According to a *Guardian* reporter:

> Police strategy was to try to plug one end of the central streets to isolate the active groups. They were also establishing vantage points in the centre of the streets and moving off in cordons in both directions to try to clear bystanders.[5]

With the outbreak of further looting, the police decided to cordon off the entire area and the Underground station was closed. In addition to the riot serials, SPG units were deployed from vans driven into the crowd at speed, and by 8.30 p.m. police authority had been re-established in the area and 42 arrests made. The level of arrests then rose sharply to reach a total of 240 during the weekend.[6] Further sporadic incidents occurred throughout Saturday and Sunday, but in the early hours of the Saturday morning it was considered safe for the Prime Minister, Margaret Thatcher, to visit Brixton police station.

On 15 July 400 officers executed search warrants in a row of 11 houses in Railton Road. Six people were arrested for drug offences and widespread damage was caused to property, including the premises owned by Lambeth Council and recently rehabilitated for youth-club use. The Chairman of Lambeth Council, Councillor Ted Knight, asserted that this was a 'revenge raid' by the police.[7] Whatever the case, further rioting broke out between 11.00 p.m. and 12.15 a.m.

Generally speaking, police strategy in Brixton depended on the physical isolation of the area and a heavy numerical presence. The April disorders differed from the July incidents in that the former came to an observable conclusion and were strictly local, whereas the latter, in the context of the national uprisings, seemed likely to continue. Police action was accompanied on both occasions by criticism from local state officials, who called repeatedly for the resignation of the chief commissioner.[8]

Pre-trial proceedings

After the disturbances of July 1981, the police arranged for 119 of their prisoners to be produced before Camberwell Green magistrates' court on the morning of Saturday 11 July, and a further 38 on the following Monday.[9] It is normal practice at the court for one or sometimes two stipendiaries to sit on Saturdays. However, according to a senior court clerk, on this occasion the arrangements were changed:

> It was thought that two would be sufficient but then a stipendiary

from Greenwich phoned up and offered to come in and help. It seemed churlish to refuse the offer and we set up a third court. I think we might have coped anyway. We were glad to have a third.

The clerk then went on to describe the importance of maintaining a sense of normality:

> I'm against treating the whole thing as a special riot court. I think it could lead to a different attitude being taken to law and justice in these courts . . . administratively our problems weren't very great. We just sat there and waited for the cases to come.

Clearly, however, an extra 119 defendants on a Saturday morning could not but create certain problems. Although the Camberwell Green stipendiaries (who also sit at the top-security court at Lambeth which deals with sensitive political cases) were particularly well used to public pressure, it is doubtful whether the rest of those attending the court could cope as easily. Practical problems encountered included the production of co-defendants in different courts and the general redundancy of the probation service.

The difference between the proportion of custodial remands after the April disorders (Fig. 8.1a) and those after the July incidents (Fig. 8.1b) is striking and needs explanation. Some practitioners believed that the bail figures argued a 'change of heart' by the bench and an increasing frustration at the apparent ineffectiveness of the more tolerant approach adopted in April. It is very probable, however, that the new strategy originated not with the magistrates but with the police. As a senior court clerk explained:

> The police used their 'deferred bail'[10] procedure in the first riot, which meant that people came a good deal later – whereas in the second riot people came straight away and this worked out as much more efficient. In fact it made us rethink the whole 'deferred bail' issue. It is more difficult to put somebody in custody for an offence if he has already been out on bail for it for a month. It was a great help not having deferred bail.

None of the July 1981 courts in the study showed any evidence of the police having used their 'deferred bail' procedure to any extent and thus most first bail decisions were made by the court in the heat of the disorders. Indeed, it appears that police bail was denied *en masse* as a matter of policy. The effect on the numbers subsequently remanded in custody by these courts (e.g., 32.9 per cent in Camberwell Green, 68.82 per cent in Liverpool) in comparison with those so remanded in April by Camberwell Green (5.15 per cent) is quite evident. What occurred was that a police decision, taken jointly by the chief constables, had the effect of co-opting the magistracy into a central position in the control strategy:

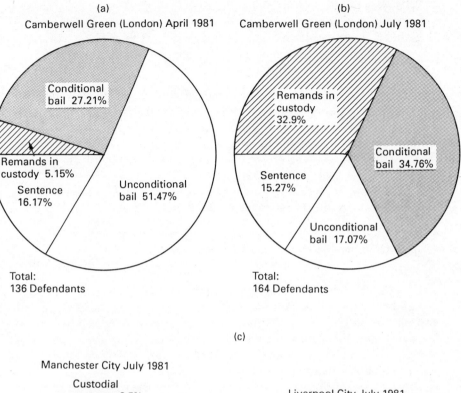

(a)
Camberwell Green (London) April 1981

Conditional bail 27.21%

Remands in custody 5.15%

Sentence 16.17%

Unconditional bail 51.47%

Total: 136 Defendants

(b)
Camberwell Green (London) July 1981

Remands in custody 32.9%

Conditional bail 34.76%

Sentence 15.27%

Unconditional bail 17.07%

Total: 164 Defendants

(c)

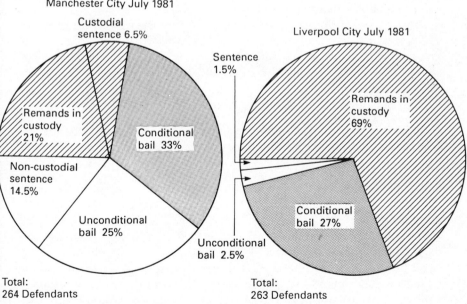

Manchester City July 1981

Custodial sentence 6.5%

Remands in custody 21%

Non-custodial sentence 14.5%

Conditional bail 33%

Unconditional bail 25%

Total: 264 Defendants

Sentence 1.5%

Liverpool City July 1981

Remands in custody 69%

Conditional bail 27%

Unconditional bail 2.5%

Total: 263 Defendants

Figure 8.1 Analysis of decisions on first appearance magistrates' courts (1981 riot defendants in survey).

What was uppermost in the minds of the police and the magistrates was the possibility of a continuance of the outbreak on Saturday night . . . the magistrates said several times that they had a duty to prevent further outbreaks of civil disturbance.

(Solicitor BY)

Faced with the artificial crisis of numbers created by police refusal to exercise their statutory discretion, it is scarcely surprising that the magistrates succumbed to the pressure. Nothing could demonstrate more clearly the organizational supremacy of the police over the magistracy. The benches had been forced to conclude, said one solicitor, that it was 'their job to stop riots' (solicitor BU).

Solicitors appearing for defendants on the first few days after the July riots were unanimous in reporting a bail 'policy'. As one put it:

For virtually all of them I would normally have expected to get bail – apart from the fact that it was a national emergency.

(Solicitor BX)

There is little evidence for the assumption that immediate custodial remand has a dampening effect on civil disorder. During the Chicago and Detroit riots in 1967, the belief that the rioters must be interned to prevent their return to the disorders was regarded by the Report to the National Advisory Commission as almost wholly without substance and potentially dangerous (Dobrovir 1969, p. 68).

One of the complicating factors produced by the central decision on bail was that 73 per cent of the July Camberwell Green defendants were first produced at court on a Saturday (Table 8.1) when hardly any of the advocates were available. The duty solicitor for the day (who unfortunately happened to be a sole practitioner) and a handful of his colleagues struggled hopelessly with the massive caseload. In his view:

The major problem was stemming the tide of people being remanded in custody without representation.

(Solicitor BY)

In fact, the duty solicitor was able to appear on behalf of approximately 30 out of the 119 defendants who were being produced continuously in the three courts.

The contrast between the April and the July proceedings was not confined merely to the early stages. The time graphs show clearly how in the April proceedings, unconditional bail predominated after the first week with custodial remand being used only in respect of a handful of defendants, some of whom were produced in the first days of July (doubtless under the impact of the renewed disorders (Fig. 8.2a)).

Since the April defendants were produced at much later stages, the work was spread over a much longer period. In July, on the other hand, there is evidence of frantic activity in the first two months, with heavy use of the custodial remand for three weeks before it was replaced by conditional, and to a lesser extent, unconditional bail (Fig. 8.2b).

Table 8.2 shows that, despite the severity of the riots, the extensive use of petrol bombs and widespread damage, the charges were of a relatively minor nature. This seems to have come as a surprise to many practitioners who had a fairly sophisticated appreciation of the strategic use of charges in civil disorder. The use of serious indictable offences to frighten benches into refusing bail had previously created problems where defendants had elected for jury trial, leaving the prosecution no option but to recharge with summary offences. One lawyer explained:

> Yes, in Lewisham for example in 1978 and in other incidents, they have charged high and then on reflection charged down. But this time [Brixton in July] they got it right and generally only charged with summary offences . . . At Southall the station officer didn't understand this but they did here. There were very few cases that weren't purely summary. I think that they probably had a circular.
>
> (Solicitor BX)

As in Liverpool and Manchester, early hearing dates were sought and one stipendiary announced that all trials would be held, if possible, within ten days (solicitor BX).

The trials

Figure 8.3b shows that the sentencing at Camberwell Green of the July defendants was completed (with the exception of committals) within 11 weeks, whereas the sentencing of the April defendants took at least 21 weeks (Fig. 8.3a). Much of this compression was obtained by the remitting of cases to Lambeth magistrates' court[11] for trial and by the relatively small number of contested cases in July (Table 8.3).

Most solicitors reported their satisfaction with the conduct of the trials and the acquittal rate, which stood at 31 per cent of magistrates' trials in April and 38 per cent in July. As is often the case in public order trials, the quality of the evidence was the chief stumbling block for the prosecution:

> there was too much exact evidence to be believable . . . The police were always in twos, always saying exactly the same things. How could it conceivably be that, whatever the lighting, time of day, however scarred the riot shields were, they always managed to have a clear view of each defendant who always managed to be in a small group of 5 people distinct from the main group – it was too much to swallow.
>
> (Solicitor BZ)

(a) Brixton (Camberwell Green Magistrates Court):
    Remands of April 1981 riot defendants

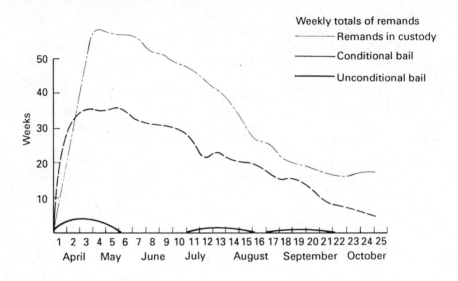

(b) Brixton (Camberwell Green Magistrates Court):
    Remands of July 1981 riot defendants

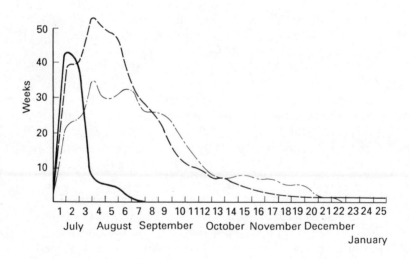

Figure 8.2

(c) Remands in Liverpool City Magistrates Court: 1981 riot defendants

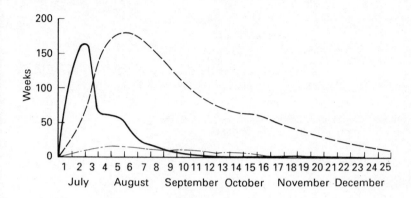

(d) Remands in Manchester City Magistrates Court: 1981 riot defendants

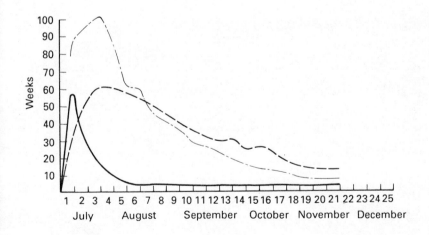

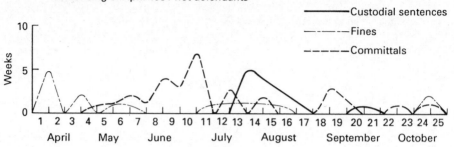

(a) Brixton (Camberwell Green Magistrates Court):
Sentencing of April 1981 riot defendants

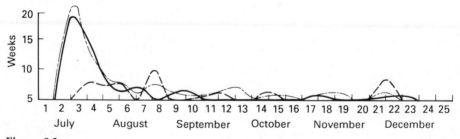

(b) Brixton (Camberwell Green Magistrates Court):
Sentencing of July 1981 riot defendants

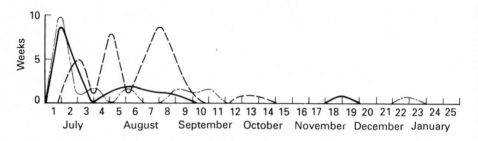

(c) Sentences in Liverpool City Magistrates Court: 1981 riot defendants

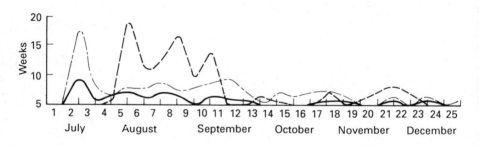

(d) Sentences in Manchester City Magistrates Court: 1981 riot defendants

Figure 8.3

Clearly many more defendants were involved in magistrates' courts trials in April, when 47.5 per cent of all cases were contested before the justices in comparison with 27 per cent of the July cases. Again this reflects the charging policy. In July more Theft Act (looting) offences were charged and fewer public order offences which made up the bulk of the July charges (see Table 8.2). Certainly, Theft Act offences present less scope for the challenge of prosecution evidence. Moreover, the reduced number of magistrates' trials may also reflect a weakening of confidence in the bench occasioned by the experience of remand decisions in the first days of July.

Conversely, sentencing policy between the two riots seems, on the face of it, to have remained remarkably stable (Table 8.4). A closer examination of the sentencing time graphs, however, reveals a custodial 'bulge' in July, which affected defendants from both sets of disorders. Custodial sentences for the July defendants were used immediately (see Fig. 8.3b) whereas for the April defendants they came 12 weeks after arrest (see Fig. 8.3a). This is not to say that the April defendants would have avoided custodial sentences at some later stage, but the impact on their cases of the subsequent rioting (for which they could hardly be held responsible) is fairly evident. It is quite clear, therefore, that the renewed disorders prompted a fresh sentencing philosophy in the Camberwell Green and Lambeth magistrates' courts. As one solicitor suggested:

> The April cases they were playing down . . . They weren't going to send anyone to prison. They weren't going to do anything inflammatory . . . Once July happened it transformed the attitude of the courts. I think they decided . . . [they] had to *brand* them all as mindless criminals and send them to prison.
>
> (Solicitor BX)

There were further interruptions of the normal processes in July. At the end of the month the Camberwell Green court received a circular to the effect that all Brixton riot cases committed for trial should be sent to the Central Criminal Court rather than to the Inner London Crown Court (senior court clerk). The temporary shift of attitudes during July can thus be seen as a response to pressure emanating from the police and from the Lord Chancellor's Department. The compliant responses of the Camberwell Green court and the clear ascendancy of policing priorities in the court at that period may have had unfortunate consequences:

> The manner in which the magistrates dealt with normal civil liberties and the Bail Act on July 12 was sufficient to give the police the encouragement that they needed to go round and smash up homes as they did in Railton Road the following week. I think that the magistrates have got to bear a large public responsibility for that.
>
> (Solicitor BV)

Nevertheless, it is clear that, after the traumatic events of early July, the court returned with equal facility to a practice of individualized process.

Southall

The background

The situation in Southall, a centre of Asian settlement, contrasts sharply with that in Brixton. As Rex (1982, p. 103) puts it:

> Relatively speaking the Indian community and Indian youth had been successful both in education and employment. True, they suffered from racial discrimination and from hardships which beset any immigrant community, but they had the cultural resources and were building the economic resources to be able to cope with difficulties.

Again, immigration had taken place largely in the 1960s in response to labour demands by newer industries in the area, including the multinationals, Nestlé and Batchelors, and smaller concerns such as Woolf's Rubber Co.

The dominance of the Sikh temple, the Indian Workers' Association and the Labour Party ensured that, despite appalling housing conditions and considerable resistance and racist provocation from the displaced white working-class community, no radical oppositional organizations were formed.

By the mid-1970s Southall had become the cultural heart of the British (and European) Asian population which now monopolized the skilled trades and services in the area. However, its quiescence and respectability made it an easy target for a series of racist attacks which culminated in June 1976 in the murder of Gurdip Singh Chaggar. The mass politicization of the Asian community dates from this period[12] with the formation of the Southall Youth Movement. In 1978, Ealing Borough Council passed to the Conservatives and the inevitable friction[13] between elements of the local state (in this case supported by the central state) and the tenacious independence of the Southall community was a crucial factor in what followed.

It was Ealing Borough Council which, in the face of considerable protest from local organizations, agreed to permit the National Front to hold an election meeting in April 1979 in Southall Town Hall. On the day, the police decided to cordon off and defend the whole town centre against the local community (Dummett 1980; Lewis 1980). The mass arrests and injuries which followed provoked almost universal revulsion and, by 1981, the radical Southall Youth Movement and Southall Rights enjoyed support from Asian communities around the world. Such was the sense of collective solidarity that Southall represented the only instance in which the magistrates' court proceedings were displaced out of their normal jurisdictions.

The disorders

The outbreak of violence on 3 July in Southall, although bearing little resemblance to what followed, was in many respects the precondition of the 1981 summer riots. Its origins were overtly political. A skinhead band, the '4 Skins', had been booked to perform at the Hamborough Tavern in Southall and, unfortunately, the implications of this booking for the Asian community appear to have been lost on both the pub manager and the police. At around 8.00 p.m. two coaches and a large number of other skinheads, totalling, in some estimates, 200, arrived in the area, many wearing national Front insignia. Shortly afterwards, a group of about 15–20 set about attacking Asian-owned shops and a hotel on the Uxbridge Road.[14]

There was an immediate response from the local community and literally hundreds of Asians rushed onto the streets to confront the skinheads. The police reaction was not quite so precipitate, and the fighting had been going on for up to two hours before substantial numbers of officers from all over West London, many equipped with riot shields, were drafted into the area. Their first act, which was deeply resented by the crowd, was to throw a protective cordon around the Hamborough Tavern from which the remaining skinheads were then 'evacuated'.[15] By 10.30 p.m. the cordon had been driven back to the point where the pub itself and a police van could be set alight. Petrol bombs and bricks were thrown at the police, who were accused of protecting the skinheads. A further cordon was set up around the police station and the area was closed to traffic while the crowd began to erect their own barricades. After a night of minor skirmishes, the disorder had died away by the morning.

The police, it seems, were taken largely by surprise, forced onto the defensive at an early stage and caught between rival groups. They were not, therefore, in a position to make many arrests despite the large numbers of people involved. Several local solicitors were nevertheless surprised at the low figures (particularly in comparison with 1979) and suggested that, once the skinheads had been forcibly removed, the experiences of 1979 taught that there was little to be gained by further confrontation with the police, and most people returned home immediately.

With the police station in a posture of siege, much of the early activities of the lawyers and Southall Rights legal advice centre workers were taken up with discovering the numbers and identities of those arrested. Lists were supplied by the police to the local Sikh temple and other groups but, pointedly, not to Southall Rights, whose offices were more or less opposite the police station.

A week later, on 10 July, there was a further, less extensive outbreak of violence of a character more consistent with those which had been taking place around the country in the interim. In this case, Asian youths were in direct confrontation with the police.

There is a great deal of confusion regarding the numbers arrested in the 1981 Southall riots. However, adopting a consensus view of the various lists of defendants, it is clear that between 21 and 23 were apprehended on the night of 3 July, and a further seven or eight in so-called 'dawn raids'. Thirteen or 14 defendants were arrested on 10 July. It seems, moreover, that only three skinheads were among those arrested on 3 July.

Pre-trial proceedings

The files of the Southall Defence Group show that 21 people charged with possessing an offensive weapon were later recharged with threatening behaviour. Indeed, well over half of these defendants had their charges altered on the same day, 20 August 1981 – a clear indication that the changes had relatively little to do with the individual merits of the cases.

This prosecutorial manoeuvre seemed to many to represent a rather clumsy attempt to defeat the right of defendants to elect for jury trial – a strategy familiar from 1979 (Dummett 1980, p. 114–15). Block re-charging to confine cases to the magistrates' courts was attacked as an abuse of process, but proceedings in 1981 in the Divisional Court to compel the police to desist from the practice were unsuccessful. Accordingly, the prosecution policy is clearly reflected in the committal rate, which was minimal in 1979 (Sweet 1980, p. 14) and 11 per cent in 1981 (see Table 8.3).

The use of bail in Southall was in marked contrast to that adopted in the rest of the country during the July disorders. Bail had been allowed almost universally to the 237 defendants appearing in the Barnet magistrates' court after the 1979 disorders. The success of this policy was demonstrated by the fact that, despite the long and difficult journey across London to Barnet, warrants for non-appearance were issued in respect of only seven defendants.

Again, in 1981 police bail was granted to all but five of the sample.[16] Conditions (curfew, residence and sureties) were imposed on a similar number of defendants appearing at Ealing magistrates' court over the period 16–23 July, but in respect of the vast majority (29 defendants) the presumption in favour of bail operated fully (see Table 8.1). As one observer put it:

> Bail was given relatively easily. I don't think the magistrates had an anti-bail policy.
>
> (Social worker SE)

It has been suggested in respect of other courts in the country where large numbers of defendants were remanded in custody that this might be attributed to the fact that many of the arrested rioters had many previous convictions.[17] In this, however, Southall was no exception, with 84 per cent of defendants having criminal records.[18] This was clearly not sufficient, however, to induce the Ealing bench to deny bail on the scale witnessed elsewhere.

It is certainly true that no one on 3 July was aware of the extent of the threat to civil order which was to follow, but by the time the majority of defendants appeared in court on 16 July this was no longer the case. One thousand other defendants had been arrested in London, and it was widely anticipated that the riots would continue.

It is perhaps also of marginal significance in this context that, in contrast with the rest of the country, no charges of looting were preferred in respect of the Southall disturbances of 3 July.[19] More important, certainly, is the fact that the Southall Asian community is remarkable for the strength of its family and social cohesion and, in this way, was radically different from, for example, Toxteth with its more fluid social composition. Moreover, once the police on 4 July had decided to release defendants on bail (at a stage before the general directive to refuse it was implemented), it would be extremely hard for the magistrates to revoke their decision. Their choice was thus free and unfettered by either of the factors which worked so potently elsewhere, the pre-existing refusal of the police and the pressure of large numbers appearing on a single day.

As in 1979, most of the cases were produced initially at Ealing magistrates' court, which was also able to deal with the extra workload (26 cases on the worst day, 16 July), with relative ease. The situation was further alleviated by the decision to remit most of the defended cases to Brentford. This decision, however, had an unfortunate resemblance to the more serious displacement of the 1979 riot trials to Barnet. One solicitor hazarded his own explanation:

> it is strange how, in 1979 [the cases] were moved from Ealing to Barnet to be tried by stipendiaries and in 1981 they were moved to Brentford . . . The only interesting factor I would say is that Ealing magistrates' court has to my knowledge 4 Asian JPs [whereas] Brentford . . . has no Asian JPs.
>
> (Solicitor SD)

In 1979 it was argued that the decision to move the trials was based upon administrative efficiency, although this view has been severely criticized by both Sweet (1980) and Dummett (1980, p. 111), who considered the decision to be 'inept and insensitive'. Much has been made of the depoliticizing effect of the displacement and the damage done to defence cases by their removal from the appropriate context (Sweet, 1980, pp. 14–16).

The trials

With significant exceptions, the conduct of the trials in Brentford was approved of by the solicitors:

> Within the strictly legal framework it wasn't like 1979. They were, with the exception of some, being treated like normal citizens.
>
> (Solicitor SG)

Many observers of the 1979–80 Barnet trials have suggested that there was a perceptible decline in the punitive attitude of the court between July 1979 and January 1980 when the trials were concluded. Sweet (1980, p. 25) suggests that it was a widespread view in Southall that the first magistrates arrived at Barnet 'determined to justify the controversial tactics of the police' but that the trials became less combative as time passed. The numbers involved in the Brentford trials in 1981 are too small for any such similar conclusions to be drawn with safety.

In two areas, however, the 1981 cases did cause concern. First, the tariff for 'threatening behaviour' offences was vastly augmented, with fines of £500 being imposed in some cases. The fine was clearly the dominant sanction, with only two sentences of immediate imprisonment imposed. The number of guilty pleas was restricted by the policy of the Legal Defence Group to challenge prosecution evidence wherever possible (see Table 8.3).

The second area of criticism concerned the Incident Control Room at Southall police station, which was accused of withholding evidence from the defence. On 30 October 1981 the Recorder of London stopped the trial of one of the Southall defendants and ordered that a transcript of the proceedings be sent to the Director of Public Prosecutions with a view to possible charges of perjury against the arresting officer.[20]

Despite these concerns, it is clear that the 1981 Southall trials were handled with considerably more tact than those of 1979 which were widely viewed in Southall as 'the final stage in a process of victimisation which began with the National Front' (Sweet 1980, p. 27). Nevertheless, it is clear that the twin strategies of containment within the magistrates' court and displacement out of the area both relate to the situation of the Asian community isolated within a somewhat hostile borough.

Liverpool

The background

The black community in Liverpool is one of the longest-established in Britain and cannot generally be categorized as immigrant. As early as 1851 racial minorities comprised 15 per cent of the population in some parts of the city[21] and they were deeply involved in the flourishing 'secondary economy' which was essential to the maintenance of the mercantile fleets (Brogden 1982, pp. 44ff.). The dominance of the port also ensured that manufacturing (as opposed to service) industries were not established until the close of the nineteenth century.

These factors have had a profound impact upon the condition of Liverpool's black community, which, by 1981, comprised 50 per cent black British and 20 per cent Chinese with only small percentages of recent West Indian and Asian arrivals.[22] Racism and inter-communal violence have been a feature of the area for centuries (Law and Henfry 1981).

Slum clearance and the blitz displaced the major part of the black population into cheap accommodation in the Abercromby and Granby wards vacated in the post-war bourgeois exodus from the central areas (Evans 1977; Simey 1988, p. 20). The concentration of the black community in the central areas indicated its dependence on the now-departed shipbuilding and dockyard industries and those other manufacturing enterprises associated with a transit port.[23] The level of unemployment among the black community in these areas was thus catastrophic (Ben-Tovim *et al.* 1980, pp. 10–18).

The black and white populations of these central wards constitute in a real sense an unemployed proletariat which has historically been subject to the disciplines and rigours of wage labour. As Rex (1982, p. 106) put it:

> the blacks in Liverpool were in every respect except their colour [*sic*] British proletarian youth . . . The Toxteth riots, therefore, more than those in Brixton, seemed to involve a confrontation of a sub-proletariat, willing as a result of their experiences to confront the police.

As in Brixton, the mid-1970s saw the foundation of a number of projects funded by Urban Aid. The creation of the 'Partnership Programme' in 1979 signalled unequivocally the linkage of the central state to local state strategies and the problems encountered by Merseyside Community Relations Council (Ben-Tovim *et al.* 1980, pp. 101–2) must be seen in the light of this relationship. Nevertheless, the Liverpool Black Organization (1979) and the Merseyside Anti-Racist Alliance (1978) had both managed to preserve their independent status and to develop radical campaigns in the black communities against racism and aggressive policing. In contrast to the case of Brixton, however, these campaigns were primarily regional and did not seek to locate themselves in a national or international context.

The attitudes of the Liverpool police to the local black communities have been well documented (Brogden 1982; Scraton 1982; 1985). For example, despite the large white presence among the 1981 rioters (as evidenced by the arrest list (Table 8.5)), the chief constable, Kenneth Oxford, was still disposed to believe that: 'It is exclusively a crowd of black hooligans intent on making life unbearable.'[24]

The complete lack of communication and the tokenism of the community liaison scheme (Ben-Tovim *et al.* 1980, pp. 76–7) is evidenced by the *Listener* incident, the Knowsley operation, and the evident surprise of the police when the riots occurred (Scraton 1982, p. 23; 1985, pp. 58–89).

The second important feature of the social context of the 1981 Liverpool riots was the fierce hostility which had existed for some time between parts of the local state and the police. In 1979 there was a considerable escalation following a policing operation in the Huyton and Kirkby areas and the death in custody of Jimmy Kelly:

> The Knowsley District Council passed a vote of 'no confidence' in the policing of its area, Harold Wilson demanded an inquiry into the policing of his Huyton constituency, the Conservative Leader of the Merseyside Metropolitan Council described Oxford as 'arrogant' in the face of criticism and the Labour group on the Police Authority stated that the Authority was powerless.
>
> (Scraton 1982, p. 22)

In the 1981 elections (see Table 7.1 on p. 102) the Labour group achieved a majority position in the Police Authority and the chief constable's foremost critic, Lady Simey, was given the chair. A crisis was clearly imminent. In the context of Liverpool, the local authority was in the position of giving expression (without the political power to do more) to the frustrations and resentments of the Liverpool 8 community (Parker *et al.* 1981, pp. 26–32; Simey 1988).

The Liverpool magistrates' courts had long attempted to maintain a balance between the police, local authority and communities. Parker *et al.* (1981, pp. 45–77) noted the prevalent atmosphere of 'pragmatic tolerance' in the courts which, they claim was based on a consensual model of Liverpool society and a healthy awareness of the limitations of custody facilities.

Clearly in July 1981 the illusion of consensus could no longer be maintained.

The disorders

The arrest and subsequent rescue of Leroy Cooper from a police van in Selbourne Street, Liverpool, on Friday 3 July 1981 (1.1)[25] is credited by Lord Scarman (1981, para. 2.27) as being the 'minor incident' which 'set off a great riot'. It was, in fact, merely one of a pattern of similar skirmishes which by 10.50 p.m. the next day had induced a group of angry youths to erect a barricade in an attempt to exclude the police from Upper Parliament Street. Shortly afterwards, this barricade was charged and dismantled by 90 policemen equipped with riot helmets, who then set about scouring the surrounding streets (2.9).

Hearing of these and earlier events, large crowds of residents appeared on the streets, expressing their hostility to the police presence by shouting and throwing stones at any officers who came too close. As a result, the police withdrew shortly after midnight and cordoned off the entire area (2.14). At this point a fresh defensive barricade was erected across Upper Parliament Street (2.17) and this was attacked by 150 officers in full riot equipment during the early hours. This attack was nevertheless repulsed and the police drew up in formation across Upper Parliament Street, facing volleys of stones and other missiles, until 6.00 a.m. when they were able to disperse the much depleted crowd with the aid of a police vehicle (2.24).

During the course of the next day, Sunday 5 July, extensive preparations were made by the police to maintain their presence in Liverpool 8. A CID Major Incident Control was set up to deal with the large number of prisoners envisaged that night (there had been only two the night before) and to liaise with the Special Branch and the Headquarters Incident Control Intelligence (Oxford 1981b, p. 41). A Force Incident Control was also established and riot equipment, including CS gas, was reviewed and prepared for use (3.6). After senior briefing and consultative sessions at 6.00 to 7.00 p.m., it was decided to deploy 373 officers into the area and, after some repeated stonings, Upper Parliament Street was again closed and the police forces drawn up in two cordons at 8.00 p.m. (3.11). Half an hour later, in response to this second mass police incursion, a further barricade was erected by the crowd (3.30)[26] and shortly afterwards the police began to advance from their lines. At the same time, the crowd was attacking and looting business premises in the area and had requisitioned milk floats from a dairy to direct against the police (3.15–16).

By 10.30 p.m. a further barricade had been constructed in Kingsley Road and, since repeated baton charges were proving ineffective against the by now vastly augmented crowd, the police were forced to retreat back along Upper Parliament Street under the collective assault of stones, petrol bombs and vehicles (3.26–30). By 1.00 a.m. it was recognized that the occupying police force in Upper Parliament Street was in danger of being routed (3.32). Therefore, under cover of a 'truce' arranged for the evacuation of Princes Park Hospital, they regrouped and called up reinforcements. At the same time the decision was taken, after an emergency telephone call to the Home Secretary (Whitelaw 1989, p. 189) to use CS gas in order to retake Upper Parliament Street. The chief constable issuing the order made no attempt subsequently to deny the questionable legality of the use of this weapon in these circumstances:

Home Office instructions had not over the past sixteen years *envisaged and authorised* the use of C.S. gas against other than armed, besieged criminals. I am fully aware that some of the equipment used (Ferret cartridges) should not be used again to deal with public disorder . . .

(Oxford 1981b, p. 3; emphasis added)

At 2.00 a.m., both frontal and flanking attacks were made on Upper Parliament Street by 800 officers under the cover of a barrage of CS canisters. No less than 59 rounds of canisters and 15 grenades were launched into the crowd (Oxford 1981, p. 3). Although many of the canisters were intended for 'barrier penetration' and designated as 'lethal', they were fired (in breach of the regulations for use) in such a way that ricochets against persons in the crowd were inevitable (BSSRS 1985, pp. 71–2; Scraton 1985, pp. 76–7). At least five persons were seriously injured in this way. Nevertheless, an hour later the police had re-occupied Upper Parliament Street and were sweeping the side streets with 'anti-looting' squads (3.41).

Although this was probably the most serious night of disorder, only 13 arrests were made in the area. 'The distance between the lines', as the chief constable maintained, made 'arrests impossible' (5.40). What is clear, however, is that the issue at stake at street level was not one of legality. There were manifest illegalities perpetrated on both sides, the majority of which were to go unpunished. The issue was, on the contrary, one of simple territorial control, as both Unsworth (1982, p. 73) and Scraton (1982, p. 28) have stressed. The Liverpool chief constable, who was later to order the inhabitants of his city to 'keep off the streets', announced on 6 July 'I will not allow no-go areas'.[27]

Later that day, full police mobilization was achieved (4.4) and a 'night operation' planned for that evening which involved dividing up the area and patrolling it in force (4.8). Again, in response to the incursion of officers 'in strength', a barricade was erected in Park Road, only to be attacked and broken up by the police.

With the police occupying Liverpool 8 in such large numbers (Fig. 8.2c), arrests became more frequent. As the chief constable reported: 'Patrols constantly engaged groups of youths, dispersing them quickly and preventing any kind of gathering' (5.4). The *Liverpool Echo* talked of a 'massive police contingent flooding the district'[28] and Peter Bassey of the Liverpool 8 Defence Committee complained 'never mind a police state, this is a police city' (Clark 1981b, p. 19). During the course of July and August, officers from 40 other forces were deployed in Liverpool 8, with each 'foreign' PSU accompanied by a 'guide' from the local force (6.5). For some considerable time afterwards 'men from Gwent, Staffordshire, the West Midlands and Hampshire, to name but a few, patrol[led] the streets in fours, armed with photocopied extracts from A to Z' (Clark 1981a, p. 3).

In Kirkby on 8 July a barricade was attacked and a crowd dispersed by officers with shields, surrounding a vehicle in a kind of police 'testudo' (6.10). The police now developed a regular 'pattern' (10.3) of light deployment during the day followed by 'high-level' saturation policing in Toxteth during the night. According to Scraton (1982, p. 28), this nocturnal presence amounted almost to a curfew. The outlying areas were covered by a mobile PSU reserve on stand-by.

By 21 July saturation policing had been reduced to levels (see Table 8.6) where the Incident Control could be stood down. However, on 26 July 1981, after further incidents, the area was again quarantined by road blocks and the police were once more driven out of Upper Parliament Street and barricades erected (14.8). The police returned in massive numbers, deploying 'a strong force of foot patrol officers in the Toxteth inner city and also on the perimeter' (Oxford, 1981b, p. 5). On this occasion the occupying force had been issued with NATO-type helmets (Oxford 1981b, p. 3) and, on the advice of the RUC, had adopted the strategy of driving vehicles at high speed into crowds to break them up (1981b, p. 5). As a consequence of such tactics one young disabled man, David Moore, was run down and killed by a police vehicle and another, Paul Conroy, had his back broken in a similar 'police traffic accident' (1981b, p. 28). After various attempts by the crowd to erect barricades, police control in Upper Parliament street was finally re-established at about 3.30 a.m. on the morning of 29 July 1981 by what amounted to a police 'armoured column': 'OSD landrovers led the sweep supported by fully equipped snatch squads on foot and followed by PSU personnel with shields' (15.13).

Pre-trial proceedings

The prisoners taken during the disturbances were moved quickly to surrounding police stations or the Main Bridewell for processing and then presented immediately before the magistrates' court. The court lists (see Table 8.1) therefore reflect numerically the ebb and flow of the various offensives in Upper Parliament Street and the surrounding areas.

The first difficulty which confronts any attempt to evaluate the conduct of the riot proceedings in Liverpool is uncertainty as to the actual number of defendants. Under continuous pressure from Conservative MP Tony Marlow and others, Home Office spokesmen made a number of announcements which, since they adopted different criteria in each case, obscured rather than illuminated the issue.[29]

The number of defendants involved in the court survey (295) was considerably smaller than the number of arrests logged by HOSD (530). The reasons for this are, first, that many of the defendants referred to in the Home Office figures were not processed at Liverpool City magistrates' court but were dealt with at neighbouring courts in Kirkby, St Helens, and elsewhere. Second, only those defendants whose cases could be identified with absolute certainty as being riot cases are included in the survey. The survey therefore concerns exclusively the operation of the Liverpool City court which dealt with the bulk of the 'Toxteth' cases. Tables 8.2 and 8.5 show that the data presented by the HOSD in relation to 'Toxteth' is, in respect of charges and outcomes, directly comparable with that of the survey. Moreover, when comparing the HOSD 'Toxteth' data and that in relation to Merseyside as a whole, there appears to be only one significant differentiating factor.[30]

Table 8.5 indicates a decided preference for Theft Act charges in 'Toxteth' as against a preponderence of Public Order Act charges in Merseyside as a whole. This doubtless reflects the incidence of looting in 'Toxteth' and the activities of the anti-looting squads. Therefore, subject to the proviso with regard to Theft Act charges and the necessary heavier penalties which such looting offences might be expected to attract, analogies drawn between the HOSD figures for Merseyside and those of the court sample may be regarded as relatively safe.

Although the HOSD figures make no distinction as to place of trial, they seem to indicate a preponderance of indictable offences (270) as against merely summary ones (260). The Report makes the point that in the 'Toxteth' incidents, three-quarters of those arrested were charged with indictable offences (20/82 HOSD (Liverpool): 12). This tends to suggest that the bulk of the offences were of an extremely grave character. However, it should be remembered that many of the Theft Act cases and those relating to violence against the person, while technically indictable, were of a sufficiently trivial character to ensure that they were dealt with summarily. Thus, for example, only 29 per cent of the Theft Act cases and only 51 per cent of the violence cases in the court survey were committed for trial or sentence. Adjusting the HOSD figures on this basis to take account of the real locus of trial, we arrive at a figure of approximately 121 cases on indictment and 409 dealt with summarily. We may, therefore, conclude that the magistrates' court was the primary mechanism for dealing with the Liverpool riot prisoners.

An examination of the charging patterns of the Merseyside police reveals similar complexities. Indeed, it will be argued that the choice of charges related directly to the dominant imperative of maintaining order on and control of the streets.

One of the noticeable tendencies in Liverpool charging was the duplication of charges. Forty per cent of defendants were charged with more than one offence. Some solicitors argued that this policy enabled the prosecution to insist on custodial remands in view of the gravity of the indictable charge and then, in the later stages of the case, to proceed only on the summary charge which gave no right of election. As one solicitor put it:

In the police's view, the main issue was to keep them in custody. They left a serious charge in to keep them in custody.

(Solicitor LD)

At the same time, the post-riot charges – particularly, as we have seen, in Merseyside as a whole – were unusual in the preponderance of Public Order Act charges.

The problem of formulating charges was further complicated by the strategic nature of policing in Toxteth. As one officer explained: 'today you make arrests, tomorrow you don't, to keep the situation quiet'. In this sense, therefore, the type of charges used at any time may as much reflect current policing objectives as the activities of the defendants.

The Liverpool City magistrates' court, as almost all those interviewed in the survey pointed out, enjoys an excellent reputation for fairness (see also Parker *et al.* 1981, p. 48). What occurred during the first seven days of the riot was therefore unprecedented. After most defendants had been held overnight at the Main Bridewell, they were produced at once, in many cases still bearing their bruises and injuries, before benches which were not inclined to mercy. Taking their lead[31] from the stipendiary sitting in court A (who remanded 22 defendants out of 23 in custody), the Liverpool City magistrates, taken together, denied bail to nearly 70 per cent of all defendants appearing during the first week (Fig. 8.1c).

On the first day, 71 defendants were dealt with, almost exclusively by three adult and three juvenile courts. The stipendiary court (A) took the bulk of the defendants and the normal list in that court of 40 defendants was distributed elsewhere to make way for the influx. By 12.30 p.m. the duty solicitor scheme was swamped and, on the clerk's initiative, three other duty solicitors were called up. It was, as the *Liverpool Echo* put it, a 'hard day's night for city magistrates'[32] who sat until 6.30 p.m. to deal with the cases.

Some advocates took the view that the unanimity of response argued that

the magistrates had already been primed before they came into court

(Solicitor LF)

or that there had been a meeting beforehand (solicitor LK). No evidence of such a meeting has been forthcoming, however, and other solicitors believed merely that there had been a 'selection of magistrates':

On the first day you didn't get an individual hearing really . . . As the cases got diffused amongst other liberal benches it changed. The hard benches were out that morning.

(Solicitor LD)

Although there was no reported problem of access, both the Bridewell and the courts were full to overflowing and the situation was highly confused. Under this pressure, bail applications had to be concise:

> if you wanted to get your application heard at all you had to be fairly quick about it.
>
> (Solicitor LD)

Moreover, it was not the clerks who were cutting applications short. It was rather the situation itself, as one advocate admitted:

> The room is full, everybody is in a hurry and you do tend to become a victim to the pressure.
>
> (Solicitor LE)

We can see, therefore, that the decision to produce all defendants together on the same day, and the concerted approach of the bench, contrived to curtail the role of the advocates to the point where they were less than useless:

> Only very, very exceptional cases were given bail – well I think of all the 26 cases I did that day I was given bail in only one . . . in the end I asked the magistrates to release me because I didn't think it was fair to the people involved to be going on with the pretence. The magistrate said . . . 'It's all right Mr——, you're doing your best.'
>
> (Solicitor LK)

The figures show that the presumption in favour of unconditional bail was operating in reverse, with only 2.5 per cent of cases enjoying the benefit of it. As the *Liverpool Echo* put it, perhaps unaware of the existence of the presumption:

> only [cases] with extra-ordinary circumstances made in their bail applications were released.[33]

Almost every solicitor interviewed insisted that he had been told by the bench that the reason for custodial remand was the endeavour to prevent defendants returning to the streets:

> They used the theory that if they put the offenders [sic] behind bars temporarily it might ease the situation in the city.
>
> (Solicitor LE)

Clearly no attempt was made to permit even those anxious to plead to do so, and only four sentences were passed amongst 263 cases appearing in the first week. It is by no means unheard of for a plea to be taken on first appearance, but the important point is that the penal sanctions available for a first offender of good character accused of a relatively minor offence such as 'picking up a packet of sweets in the street' (social worker LH) were

considerably less potent than those given by the power of custodial remand. Quite clearly in many cases the remand had become much more
than a containment strategy – indeed, it was the punishment itself.

The magistrates imposed a total of 86,856 man-hours' custodial remand
on the defendants in the survey, whereas they awarded only 55,104 man-
hours' custodial sentence (allowing for remission).[34] The latter figure is,
of course, clearly overstated since it does not take account of the discount
allowed for time already served on remand. On this basis we can safely
assume that the Liverpool magistrates imposed custodial remands in
respect of the riot defendants which almost doubled the total immediate
custodial penalties imposed by them following convictions.

The relationship between the use of custody and of unconditional bail
for untried defendants is significant. Clearly, some time during the second week of the disorders the decision was taken to release the majority
of prisoners on conditional bail with curfews, residence and surety conditions in almost every case (Fig. 8.2c).

It is highly improbable that this radical change in approach may be
attributed to a sudden improvement in the quality of the terms of the bail
applications. Rather, the initiative came from the prosecution:

> [The prosecution] actually said 'We don't object to bail any more but
> would ask for a curfew to be imposed'. One of the reasons for that –
> well, I know there were behind-the-scenes discussions – one of the
> reasons was that Risley couldn't take the pressure . . . it's always full,
> but the population just doubled for that week so they had to do
> something.
>
> (Solicitor LG)

Certainly chronic overcrowding at Risley remand centre must have
played a part in the decision,[35] but it is suggested that the figures in Fig.
8.2c must be read against those in Table 8.6 which indicate the level of
police deployment in Liverpool 8 during the same period. It was only
when the re-occupation of the area had been consolidated during the
period of 12–20 July that it was considered safe to release defendants. In
these circumstances we see the population of custodial remands decreas-
ing from 165 on 12 July to 60 eight days later, and the numbers of those on
conditional bail rising from 65 to 170 over the same period.

It might be argued that the relationship between these two sets of
figures indicates merely that the police and courts reacted independently,
but in similar ways, to the level of criminal activity in the area. However,
this does not explain the violent reversal of custody and conditional bail
rates in Fig. 8.2c. The factors which are relevant to benches attempting to
make judicial decisions under the Bail Act 1976 must relate to the individual defendant rather than to policing strategies which are outside the
immediate circumstances of the defendant.

The trials

The approach to bail in the Liverpool City magistrates' court in the riot cases is mirrored by their approach to the trials and sentencing. It was evident, for example (Fig. 8.3c), that the heavier sentencing was taking place in the early days of July:

> They were behaving like Christmas shopping courts, giving heavier sentences for publicity.
>
> (Solicitor LG)

The proceedings in the crowded courtrooms in July were tense and emotional. The *Liverpool Echo* described a scene on 13 July when two women and a man were sentenced for looting:

> There were gasps from a crowded public gallery as the magistrates announced: 'Because you are in no position to pay the sort of fine that this court is expecting you will go to prison for 3 months'. There were shouts of 'seven children in care' and other marks of derision as the three prisoners were led out of the dock. Officials were threatening to clear the court before their attention was drawn to a woman aged about 60 slumped unconscious in her chair at the back of the courtroom. Another observer in court said that she fainted when she heard the sentence imposed on her daughter. From the beginning of today's hearings at Liverpool magistrates' court extra police were on duty around the various courts.[36]

Conviction rates were also higher in the period immediately after the disorders. Figure 8.4a shows that convictions and defended trials were rising steeply from the end of July to a peak in mid-August, while acquittals did not show a similar rise until the early part of September:

> I think their minds were clouded by political and general opinions and views . . . it would be stamped as a riot case. The prosecution would open on that basis and it was always very difficult to treat it as a normal case.
>
> (Solicitor LE)

Some advocates indulged in deliberate delaying tactics to ensure that the maximum time had elapsed after the traumatic events of July. By the late autumn, however, the situation had improved to the extent that riot cases were, if anything, being given preferential treatment, and the acquittal rate often exceeded the conviction rate.

Thus it is evident that the collective panic in the court which affected remand and acquittal rates and sentencing had subsided by the middle of August 1981, and the court had re-established itself relatively quickly and dispersed the riot cases among the normal business. It is true that these cases still tended to have a contaminating effect on other cases:

(a) Outcomes of trials in Liverpool City Magistrates Court: 1981 riot defendants

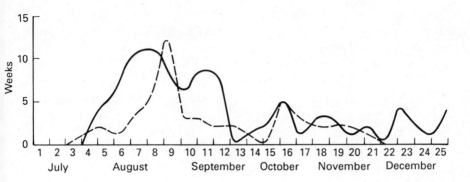

(b) Outcomes of trials in Manchester City Magistrates Court: 1981 riot defendants

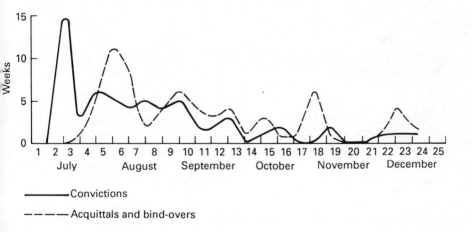

Figure 8.4

When dealing with non-riot cases arising in Liverpool 8, especially if [the defendants] are black I must draw a distinction and point out to the magistrates that this was not related to the riot.

(Solicitor LF)

However, no longer was there a distinct body of rioters representing an apparent threat to the authority of the police, but occasional rather problematic cases to be dealt with in the normal way. It was then that the quality of the evidence began to come under closer scrutiny and for the rushed procedures and charging of July to take effect:

The difficulty was that you cannot always pinpoint who did what to whom because of all the muddle – you cannot say that 'defendant X threw a lump of concrete at constable Y and I saw him do it and I have no doubt whatsoever'; so they rounded them up and put a blanket charge on them.

(Solicitor LE)

The extremely high committal rate of 26 per cent is further evidence of disquiet during the early period at the operation of the magistrates' court in the riot cases:

I think mainly they didn't expect to get decent justice in the magistrates' [court]. There was a feeling that there was no hope.

(Solicitor LE)

It is fairly clear that the high election rate was reflected in the acquittal rate overall. Thus, when the Crown Court figures are added, the percentage rate almost doubles.

Two further factors facilitated this flexible response by the magistrates' court to the disorders. The first was the physical organization of the court, and the second was the nature of the local legal profession.

We have already seen that it was possible for the courts to absorb an extra 300 defendants in the space of a week. For the first time in living memory courts were scheduled for a Sunday (which unfortunately coincided with Orange Day). Extra courts were actually held on Saturday. As a senior court clerk said: 'we had a few hairy days. I wouldn't like to go through this very often.' He went on to suggest:

I said you have an easy way to speed things up. Stick a red star on riot cases and you can more or less process them in a different way. We tried to get the vast majority of s.1 committals to the Crown Court by mid-August.

The figures reveal a remarkably concerted and successful effort to achieve this (see Fig. 8.3c), and defence advocates complained bitterly that they were not given time to examine committal papers or to prepare cases properly.

The nature of the legal profession in Liverpool did not assist matters. Competition for clients has always been fierce in the city. As one practitioner put it:

> Oh yes, there are far too many solicitors in Liverpool. People never go unrepresented here – solicitors fight with each other for clients. It is a dreadful place.
>
> (Solicitor LE)

In this situation, the riots were generally viewed as an unexpected windfall for the profession and competition for clients was intense. Most of those interviewed expressed extremely strong feelings regarding the activities of their fellow advocates, and accusations of touting and of 'cell bar rattling' were fairly universal:

> There were some people in court writing down names and addresses of defendants and who represented them – there was definite pressure to go to a *certain* solicitor.
>
> (Solicitor LG)

Another solicitor claimed:

> There were big scraps going on. One solicitor got himself appointed to the Liverpool 8 Defence Committee and all the others started getting very upset about it . . . it was really very bad and there were solicitors trying to report other solicitors for touting and advertising.
>
> (Solicitor LE)

The solicitor referred to, vehemently denied the charge, insisting that only three of his 30 or so cases were referrals from the Committee and he was very far from being 'appointed'. Nevertheless, tempers ran extremely high, with documents of complaint circulating, and it was alleged that two solicitors had been involved in what amounted to a physical contest over a client. Thus, in a time of crisis, the Liverpool legal profession was scarcely able to develop the kind of mutuality necessary for conducting defences arising from large-scale disorder.

To recapitulate, it has been argued that the riots in Liverpool, although arising from a complex of issues, concerned essentially the right to control territory in Liverpool 8. This concern for territorial control was reflected in the charging and bail policies of the Merseyside police, who sought physical containment for a short period on a large scale. In the event, this was achieved by flooding the court with defendants during the first week of the crisis and thus making impossible its operation as an adversarial tribunal.

In these circumstances, the presumption regarding bail became reversed, and the major, most severe single punishment inflicted by the court became the custodial remand rather than post-conviction sentence.

The almost complete surrender of the magistrates to policing rather than judicial priorities, for a strictly limited period during the crisis, indicates both a remarkable flexibility within the court structure and the clear operational ascendancy of the police.

Manchester

Background

In the Moss Side area, as in Brixton, the establishment of the black population (see Table below) had taken place largely during the post-war period, particularly in response to demand for labour in the cotton and synthetic fibres industries. With the amalgamation of the major employers into four or five large combines and their subsequent relocation, 40,000 manufacturing jobs were lost between 1966 and 1975 (Lloyd 1980; Rogers 1980). At the same time there was a massive decentralization of retail and small manufacturing to the peripheries. The balance of the various communities who remained, the level of unemployment and the shift from manufacturing to service industries are also not dissimilar to Brixton.

Racial composition of wards in Manchester riot areas (per cent)

	White	*W. Indian*	*African*	*Indian*	*Others*
Hulme	71	20	4	2	3
Moss Side	64	25	–	7	4
Lloyd Street	82	8	–	7	3
Rusholme	84	3	1	6	6
Alexandra	72	6	1	14	7

Where the area differs sharply is in the relative status of the autonomous black organizations. Despite the political activity surrounding the Darcus Howe case in Manchester in 1978 and the establishment of the Black Parents Movement, most black activists have been involved to a greater or lesser degree in state-funded projects. The contrast with Brixton, Southall and Liverpool is perhaps best exemplified by the fact that after the disorders on 12 July 1981, legal defences were co-ordinated by the Moss Side Community Action Group, composed largely of local state community workers, and it was not until 5 August that an independent group (the Moss Side Defence Committee) was formed. In other areas the formation of independent defence committees had been immediate.

The intervention of the local state in the area is evident also in the housing, shopping and community centre projects. This is not to suggest that these schemes were necessarily appropriate to the condition of the local community (Hytner 1981). Indeed, the Hulme–Moss Side urban renewal scheme was grandiose, the largest urban renewal scheme in Europe, but at least involvement was more than merely cosmetic. It is perhaps also significant that the Moss Side community, unlike that in Liverpool, was able to call on the services of a group of radical and committed lawyers, the Haldane Group.

In 1981 the local Labour Party made massive gains in the Greater Manchester council elections (Table 7.1 on p. 102). Despite the contentious character of Manchester policing under the chief constableship of James Anderton, and the many complaints of harassment from the black community, the new police authority did not, either before or during the riots, move into a position of confrontation with the police. The chairman of the authority reported in late 1981 that relations were good (Hytner 1981, para. 4.13), and the whole tone of the Hytner Report (adopted *in toto* by the committee) is that of submission to the authority and superior skill of Mr Anderton and the strenuous avoidance of points of contention. In contrast to Liverpool and Brixton, support for the police by the local authority during the riots was extensive.

Nevertheless, the contempt of the police for the local state authority under its Labour majority is evidenced by the incident of 8 July 1981 (see below), the peremptory refusal of the chief constable to co-operate with the local authority inquiry, and a series of clashes which resulted in the complete breakdown of relations after the riots.[37] However, the unity of police, local authority and magistracy at the time of the riots was of the greatest significance.

The disorders

The disorders in Manchester fell into three distinct phases which must be considered in turn. From Sunday 5 July for two days Manchester police had been involved in 'mutual aid' in the Liverpool 8 riots and had suffered heavy casualties (Anderton 1981, p. 4). Therefore, when local fighting first took place in the early hours of Wednesday 8 July and ten shops in Princess Road and the Moss Side shopping centre were attacked with stones and petrol bombs, it was widely believed that the police were under strength:

> We had transferred nearly everyone to Liverpool to stand by for more trouble there, but as soon as news of the Manchester attack filtered through, the force swiftly recalled the men to deal with its own problems.[38]

Be this as it may, only seven arrests were made at the time[39] and, as chief constable Anderton put it, 'there was no direct confrontation'.[40] However, officers in sufficient numbers to dispel the crowd were drafted into

Moss Side in accordance with a previously prepared plan (Anderton 1981, p. 1).

The second stage, which includes broadly the events from the afternoon of 8 July to the early hours of the next morning, has provoked sharp controversy. In examining these events it must be borne in mind that the police had been deeply influenced by their 'mutual aid' experiences and casualties in Liverpool, and the need at all costs to avoid set-piece confrontation (Anderton 1981, p. 4).

Some time in the morning of 8 July, chief superintendent Albert Leach, divisional commander of 'E' division (Manchester South-West), acting doubtless on the authority of the chief constable, called a meeting at Moss Side police station with local community leaders. The major concern of the civilians attending the meeting (which included Councillor Cox, the deputy chair of the police committee, and Limbert Spencer, later of the Hytner committee) was to inquire into the well-being of the seven arrested youths in order to calm widespread fears that they had been improperly detained. Superintendent Leach absented himself from the meeting 'at an early stage' (Hytner, 1981 para. 34.4) to confer, as he subsequently maintained, with other officers. Whatever the case, his action was viewed as a deliberate snub to the group, two of whose members were sufficiently incensed to suggest to the chief constable privately that there should be an apology and that, in view of the history of the affair, Leach should be moved from his present post. The response of Mr Anderton was characteristic: 'We hear a lot nowadays about the much heralded concept of "democratic community policing" . . . Well, if this is a practical example then all I can say is . . . God help us!'[41] Although offering fulsome apologies at the time, the chief constable had clearly formed the view that the abortive meeting was merely a trap set for him by community leaders:

> All the questions put to me personally were obviously designed to discover the intended level of policing in Moss Side, the numbers of police who would be held in reserve and the capacity of the police to respond to any disturbances . . . a guarantee of virtually unpoliced streets . . . suited some terrible ulterior purpose.[42]

As Hytner (1981, para. 34.12) pointed out, this was tantamount to suggesting that the vice-chair of the police committee and others were 'contemplating rioting and were spying for the rioters'.

There is some dispute as to who suggested 'low-profile policing' for the night. Hytner (1981, para. 34.5) clearly felt that it was Mr Anderton: 'In particular it is apparently common ground that the Chief Constable proposed "low profile" policing on Wednesday and this was widely supported.' Mr Anderton vehemently denied responsibility for any such proposal: 'I was asked to maintain a low police profile and I agreed this would be done.'[43] Nevertheless, after the meeting, contingency plans were drawn up and a large number of officers placed on 'stand-by' at each divisional HQ. An observation post was established in Moss Side shopping centre. Clearly the chief constable had now taken the view that further disorders were almost inevitable (Anderton 1981, p. 2).

By the mid-afternoon of 8 July rumours of preparation for an armed siege at Moss Side police station, resentment at the new arrests, and general excitement had drawn a crowd of 500 to the 'Meadow' near Princess Road. By 10.00 p.m. feelings were strong enough to provoke a direct attack upon Moss Side police station. In an outburst of anger against the police, windows were broken and serious damage done to the property and to vehicles in the yard. One police inspector was apparently struck by a cross-bow bolt. At this stage the picture became somewhat confused.

Hytner (1981, para. 38.1) concludes that an attack on the Princess Road shops by black and white youths began at 10.40 p.m. and that, before that period, the crowd had been calm. Anderton (1981, p. 2), on the other hand, times the outbreak of rioting 40 minutes earlier in Wilmslow Road: 'At 10.00 p.m. another group of 200 youths, almost exclusively coloured, left a Community Centre about a mile and a half away and immediately commenced rioting in a nearby shopping area causing extensive damage.' In his account, this group then joined the main group (1,000 strong) to converge on Moss Side police station. What is agreed in all accounts, however, is that the attacks on the Princess Road and other shops were accomplished in the almost complete absence of police officers who were, at the time, installed in large numbers in waiting vehicles and on stand-by in Platt Lane and neighbouring police stations. As the *Manchester Evening News* put it: 'A thousand strong mob of screaming looters invaded a street of shops with not a policeman in sight.'[44]

Hytner (1981, para. 38.7) recorded the anger of local shopkeepers, 'among the best friends of the police in the area', at the absence of the police:

> During this period looting continued unhindered on Princess Road. Much bitter comment was made about the absence of police officers from the Princess Road and Claremont Road areas for a period of two hours and also from the Rusholme area. It was said that the police had adopted a 'no profile' approach instead of the 'low profile' approach promised.

Large numbers of reserves were certainly available. Indeed, a substantial force of officers was observed in transit between Longsight and Platt Lane police stations.[45] When the police offensive did come at 11.40 p.m., it was accomplished with extraordinary efficiency and speed: 'The police swept into the area in force equipped with riot shields, new protective head gear and shin pads.'[46] The rapidity of the deployment and the number of officers involved after the order had been given, clearly impressed the *Manchester Evening News* reporter:

> 11.40 p.m. Police entered the devastated Princess Road area in massive numbers . . . Within minutes hundreds more police were drafted into the area . . . By midnight the Princess Road parade of shops was closed off. 11.55 p.m. Simultaneously squads of riot police poured from transit vans in Moss Lane East and formed cordons behind shields on grassland between Princess Road . . . and Quinney Crescent.[47]

This was, without doubt, a well-prepared operation.

If Mr Anderton's assertion that rioting began at 10.00 p.m. is accepted, it is hard to understand why the police reaction was delayed by 1 hour 40 minutes, during a period in which most of the damage was done. Clearly the chief constable was aware of the attacks since he was receiving 1,600 emergency calls every hour (Anderton 1981, p. 8).

Hytner (1981, para. 38.8) dismissed as 'a wild allegation' the idea that 'the police as a matter of policy had decided to "let Moss Side burn to teach the community a lesson"'. No evidence is produced for this dismissal, and indeed the only alternative offered is that there was a 'misunderstanding between Mr. Anderton and the community leaders as to what policing was required' (1981, para. 38.8). This seems a doubtful proposition. It is scarcely likely that Mr Anderton would knowingly neglect his statutory duty out of respect for the views on policing of a group of people he had decided by the afternoon were bent 'upon some terrible ulterior purpose'. Nevertheless, the clear effect of Mr Anderton's strategy was to enlist popular support for heavy policing operations in Moss Side, and to ensure that the local authority would not dare make any further intervention.[48]

By 1.00 a.m. the crowd of bystanders had been pushed off the grassland and 'wielding batons and riot shields yelling officers surged into the crowd, scattering them into the tangled maze of council flats and houses'.[49] A barricade was swept away and, despite petrol bombs and vicious fighting which included a charge into the crowd at speed by police vans, the police had occupied the estate 'in massive numbers' by 3.00 a.m. At least 44 arrests were made by snatch squads. According to the Manchester Haldane Society:

> As a result of the damage on the evening of 8th July and the early hours of the morning of the 9th July the police tactics then changed on Thursday 9th July leading up to the mass arrests on the evening of 9th July.[50]

Anderton (1981, p. 3) seemed to confirm this view by stating categorically that the new strategy of rapid deployment was devised *after* the events of the night of 8–9 July 1981. This seems, however, to be wrong. Quite clearly, if the *Manchester Evening News* and Hytner are accurate in their observations, the new style of policing involving groups of officers deployed from vans was in operation well before midnight on 8 July.

The preparations made by the chief constable during the course of the next day, 9 July, unlike those of the previous day, are detailed in his Report. A total of 560 reserves were stationed at four police stations in such a way that the city was, in Anderton's (1981, p. 3) words, 'virtually encircled'. Throughout the day Manchester had the appearance of a city under occupation: 'in the city centre this afternoon police with dogs are standing guard at most street corners. Patrol vans are cruising the main shopping areas.'[51] A total of 1,600 men was made available by altering shift arrangements, and mobility was increased by the hiring of extra personnel-carrying vehicles to enable the riot zone to be 'swamped'.[52] Anderton held a press conference to deny that he was 'declaring war' and to stress that low-profile policing and community co-operation had been given their chance and failed:

> They have had their chance – I am convinced that the vast majority of the public want to see policemen on the street to prevent disorder and from here on that is where they are going to be.[53]

What the citizens of Manchester were going to see (and in Moss Side had already seen) was 'a positive police response [by] the determined arrest of offenders to regain the initiative from the rioters' (Anderton 1981, p. 3). 'Mobile charging centres' were set up to facilitate the containment of the large number of prisoners envisaged. Here, then, was the philosophy of mass arrest which was to cause such problems for the courts in the days to come.

The events of the evening, which involved approximately 150 arrests, are confused. Anderton (1981, p. 4) offers no description, merely stating that the 'strategy herein described was used to good effect'. Hytner does little better, while the local newspapers confined themselves to remarks such as: 'Flying squad tactics by Manchester Police paid off in the streets of Moss Side during the night.'[54]

The Haldane Society had this to say:

> On the 9th July the police were parading through South Manchester in convoys. They had large black vans with approximately six officers in each van. Many of them had crash helmets with visors and they had their batons in their hands. The back doors of the vans were open and complaints had been made that they were picking people up at random and arresting them, or in other cases putting them back on the streets in another area.[55]

This account is corroborated by Hytner (1981, para. 42.2), who for once abandoned his policy of withholding comment on operational police matters:

> we think that it is in the public interest that we should record that we heard a great deal of evidence, much of which came from apparently reliable and respectable people, white and black, that many police-men in Moss Side in vehicles on the 9th July were actively spoiling for trouble with young blacks.

In these circumstances, violence was clearly inevitable and arrests, it was alleged, were made with a certain lack of discrimination (1981, para. 41.2) in a series of 'sweeps' of the area.

Community fears rose to a point where youth-club leaders kept their charges indoors all night rather than let them face police action on the streets (1981, para. 42.3). In many instances, alleged the Haldane Society, 'mere presence at the scene of disorder seems to have been sufficient for a person to have been arrested and charged'.[56] The initiative had passed to the police with a vengeance. The next day the Home Secretary visited the area, remarking with uncharacteristic hawkishness, 'it was good last night, wasn't it?'[57]

Of those arrested, over half were charged with offences of obstruction or under s.5 of the Public Order Act 1936 (see Table 8.2). The contrast with Liverpool 8, where looting charges predominate, is marked. In comparing the figures for arrests and police injuries in Manchester and Liverpool (Table 8.7) it is clear how much more effective was the strategy adopted by Mr Anderton. The Liverpool police suffered 15 times the number of injuries and ten times the number of vehicles damaged as the Manchester police, and yet the arrest rates were not dissimilar (530 in Merseyside, 475 in Manchester) over a considerably shorter period.

Arrested defendants were taken to the 'mobile charging centres' which were driven, when full, to local police stations where the occupants were subjected to a 'streamlined charging procedure'[58] (Anderton 1981, p. 4). Altogether 475 people were arrested and the whole problem was handed over to the magistrates' courts.[59]

Two questions arise from these accounts of the riot in Manchester. The first concerns the absence of any coherent explanation for the apparent police inactivity during nearly two hours of the most severe looting on the night of 8 July at a time when a substantial and well-equipped force was apparently on stand-by. Second, it has not been made clear why Mr Anderton sought to give the impression that the decision to adopt the new strategy of policing was taken *after* the events of the night of 8–9 July, when quite clearly it was in operation 24 hours earlier.

Certainly, the events of the night served to discredit what is best de-scribed as a caricature of community involvement in policing, and to

present the strategy of mass arrest as a natural and inevitable consequence of the breakdown of liberal policing. Whether or not this was
Anderton's intention at the time it is impossible to say. However, the
policing strategies adopted in Manchester in 1981 pointed the way clearly
forward to the massive revaluation subsequently undertaken by the
ACPO (see Chapter 7).

Pre-trial proceedings

Two factors dominated the conduct of proceedings during the first few
days. The first was political, and the second organizational.

There is no doubt that the magistrates, particularly on the first day of
the riot proceedings, were keenly aware of their expected role in the city.
They were, as a court clerk has said, 'very much on trial themselves'. He
went on:

> I don't know if they were frightened of being criticized for leniency
> but the bench would know that its actions would have an effect on
> the mood of the city and you would have frustration among the
> citizens if the magistrates were seen not to act quickly and firmly to
> reassure the public that the authorities were looking after them.

When Stuart Tendler of *The Times* wrote that 'the words "civil disorder" seemed to hang over Manchester's plush new Court complex',[60] this
was not merely a journalistic flourish. There was clearly a common
awareness among the magistrates that these were not ordinary cases.
There was no need, for example, for the context of cases to be described in
detail:

> The magistrates did know throughout the background of the matter.
> That's the thing you have to understand.
>
> (Solicitor MK)

According to Gus John, a community worker, 'even defence lawyers were
making certain assumptions about what had taken place in Moss Side'
(John 1982, p. 6). This common understanding must, of course, have been
based in the main on press reports. However, without it the court would
have been unable to cope with the extra cases.

The pressure on all concerned was heightened materially by the organizational factors – the desire to cram an extraordinary number and variety
of cases into an ordinary day's business with no special courts sitting.
Comments by court personnel reveal a certain pride in this normalising
approach:

> We in Manchester have done as well, if not better than other
> Benches.[61]

[We were] very interested in seeing that it did go through very smoothly and quickly. I didn't detect any strain . . . we didn't go to the extremes they did in other cities where they came in on Saturdays and Sundays.

(Senior court clerk)

Many advocates, however, certainly felt the strain, describing the scene as

total pandemonium . . . total bedlam. Nobody knows which court he is in . . . some of the prosecution were reading the file for the first time when giving the magistrates the description.

(Solicitor MK)

There was no time for discussions with the defence and, in the Criminal Detention Centre, the duty solicitor was in grave difficulties:

They kept on being brought in from outlying police stations. We found it was like a factory conveyor belt . . . we had almost got to the stage of going into the holding cages and saying 'hands up all those who are on s.20 assault' . . . so many hands . . . 'Right, you lot over there!' None of us had ever had the experience of coping with so large a number of people.

(Solicitor MJ)

In Manchester, the 'duty solicitor scheme' was based on a rota of firms. Some practitioners had developed fairly sophisticated systems for dealing with large numbers of defendants on their duty day, ensuring that instructions were taken by the advocates and form-filling by their assistants. The duty solicitors on 10 July were quite unprepared for the massive workload and managed to interview no more than 30 defendants out of at least 136 appearing.

The approach of the court to bail was marked by the fact that by the time cases began to arrive at the court it was apparent that the police were very much in control of Moss Side. Of the defendants in the sample, 189 (71 per cent) were produced on the first four days (10–14 July), and it is certainly true that a much higher proportion of this group (see Table 8.1) were imprisoned (either on remand or by sentence) than of that which appeared subsequently.

There were further allegations by the Haldane Society that custodial remands were made even where no prosecution objection to bail was offered.[62] However, among the advocates in general, there was none of the universal sense of outrage at the denial of bail experienced by their Liverpool colleagues. Figure 8.2d reveals that the use of mass custodial remand was neither as extensive nor as long-lasting as in Liverpool, and that unconditional bail was introduced at a fairly early stage. A duty solicitor noticed the contrast during the second week:

I'd say we were lucky that week. I'm not going to say we'd be talking like this if we were duty solicitor on the Friday . . . by and large everybody who should have had bail got it by the end of the week.

(Solicitor MK)

The key to the situation was the use of the bail curfew condition. Table 8.1 reveals an astonishing unanimity in the use of curfews (applied in almost all cases of conditional bail) particularly on the first day, 10 July. Some advocates and probation officers felt that the co-ordination was more than coincidental and alleged that there had been a bench meeting beforehand, possibly in the presence of police representatives. This was emphatically denied by a senior court clerk:

It is a lot of nonsense to say there was a meeting between magistrates and police to tie things up . . . it's just untrue. I mean we met in the morning and we knew what was happening, so you do see the magistrates and it was obvious . . . we didn't say to the magistrates what they had to do but they knew we had to clear the streets. And the one thing that couldn't be allowed to happen was that people who were on bail had the opportunity to go back onto the street.

The use of the curfew, then, was a fairly concerted attempt to maintain the initiative which the police had won on the streets, and its prevalence in Manchester is a reflection of the success of the police action there. The point is that, once defence advocates became aware that bail was obtainable only with curfew conditions attached, they could be relied on to take the initiative.

Thus, the hierarchical structure of the court itself produced an inevitable effect upon its dispositions. Once a lead was given, it became policy by a kind of snowball effect. With nearly 50 per cent of defendants receiving curfews on first appearance, it was apparent that many minor offenders – for example, young persons allegedly obstructing the highway – were being subjected to severe restrictions, often lasting in excess of four months in respect of an offence which carried a maximum penalty of a £50 fine.

The bail curfew may in many respects mark a crossing of the line by the court into an area which more properly belongs to the police. Its use illustrates the painful dual demands on a magistrates' court in civil disorder to keep the peace and to adjudicate in an unbiased way. As one clerk put it:

They [the magistrates] are sworn to uphold the Queen's Peace, aren't they, and if [curfews] are the best way to do it they are going to do it.

Answering criticism, the chairman of the bench, Robert Carlyle, said:

It seems to say that the court should not have processed cases fairly quickly and the use of deterrent sentences was not called for. I should have thought it perfectly plain that these steps were precisely what was required when the citizens of Manchester were extremely concerned about serious incidents in their midst. Justice has to be administered promptly, I thought so then, and I think so now . . .[63]

Unfortunately, by its very nature, 'prompt justice' tends to blur distinctions. The view that mere presence at the scene of the disorders was sufficient for conviction seems to have spread from the police to the bench. Some solicitors, too, felt that there was something to be said for this approach:

there were enormous numbers of them who had been told to move on, given four seconds and then they were inside the black maria. They were regarded by the magistrates, rightly in my view, as having offended by being there.

(Solicitor MR)

One community officer overheard a duty solicitor giving pragmatic advice to a client:

Look, once you are prepared to admit that you were there, the magistrates are unlikely to believe you didn't do it.

(Community worker MQ)

The trials

Some of the earlier trials took place in an atmosphere of extreme antagonism. On 24 July, the chairman of the bench retired from one court in mid-trial to allow, he maintained, 'tempers to cool down', after he had rebuked a solicitor for being 'awkward'.

However, as in Liverpool, this atmosphere dissipated within a few weeks (solicitor MM). Figure 8.4b shows a concerted spate of convictions in July being overtaken and surpassed by acquittals and bind-overs for the remainder of the period. August was a particularly good month from the point of view of the defence advocates dealing with riot cases. Much of this improvement may be attributed to the decision by the prosecution (which had already shed at least 25 of the Moss Side defendants before charge)[64] to offer substantial numbers of bind-overs in line with the policy on curfews. With the police well in control, there was no need to incarcerate and 12 per cent of all defendants in the sample were bound over (see Table 8.4). It was also recognized by prosecutors that, outside the immediate context of the riots, many of the allegations did not look particularly substantial:

it doesn't sound as serious as the matter probably was because you

are pinpointing one incident . . . the difficulty is very much giving
the court the feeling that this is really a serious situation.

(Prosecutor MP)

Moreover, since the Moss Side disorders occurred at a late stage in the
national crisis, and the court proceedings were interrupted after only one
day by a trouble-free weekend, the Manchester bench never lost its credibility in the way which others had done. This is reflected in a committal
rate which is approximately half that of Liverpool (see Table 8.4).

Almost every advocate interviewed spoke of the fairness with which
trials were conducted after the initial panic had subsided:

we received very fair treatment. I keep saying this because I think it
is to the credit of the bench . . . when we wanted a good chew at the
prosecution . . . we were allowed a good chew.

(Solicitor MK)

Indeed, even the prosecution felt that cases were being defended with no
more acrimony towards the police than usual (prosecutor MP). Figure
8.3d shows that very much the same can be said for sentencing, which
was deterrent only in mid-July but, as one solicitor observed,

they got that out of their systems fairly quickly.

(Solicitor MI)

There was considerable pressure at first from the prosecution to list
cases for extremely early trial dates. In one case,

the chief prosecuting solicitor stood up and made a speech about
serious public disorder and how it was important for matters to be
dealt with as soon as possible.

(Solicitor MN)

However, resistance to this approach by defence solicitors eventually
prevailed and over 65 per cent of trials took place after the expiry of one
month from the disorders.

On the other hand, conflict between the lawyers themselves, although
not as marked as in Liverpool, continued to impede any collective response. Most solicitors felt considerable resentment towards the Moss
Side Defence Committee who, they considered, were standing between
them and their clients:

they take the view that we are here just trying to make money out of
the thing.

(Solicitor MH)

The Committee was indeed bitterly critical of certain lawyers:

on the performance of particular solicitors there was no way defendants could afford to risk their freedom with them . . . and we would refer them to some others . . . and you can't imagine the resentment there was. I got threatening letters myself . . . threatening phone calls from solicitors.

(Community worker MQ)

Manchester, therefore, is an example of a court which not only managed a rapid transfer back to normality, but even in the early stages never entirely abandoned its commitment to individualized process. Particularly important in this context is the reliance on sentence as opposed to the custodial remand as the major form of control (Table 8.9). Although this did entail much earlier and more hurried sentencing, it gave a comparatively greater prominence to the role of the advocates and to the principles of adversarial process.

An important factor here is certainly the radically different policing tactics adopted by Mr Anderton, which quickly achieved control of the streets and hence did not rely so heavily upon mass pre-trial internment for deterrence. As a result, the police had no need to call in the support of the courts in so complete a manner as had been required in Liverpool.

Tables

Table 8.1   Distribution of cases on first appearance (1981 riot defendants in survey)

(a) Camberwell Green Magistrates' Court (April 1981 defendants)

Date	Total	Custody	Cond. bail	Uncond. bail	Plea
April					
11	8	–	1	4	3
13	57	3	27	18	9
14	2	–	1	1	–
22	13	–	–	12	1
23	14	2	3	9	–
27	1	–	1	–	–
Sub-total	95	5	33	44	13
May	28	2	–	22	4
June	3	–	2	1	–
July	8	–	2	2	4
Aug–Oct	2	–	–	1	1
Total	136	7	37	70	22

Table 8.1   (*cont.*)

(b) Camberwell Green Magistrates' Court (July 1981 defendants)

Date	Total	Custody	Cond. bail	Uncond. bail	Plea
11 July[1]	119	34[2]	50	14	21
13 July	38	18	5	12	3
14 July to September	7	2	2	2	1
Total	164	54	57	28	25

[1] Three courts sitting.
[2] Includes total of seven custodial sentences.

(c) Liverpool City Magistrates' Court

Date	Total	Custody	Cond. bail	Uncond. bail	Sentence
6 July	71	52	18	1	–
7 July	72	52	18	1	1
8 July	31	20	8	3	–
9 July	34	25	8	1	–
10 July	25	8	16	–	1
11 July	30	24	3	1	2
Total	263	181	71	7	4

(d) Manchester City Magistrates' Court

Date	Total	Custody	Custod. sentence	Cond. bail	Bail	Other sentence
10 July	108	26	6	47	12	17
11 July	24	12	1	7	4	–
13 July	45	14	4	12	4	11
14 July	12	1	6	2	3	–
16 July	21	1	–	13	7	–
17 July	7	1	–	–	4	2
20 July	23	–	–	4	15	4
21/31 July	19	–	–	2	13	4
August/ September	5	–	–	–	5	–
Total	264	55	17	87	67	38

Table 8.1   *(cont.)*

(e) Ealing Magistrates' Court

Date	Total	Custody	Cond. bail	Uncond. bail	Plea
11 July	1	1	–	–	–
13 July	2	2	–	–	–
16 July	26	2	1	20	3
17 July	1	–	1	–	–
20 July	7	–	2	5	–
23 July	1	–	1	–	–
13 August	1	–	–	1	–
9 October	1	–	–	1	–
23 October	1	–	–	1	–
7 December	1	–	–	1	–
Total	42	5[1]	5	29	3

[1] Of the five remands in custody, four had been released on bail or dealt with by the end of the month.

Table 8.2   Principal offences charged (1981 riot defendants in survey)

	Brixton (April)	Brixton (July)	Southall (1979)	Liverpool	Manchester
Minor summary	–	1	4	–	1
Obstruction (highway)	10	4	20	2	46
Obstruction (police)	–	–	33	–	–
Criminal damage	8	15	11	17	22
Theft	20	58	–	54	63
Burglary	19	37	–	71	–
Threatening words etc.	32	32	85	74	91
Offensive weapon	21	8	33	36	24
Assault	2	–	63	2	1
Assault/police	15	7	1	6	4
Wounding/GBH	1	2	–	16	6
Explosives	8	–	–	17	7
Totals	136	164	250	295	265

Table 8.3   Table of outcomes as percentages of sample (1981 riot defendants in survey)

	Brixton (April)		Brixton (July)	
Guilty pleas		18.5		34
Not guilty pleas:				
Convicted	(32.5)		(16.5)	
Acquitted	(15)		(10.5)	
NEO				
Bound over				
Total	———	47.5	———	27
Remitted		5		17
Failed to appear etc.		4		2.5
Committed		25		19.5
Total (%)		100.0		100.0
Numerical totals:		136		164

	Liverpool		Manchester	
Guilty pleas		28		34.5
Not guilty pleas:				
Convicted	(29)		(25)	
Acquitted	(12)		(15)	
NEO			(5.5)	
Bound over			(8.5)	
Total	———	41		54
Remitted				
Failed to appear etc.		7		
Committed		24		11.5
Total (%)		100.0		100.0
Numerical totals		295		265

	Southall	
Guilty pleas		24
Not guilty pleas:		
Convicted	(43)	
Acquitted	(22)	
Total		65
Committed		11
Total (%)		100
Numerical total		42

Table 8.4   Table of disposals as percentages of sample (1981 riot defendants in survey)

	Brixton (April)		Brixton (July)	
Custodial				
Prison: over 3 months	(4.5)		(3.0)	
Prison: under 3 months	(5.5)		(9.5)	
Committed Borstal				
Detention Centre	(2.5)		(1.0)	
Total		12.5		13.5
Suspended sentence		6.0		8.0
Committed for sentence		1.5		2.0
Committed for trial		26.0		20.5
Fines				
Over £250			(2.0)	
Under £250	(13.0)		(12.0)	
Total		13.0		14.0
Other				
Care				
C.S.O.	(1.5)		(3.1)	
Probation	(2.5)		(1.0)	
Conditional discharge	(10.0)		(4.5)	
Attendance centre			(2.5)	
Bound over	(4.5)		(1.0)	
Total		18.5		12.0
Dismissed		15.5		11.5
Remits to other courts		7.0		18.5
Total (%)		100.0		100.0
Numerical size of sample		136		164
	Liverpool		*Manchester*	
Custodial				
Prison: over 3 months	(7.5)		(1.5)	
Prison: under 3 months	(1.5)		(5.0)	
Committed Borstal	(1.5)			
Detention Centre	(2.0)		(7.5)	
Total		12.5		14.0
Suspended sentence		5.0		5.5
Committed for sentence		2.0		0.5
Committed for trial		26.0		11.0
Fines				
Over £250	(3.5)		(1.0)	
Under £250	(20.0)		(24.0)	
Total		23.5		25.0

Table 8.4 *(cont.)*

	Liverpool		Manchester	
Other				
Care	(1.0)			
C.S.O.	(2.5)		(1.0)	
Probation	(3.0)		(1.5)	
Conditional discharge	(2.0)		(5.5)	
Attendance centre	(3.5)		(5.5)	
Bound over	(5.0)		(12.0)	
Total		17.0		25.5
Dismissed		14.0		18.5
Total (%)		100.0		100.0
Numerical size of sample		295.0		264.0

Table 8.5 Comparison of defendants included in HOSD Merseyside and Toxteth samples (riot cases) by percentages

		Merseyside	Toxteth
Table 2 (Sex)	Male	88	82
	Female	12	18
Table 4 (Ethnic origin)	White	84	71
	West Indian	4	7
	Asian		
	Others	12	22
Table 5 (Employment)	Employed	19	14
	Unemployed	50	51
	Student	10	16
	Housewife	3	6
	Unknown	18	13
Table 7 (Addresses)	Area	53	61
	Adjacent	35	23
	Elsewhere/Liverpool	9	14
	Elsewhere/Merseyside	1.5	
	Not in Merseyside	0.5	1
	Not known	1	1
Table 9 (Offences)	Violence	12	15
	Theft Act	31	56
	Criminal Damage £200+	4.5	3
	Riot etc.	3.5	
	Total Indictable	51	74
	Public Order Act	37.5	24
	Disorderly Behaviour	4	0.5
	Criminal Damage £200–	6.5	1.5
	Other Summary	1	
	Total Summary	49	26

Source: HOSD 20/82 (Merseyside)

Table 8.6   Total deployment of police officers in Toxteth area (July 1981)

July	Number
7	2,321
8	1,972
10	2,104
11	2,330
12	1,890
13	1,631
14	884
15	612
16	374
17	578
18	578
19	578
20–25	207

Source: Oxford 1981.

Table 8.7   Comparison of Merseyside and Greater Manchester arrests etc.

	Merseyside	Greater Manchester
Number of arrests	530	475
Number of police injured	781[1]	52[2]
Number of police vehicles damaged	214[3]	22[4]

[1] Oxford 1981a: 39.
[2] Appendix 7.
[3] Oxford 1981a: 52.
[4] Appendix 9.

Table 8.8   Comparison of man-hours spent on remand and following custodial sentence: as imposed by Manchester City and Liverpool City magistrates' Courts on July 1981 riot defendants

	Manchester City Court	Liverpool City Court
Number of man-hours of custodial remand	28,224	86,858
Number of man-hours of imprisonment ordered	45,041[1]	50,400[1]

[1] These figures may be slightly over-stated as they do not take account of the allowance against sentence for time spent on remand. The reduction of the Manchester figures would, in any event, be less since nearly 63 per cent of sentenced man-hours were to Detention Centre (where there was no reduction for time served on remand) whereas the figure was only 27 per cent for Liverpool.

9 Police and magistracy in contemporary civil disorder

The climax of the rioting in early July 1981 resulted in calls at Cabinet level for the creation of a separate summary institution, a 'special' or 'riot' court in which rules of due process would be suspended. In addition, a new summary Riot Act would free the courts, it was argued, from the formal requirements as to proof of intention.[1]

By mid-July, however, it had become clear that the magistrates' courts had been able to adapt effectively to the new conditions without legislative assistance and without the organizational breakdown experienced by the US courts in the 1960s (Dobrovir 1969; Balbus 1973). The demand for 'special courts' was accordingly silenced. As *The Times* conceded: 'The so-called "special riot courts" being urged from some quarters mean little more than many magistrates' courts, at least outside London, are already doing.'[2] The Home Secretary also concluded that 'the response of the system at the time [has] demonstrated its ability to react to changing circumstances'.[3]

What was the basis for this growing confidence in the serviceability of the magistrates' courts under these conditions? First, it must be made clear that there was no evidence from the 1981 research that any of the actions of the courts were influenced substantially by pressure from the central state other than by vague governmental encouragement for prompt and positive action. Similarly, at the local level, there was no evidence of the magistrates having been briefed beforehand by any other agency. If the magistrates' courts reacted to the crisis in a certain way, it was simply because of their own organizational structure and mode of operation. As

Skyrme (1979, p. 7) puts it: 'Justices . . . appeal to the government because their system is flexible.'

Relations between the agencies

For the reasons already outlined, participation by the army in the civil disorders of 1981 was almost non-existent. Military liaison officers were certainly in attendance in some areas[4] but contingency plans were not put into operation.[5] It was rather the institutional relationship between police and magistracy which dominated the conduct of proceedings. Moreover, it is argued here that it was the priorities of the police which prevailed. These were not communicated to the magistrates by any overt institutional directives or briefings, but by the use of organizational techniques.

The first major technique was the manipulation of the flow of cases. By flooding the courts with defendants, the police could ensure a temporary transition to bail refusal as the dominant sanction. Since bail proceedings are non-adversarial, discretionary and with no burden of proof, the involvement of the legal profession and legal ideologies was limited. Moreover, para. 2(b) of Part I of the Bail Act 1976 (pre-emptive detention) allowed benches to make policy decisions with regard to the future prevalence of certain offences in defined areas (Vogler 1982; 1983). In contrast to the normal sentencing process, custodial remand is quick, flexible and subject to reversal as soon as the policing situation changes. It was not necessary for the character of the disorders to be described in general terms to the bench (a rather dubious procedure adopted in Nottingham)[6] since the cumulative effect of successive prosecution summaries communicated understandings and perspectives held by the police. In Southall and in Brixton (in April 1981), where territorial control had been established and rioting was not expected to continue, full bail was almost universal. By contrast, in Liverpool in July 1981 the police felt their authority under threat at the time of the first remands and thus sought and obtained from the courts temporary 'internment' of their prisoners by refusing to exercise their deferred bail procedure. In Manchester, where police domination of the area had been decisively established (but only on the basis of heavy numerical presence and surveillance) conditional bail predominated.

The second way in which the police were able to influence proceedings was through charging strategies. Nearly half (48 per cent) of those arrested in July 1981 were charged with Public Order Act offences[7] and very much in excess of 75 per cent of all defendants' cases were concluded in the magistrates' courts. Only 1 per cent of defendants were charged with riot offences.[8] Not only were there obvious attempts, as in Southall, to re-charge in order to prevent jury trial, but the practice was widespread of charging high initially to obtain custodial remand and then proceeding on a lesser alternative to ensure summary trial.

In short, the organizational domination of the magistracy by the police was achieved through control of the flow of work, the first bail decision and initial charging. Thus, although the police retain, in court at least, their formal, historical deference to the bench, it is evident that, at a time of crisis, the balance of authority is tilted firmly in their direction.

The precise character of this relationship has important implications for the theory of the state. Poulantzas has argued that the recent period had seen the imposition of 'new forms' of state committed to the extension of control over every sphere of economic life, the dismantling of the institutions of popular democracy and the destruction of formal (rhetorical) liberties. He describes this tendency as 'authoritarian statism' (Poulantzas 1978, pp. 203–5). Central to this concept is the supposed fusion of legislature, executive and judiciary and the 'irresistible rise of state administration' (1978, pp. 217–31). Criminal justice becomes executive action:

> From the punishable offence laid down by a universal and general act of parliament, we are moving towards the suspicious circumstance whose contours are administratively defined by supple, malleable, particularistic regulation . . . Thus, while the law is evidently not defunct, it is undergoing a clear *retreat*.
>
> (Poulantzas 1978, p. 220)

In this pessimistic account of the role of the law in the advanced capitalist state, Poulantzas seems to ignore much of his own analysis. As he has demonstrated elsewhere, institutional change is scarcely irresistible, nor can it be generalized in the manner he suggests (Jessop 1985, p. 360).

Hall *et al.* (1978, p. 255) develop the argument to a further stage, suggesting that the early 1970s have seen a crisis of hegemony brought about by the exhaustion of strategies of consent during a 'profound restructuring of the inner organisation and composition of capitalist relations'. With the disappearance of the last vestige of the hegemony of consent (1978, p. 262), the advent of the exceptional or 'strong' state becomes inevitable. This approach has unfortunately led to some rather sterile debates as to the nature of 'authoritarian populism' (Jessop *et al.* 1984; Hall 1985), which have tended to overidentify the conjunctural phenomenon of 'Thatcherism' with structural changes in the state form. The state, in some more extreme versions, has been 'Thatcherised' (Jessop *et al.* 1984, p. 50).

These accounts are in many respects both inadequate and misleading. Not only do they ignore the regional and local specificity of particular modes of control and institutional practice, but they also tend to minimize the complexity of inter-institutional relations. It is not sufficient merely to assert the identity of interest between police and magistracy – the executive and judicial aspects of the local state. The ability to concert action in a crisis, such as that of 1981, does not imply that such unanimity is permanent. To take an analogous example: the police appropriation of fire equipment to direct against the 1981 Brixton rioters (Scarman 1981, 3.70–1) did not involve the permanent co-option of the local authority fire services as a coercive agency. The annexation of magisterial authority was equally temporary. The argument that has been made here is not that the two agencies have fused into a new local form of 'strong state', but that in certain areas, and for certain crucial,strategic purposes, the operational action of the magistrates may be almost entirely dominated by the police. The relationship of dependency can, as it were, be enforced. By demonstrating the mechanisms by which this relationship is maintained, it has been possible to show how the distance between the two agencies can be narrowed or widened in accordance with the current priorities of the dominant agency, the police.

The petty sessional jurisdiction

The forms of surveillance/control advocated for inner cities make intense use of police labour. It is inevitable, therefore, that their operation will not be distributed evenly but targeted on certain zones of 'high crime'. The physical isolation of such territorial zones, often by road-block or cordon (Kirsch 1981, p. 6; Bridges and Bunyan 1983, pp. 87–8) has become a feature of policing which, as we have seen, is at its most intense in periods of civil disorder when transport services are also modified (Applegate 1969, pp. 59–64).

The location, moreover, of such areas corresponds to the zones of multi-deprivation described by Peet (1975, p. 570) as 'internal reservations for the reserve army' and associated in the previous chapter with developments in the international sphere of productive relations. To Poulantzas (1978, p. 103), such territorial inequality, 'the serial, fractured, parcelled, cellular and irreversible space' created by international monopoly capitalism, is derived ultimately from a Taylorist division of the workforce. Crucial to the maintenance of this authority are the jurisdictional boundaries of the local states themselves. Dear and Clarke (1978, p. 181) go so far as to suggest that 'it is likely that the plethora of local state jurisdictional boundaries is itself a functional source of inter-regional inequality'.

It has been suggested above that the justices, imprisoned within their jurisdictions, were not in a position to co-ordinate forces in response to disorder occurring in and around the premises of national corporations dispersed across large areas in the late nineteenth century. The benches therefore suffered a decline in authority in relation to the other agencies which were better able to develop national 'corporate' organizations.

Under contemporary conditions, however, in the period of the international centralization of capital, the petty sessional jurisdictions may take on a new significance. If it is correct that the international socialization of production has resulted in a 'balkanized' labour force, then two conclusions follow. First, each geographical area, each community, will experience a mode of policing and adjudication which is distinct and which corresponds to the degree and nature of the integration of the community in the production process and the level of state intervention. Nothing could be more suited to this structural diversity than the petty sessional jurisdictions with their distinctive local characteristics and policies (Hood 1962). Tarling (1979, p. 10) and Burney (1979, pp. 125–45) have both pointed out the extent to which different benches have developed their own characteristic sentencing policies, and the sharp differences between benches was also clearly evident among the riot courts.

Second, the post-war magistracy has succeeded – largely through secrecy in its self-selection procedures and the achievement of a quasi-professional status – in rendering itself almost immune to democratic pressure (Vogler 1990). Middle-class and professional interests can be concerted and projected (under the auspices of the police) into the inner-city areas with relative anonymity. This has, as Skyrme (1979, p. 9) puts it, exercised a 'stabilising influence' on local communities. In short, we may conclude that the recently revived importance of the magistracy in civil disorder is likely to be both general and long-lasting.

Notes

1 Reading the Riot Act: local state power and social class

1 Proclamation under the Riot Act 1715, s.ii, 1 George I, c.5.
2 Ashton J., *Trial of Gillam* (1768), quoted in Clode (1869, p. 633).
3 *Parl. Hist.* vii, 18 July 1715, 110.
4 *Pltry. Debs.* cccxvi, 23 June 1887, 768.
5 *Report of the Select Committee on Employment of Military in Cases of Disturbance etc.*, PP 1908, 236 (minutes), p. 424.
6 *The Times*, 23 February 1967, p. 1.
7 *Guardian*, 19 August 1981, p. 22. See also renewed calls by the police in 1985, *The Times*, 8 August 1985, p. 2.
8 At various stages in his career Poulantzas has been identified as an Althusserian (Petras and Gundle 1982), a Gramscian (Jessop 1982, pp. 153–8), a disciple of Foucault (Hall 1980a) and even as a proponent of 'stamocap' theory (Jessop 1982, pp. 189–90).
9 The concept is not used in the sense familiar to political scientists to denote the *form* of state involved in social and economic intervention (see, for example, Williamson 1985).
10 The importance of the distinction between town and country was, of course, also of great significance to Marx and Engels.
11 Honourable exceptions here might include Cockburn (1977); Broadbent (1977); Dear and Clarke (1978).
12 The extensive literature on central state forms requires no addition here. The term is used in this context to denote the supreme legislative, judicial and executive authorities (Parliament, Home Office, Superior Courts of Appeal, etc.) whether or not located in London.

13 Capital is defined here as exchange value which seeks a further accretion of value, and, by extension, the interest of the classes which monopolize the capital mode of production.

14 The terms 'nationally' and 'locally centred' forms of capital broadly conform to the typology of 'competitive' (liberal) and 'monopoly' (imperialist) forms.

2   The magistrate as state servant

1 Quoted in Hamburger (1963, p. 209n). See also Philips (1976, pp. 176–7) on the activities of the coal-owning Justices during strikes in the 1850s.

2 Lord Francis Egerton, 22 August 1839, Lancs Record Office DP 378; quoted in Gattrell *et al.* (1980, pp. 271–2).

3 34 Edward III, c.1.

4 *Per* Holroyd J. in *Redford* v *Birley* (1822) 1 St. Tr. (N.S.) 1071.

5 17 Rich. II, c.8.

6 Special Constables Act 1831, 1 & 2 Will. IV, c.41, s.1.

7 Riot Act 1715, 1 Geo. I, c.5.

8 *Trial of Pinney* 1832, pp. 39ff.

9 Of the magistrates indicted for their part in riots, Gillam in 1766 was a victim of the Wilkites, Barkley Kennet in 1781 of the anti-Gordon party, Charles Pinney in 1832 of the Bristol commercial interest and Badger in 1843 of the Chartists. They were all eventually exonerated.

10 Quoted in Hobsbawm and Rudé (1969, p. 255).

11 Marx, quoted in Mack (1969, p. 2).

12 All references to Bentham's works are to the Bowring (1843) edition.

13 Who obtained covert central state sponsorship for a small integrated force of magistrates and police with a metropolitan jurisdiction as early as 1750 (Critchley 1978, pp. 32–5).

14 *Pltry. Hist.* xxv, 23 June 1785, 896.

15 Draft Bill, Part 29.

16 *Pltry. Hist.* xxv, 23 June 1785, 888–90.

17 *Pltry. Hist.* xxv, 29 June 1785, 911.

18 *Pltry. Hist.* xxi, 19 June 1780, 698.

19 *Pltry. Hist.* xxi, 1 March 1781, 1319.

20 Draft Bill, Part 58.

21 *Pltry. Hist.* xxv, 23 June 1785, 890.

22 'An Inhabitant of Westminster', *Defence of the Police Bill etc.* (1786, p. 17).

23 *Pltry. Hist.* xxv, 23 June 1785, 895.

24 *Pltry. Hist.* xxv, 29 June 1785, 907.

25 The Dublin Police Act 1786 (26 Geo. III, c.24) extended subsequently to the whole of Ireland. See Palmer 1988, pp. 92–140.

26 See *Journal of the House of Commons* 47, 25 May 1792, pp. 813–14.

27 *Pltry. Hist.* xxix, 25 May 1792, 1477.

28 36 Geo. III, c.8.

29 *Pltry. Hist.* xxxii, 10 November 1795, 281.

30 *Pltry. Hist.* xxix, 21 May 1792, 1464.

31 New Annual Register, 31 July 1797, pp. 120–1.

32 Francis Burton, *Pltry. Hist.* xxix, 16 March 1792, 1036.

33 39 & 40 Geo. III, c.87.

34 See also *Report from the Select Committee on the State of the Police of the Metropolis*, PP 1816 (510), v, p. 36 on 'a purer and better informed magistracy'.

35 2 *Pltry. Debs.* xii, 21 March 1825, 1128.

36 42 Geo. III c.76.

37 2 *Pltry. Debs.* xii, 21 March 1825, 1129.

38 Lord Stowell to Lord Sidmouth, quoted in Pellew (1847, p. 365).

39 Quoted in Reith (1943, p. 226).

40 See, for example, evidence of W.A. White to the *Select Committee on the Police of the Metropolis*, PP 1834 (600), xvi (minutes), para. 1770.

41 PP 1834, para. 1426.

42 Sir Frederick Roe, ibid., para. 1471.

43 Ibid., para. 1464.

44 Ibid., para. 1546.

45 Ibid., para.1459.

46 *Report of the Select Committee on Policemen as Spies*, PP 1833 (627), xiii, evidence, p. 181.

47 Sir Frederick Roe, *Report from the Select Committee on Metropolis Police Offices etc.*, PP 1837 (451), xii (minutes), para. 193.

48 Ibid. and *Report from the Select Committee on Metropolis Police Offices etc.*, PP 1837–8 (578) xv.

49 John Buckle, PP 1837 (minutes), para 834.

50 *Pltry. Debs.* 1, 20 August 1839, 446.

51 PP 1837–8, p. 19.

52 W. Ballantine, PP 1837 (minutes), para. 913.

53 3 *Pltry. Debs.* xlix, 20 July 1839, 549.

54 PP 1837–8, p. 26.

55 3 *Pltry. Debs.* xlvii, 3 June 1839, 1291.

56 See, for example, *The Times*, 7 August 1839; 9 August 1839; Taylor in the *Morning Herald*, 25 May 1839.

57 *The Times*, 18 October 1839, p. 4. Thereby making good the threat issued by Lord Duncannon for the government that if the Bill failed 'every petty case must be sent to the Central Criminal Court for trial' (3 *Pltry. Debs.* xliv, 12 August 1839, 185).

58 5 & 6 Will. IV, c.76.

59 *Quarterly Review* lxxi, December 1842, p. 249.

60 Ibid.

61 Ibid., p. 295.

62 See, for example, Stevenson (1979, pp. 253–7).

63 3 *Pltry. Debs.* xlix, 16 July 1839, 371–5.

64 Ibid., 381.

65 3 *Pltry. Debs.* xlix, 19 July 1839, 535.

66 *The Times*, 9 August 1839, p. 6.

67 3 *Pltry. Debs.* xlix, 6 August 1839, 1386.

3 Two versions of magisterial authority: Bristol and Hyde Park

1 *The Times*, 7 November 1831, p. 2.
2 Charles Pinney, the mayor, was a Liberal, elected shortly before the riots and almost certainly selected as a Liberal scapegoat by the Tories in anticipation of disorder (see *The Times*, 7 November 1831, p. 3; Amey 1979, pp. 110–11).
3 Reprinted in *The Times*, 4 November 1831, p. 3.
4 *Baillie and Bristol Forever*, Bristol elections 1830, Bristol Ref. Library.
5 Pinney, the mayor, had withdrawn from his slave plantation interests by the mid-1830s and diversified his capital and compensation into railway stock (Marshall 1975, p. 27).
6 *The Times*, 23 November 1831, p. 3.
7 *The Times*, 2 November 1831, p. 2; *Trial of Pinney* 1832, p. 87.
8 See Sir James Scarlett, *Trial of Pinney* 1832, p. 312.
9 See, for example, Thomas (1974, pp. 9, 14); *Trial of Pinney* 1832, pp. 39, 47.
10 *Trial of Pinney* 1832, p. xvii. See also Eagles (1832, p. 2); Thomas (1974, p. 5).
11 *The Times*, 1 November 1831, p. 2.
12 Quoted in Eagles (1832, p. 215).
13 *The Times*, 3 November 1831, p. 2.
14 Ibid.
15 *The Times*, 9 November 1831, p. 2.
16 Ibid.
17 *Bristolian*, 20 June 1827, p. 2.
18 *The Times*, 4 November 1831, p. 3.
19 *The Times*, 7 November 1831, p. 3.
20 *Annual Register* (1831, p. 177); *The Times*, 9 November 1831, p. 2.
21 *The Times*, 7 November 1831, p. 3.
22 Quoted in Eagles (1832, p. 220).
23 *The Times*, 11 November 1831, p. 3.
24 3 *Pltry. Debs.* ix, 6 December 1831, 66.
25 *Trial of Pinney* 1832, p. vii.
26 *The Times*, 23 November 1831, p. 3.
27 *Trial of Pinney* 1832, p. 189.
28 Ibid., p. xxii.
29 At the first set of incidents on 24 June 1855, see Payne (1968, pp. 297–9).
30 *Report of Her Majesty's Commissioners appointed to Inquire into the alleged Disturbance of the Public Peace in Hyde Park on Sunday 1st July etc.*, PP 1856 (2016) xxiii.
31 And by *The Times* (2 July 1855, p. 12) and Marx (1980, p. 324) at 150,000.
32 *The Times*, 29 June 1855, p. 10.
33 Marx (1980, p. 324) maintained that there were 800 police hidden in 'buildings and ambuscades' on 1 July.
34 He claimed to the Inquiry that he was 'one of the first' in the police charge at Calthorpe Street; see PP 1856, xxiii (minutes) para. 12785.
35 Edward Ayrton, PP 1856, xxiii (minutes), para. 4366.
36 PP 1856, xxiii, p. xxx.
37 *The Times*, 6 July 1855, p. 7.

38   G. Dundas announced in the Commons, 'Nothing will frighten a mob more than the crash upon pavement of the trail of a six-pounder (cries of "Oh!" and some sensation)' (3 *Pltry. Debs.* cxxxix, 6 July 1855, 530).

39   3 *Pltry. Debs.* cxxxix, 7 July 1855, 368.

40   *Spectator*, 7 July 1855, p. 705.

41   *The Times*, 3 July 1855, p. 8.

42   PP 1856, xxiii, p. xxix.

42a 10 Geo. IV, c.44.

43   *Spectator*, 7 July 1855, p. 697.

44   *The Times*, 3 July 1855, p. 12.

45   PP 1856, xxiii (minutes), para. 6561.

46   Ibid., para. 6307.

47   Ibid., para. 6308.

48   Ibid., para. 6561.

49   *The Times*, 3 July 1855, p. 12.

50   PP 1856, xxxiii (minutes), para. 6582.

51   *The Times*, 4 July 1855, p. 12.

52   *The Times*, 3 July 1855, p. 12.

53   Ibid.

54   *The Times*, 4 July 1855, p. 12.

55   3 *Pltry. Debs.* xxxix, 2 July 1855, 371.

56   PP 1856, xxiii (minutes), para. 6543.

57   *The Times*, 6 July 1855, p. 7.

58   PP 1856, xxiii (minutes), para. 3636.

4   Provincial magistrates and local power

1   See, for example, *Westminster Review* 4, 1825, pp. 315–36; Edwards (1825, p. 82); Bird (1828).

2   *Select Committee to Inquire into the execution of the Criminal Law especially relating to Juvenile Offenders and Transportation*, PP 1847 (447), vii.

3   *The Times*, 9 August 1839, p. 6.

4   *The Times*, 12 August 1847, p. 5.

5   See, for example, Webb and Webb (1963, p. 553); Mullins (1836, p. 16) on political recruitment.

6   See Clarke (1955, p. 59) for a list of the statutory authorities created between 1833 and 1888.

7   The increase in the value of land in the nineteenth century made a few acres sufficient qualification. In 1875 it was reduced to leasehold property with a rateable value of £100 per annum (38 & 39 Vict. c.54) and in 1906 abolished (6 Edward VII, c.16).

8   *Blackwood's Magazine*, 1888, p. 70.

9   *Maidstone Gazette*, 10 March 1840, quoted in Steedman (1984, p. 18).

10   18 & 19 Vict. c.126.

11   *Justice of the Peace* xix, no. 35, September 1855, p. 545.

12   42 & 43, Vict. c.49.

13   Summary Justice Act, 62 & 63 Vict. c.22.

14 Criminal Justice Administration Act, 4 & 5 Geo. V, c.58.

15 Criminal Justice Act, 15 & 16 Geo. V, c.86.

16 4 *Pltry. Debs.* ccxiv, 13 April 1888, 1231.

17 *The Times*, 4 April 1888, p. 6.

18 *Pall Mall Gazette*, 5 April 1888, p. 1.

19 4 *Pltry. Debs.* cccxxix, 6 August 1888, 1654.

20 Ibid., 1653.

21 4 *Pltry. Debs.* xcviii, 2 August 1901, 1071.

22 Ibid., 1072.

23 *Report of the Interdepartmental Committee on Riots*, PP 1895 (C.2016), xxxv.

24 Ibid., paras 6–8.

25 See, for example, the snubbing of the chief constable of Denbigh in 1887, HO 144/1022/A47143/4.

26 *Report of the Select Committee on the Employment of Military in Cases of Disturbance*, PP 1908 (236) vii.

27 Ibid., para. 361.

28 C. Russell and J. Rigby, HO 45/9974/X44685.

29 See proposal by Balfour, 4 *Pltry. Debs.* xcviii, 2 August 1901, 1071–81.

30 *Report of the Select Committee on the Employment of Military in Cases of Disturbance*, PP 1908 (365), minutes, p. 256.

31 See, for example, correspondence between General Wilkinson and the Mayor of Hull in April 1893, HO 144/494/X41472.

32 See HO 144/1022/163219.

33 See HO 144/494/X41472.

34 4 *Pltry. Debs.* xcix, 8 August 1901, 50.

35 In evidence to the PP 1908 (236) para. 379.

36 5 *Pltry. Debs.* xxix, 22 August 1911, 2285.

37 See also *Daily Chronicle*, 7 July 1911, p. 5; and *The Times*, 23 August 1911.

38 5 *Pltry. Debs.* xxix, 22 August 1911, 2286 (emphasis added).

39 Ibid., 2296.

40 Ibid., 2335.

41 *Justice of the Peace* lxxxiv, 15 May 1920, p. 215 (emphasis added).

42 MEPO, 2, 3135.

43 Ibid.

44 See, 5 *Pltry. Debs.* 196, 10 June 1926, 1678; 202, 10 February 1927, 262–3 and *Judicial Statistics for England and Wales* (Cmd. 30551) xxv. For the extreme partiality of the police courts in support of the police see Solicitor (1932, pp. 73–4).

45 The deterrent strategies of the pugnacious Glamorgan chief constable, Lindsay, between 1891 and 1936 may also have played a part in this policy.

46 CC, 4 Division, MEPO, 2, 3135.

47 MEPO 2, 8132.

48 *Police Journal*, 1929, p. 197.

49 The term fell out of official favour after a vigorous campaign by Herbert Morrison during the war.

50 These impressions were confirmed by J.A. Cairns, a metropolitan magistrate.

51 *Justice of the Peace* ciii, 20 May 1939, p. 333.

52 *Justice of the Peace* cxiii, 12 February 1949, p. 108.
53 *Police Journal* xxix, no. 1, January–March 1946, p. 62.
54 Sir Joseph Simpson, *Royal Commission on the Police* (Cmnd. 1728) (minutes), 20, para. 4104.
55 Sched. 3 part III.
56 5 *Pltry. Debs.* 909, 8 April 1976, 616.
57 *Howard Journal*, 1 October 1921, p. 60.
58 *Report of the Working Group on Magistrates' Courts* (1982), Annex S.
59 Justice of the Peace Act 1949, s.27.
60 *The Times*, 18 January 1989, p. 2.
61 *The Magistrate* 45, no. 12, 20 October 1989, pp. 213–14.
62 See, their own proposals in *Administering Magistrates' Courts – the Role of the Justices' Clerk* (1989); and *The Times*, 26 September 1989, p. 32.

5   Shifts in the relations of power: Trafalgar Square, Featherstone and Tonypandy

1 *Saturday Review*, 12 November 1887, p. 649.
2 Engels (1960, p. 334) considered that this was a deliberate policy to provoke disorder.
3 It was the police and the magistrates who were responsible for co-ordinating welfare relief. See, for example, *Illustrated London News*, 29 October 1887, pp. 511–12.
4 *The Times*, 18 October 1887, p. 9.
5 *Daily Telegraph*, 18 October 1887, p. 5.
6 *The Times*, 18 October 1887, p. 10.
7 Ibid., p. 9.
8 *Pall Mall Gazette*, 21 October 1881, p. 1.
9 *Commonweal*, 29 October 1887, p. 345.
10 *Pall Mall Gazette*, 20 October 1887, p. 4.
11 *The Times*, 25 October 1887.
12 *The Times*, 7 November 1887, p. 7.
13 *Pall Mall Gazette*, 10 November 1887, p. 4. The newspaper wanted to know why Hyndman of the SDF could not be similarly accommodated.
14 *Daily Telegraph*, 26 October 1887, p. 3.
15 HO 144/198 46 998/34.
16 HO 65 93.94.
17 *Daily News*, 9 November 1887, p. 4.
18 *The Times*, 18 November 1887, p. 4.
19 *Pall Mall Gazette*, 22 October 1887, p. 1.
20 *Commonweal*, 29 October 1887, p. 345.
21 *Pall Mall Gazette*, 15 November 1887, p. 4.
22 M. Andrieux subsequently 'expressed surprise that the London police should display such violence towards peaceably disposed crowds': *Daily News*, 16 November 1887, p. 6. See also *Saturday Review*, 19 November 1887, p. 690.
23 *The Times*, 17 November 1887, p. 4.
24 *Daily Telegraph*, 15 November 1887, p. 5.

25 In particular to the recent Mitchelstown incident (Annual Register, 1887, p. 159).
26 Annual Register, 1887, p. 177.
27 *Daily Telegraph*, 24 October 1887, p. 5.
28 *Pall Mall Gazette*, 23 November 1887, p. 1.
29 *Daily Telegraph*, 14 November 1887, p. 6.
30 *Illustrated London News*, 19 November 1887, p. 605.
31 *The Times* 14 November 1887, p. 6; see also *Illustrated London News*, 19 November 1887, pp. 605–6.
32 *Remember Trafalgar Square, Pall Mall Gazette* 'Extra', 1887, p. 8.
33 Troops had to be restrained by their officers from using their bayonets on the crowd (*Illustrated London News*, 19 November 1887, p. 606).
34 Annual Register, 1887, p. 176.
35 *Daily News*, 14 November 1887, p. 5.
36 *Daily Telegraph*, 14 November 1887, p. 5.
37 *Daily Chronicle*, 14 November 1887, p. 4. The *Illustrated London News* (19 November 1887, p. 606) claimed 300.
38 *Daily Telegraph*, 14 November 1887, p. 3.
39 Ibid.
40 For T. Cantwell's account of his arrest see *Commonweal*, 3 December 1887, p. 389.
41 Ibid.
42 *Pall Mall Gazette*, 15 November 1887, p. 2.
43 *The Times*, 16 November 1887, p. 6.
44 *The Times*, 14 November 1887, p. 8.
45 Ibid., p. 6.
46 *Daily News*, 15 November 1887, p. 2.
47 See also Besant in *Pall Mall Gazette*, 18 November 1887, p. 5; and *Daily News*, 15 November 1887, p. 2.
48 *Pall Mall Gazette*, 2 December 1887, p. 1.
49 *Pall Mall Gazette*, 10 November 1887, p. 11.
50 In the case of Robert Burrell, Bow Street police court. See *The Times*, 8 November 1887, p. 3.
51 *The Times*, 18 November 1887, p. 4.
52 *Pall Mall Gazette*, 18 November 1887, p. 1.
53 *Daily News*, 15 November 1887, p. 2.
54 *Commonweal*, 10 December 1887, p. 1.
55 *Pall Mall Gazette*, 15 November 1887, p. 2.
56 *The Times*, 14 November 1887, p. 9.
57 *Saturday Review*, 19 November 1887, p. 685.
58 Letter to *Pall Mall Gazette*, 16 November 1887, p. 11.
59 *Pall Mall Gazette*, 24 March 1888, p. 1. See also Firth in 4 *Pltry. Debs.* cccxxiv, 19 April 1888, 1762.
60 *Saturday Review* 19 November 1887, p. 685.
61 See also *Illustrated London News*, 26 November 1887, p. 616.
62 *Daily Graphic*, 7 September 1893, p. 7.

63 *Report of the Committee appointed to Inquire into the circumstances connected with the disturbances at Featherstone on 7th September 1893*, PP 1893 (C.7234) xvii, p. 6.

64 Ibid. (minutes), para. 5295.

65 Ibid., p. 395.

66 4 *Pltry. Debs.* xx, 10 January 1894, 1294.

67 4 *Pltry. Debs.* xvi, 22 August 1893, 764–5.

68 Ibid.

69 Ibid.

70 Motion at 14th conference of the Mine Workers' Federation of Great Britain.

71 4 *Pltry. Debs.* xviii, 6 November 1893, 227–8.

72 4 *Pltry. Debs.* xvii, 20 September 1893, 1731.

73 Francis Allen Darwin, Wakefield, 12 September 1893.

74 *Daily Graphic*, 12 September 1893, p. 9.

75 *Daily Chronicle*, 11 September 1893, p. 7.

76 4 *Pltry. Debs.* xvii, 20 September 1893, 1722–3.

77 *The Times*, 21 September 1893, p. 5. By October the situation had improved sufficiently for Asquith to 'accept responsibility for everything that had been done'. *The Times*, 18 October 1893, p. 10.

78 *Daily Chronicle*, 14 September 1893, p. 3.

79 4 *Pltry. Debs.* xvii, 20 September 1893, 1719.

80 Ibid.

81 4 *Pltry. Debs.* xx, 10 January 1894, 1301.

82 Ibid., 1305.

83 *Leeds Mercury*, 16 October 1893, p. 3.

84 *Leeds Mercury*, 15 December 1893, p. 3.

85 4 *Pltry. Debs.* xxv, 22 December 1893, 199.

86 *Leeds Mercury*, 5 December 1893, p. 6.

87 4 *Pltry. Debs.* xx, 10 January 1894, 1301.

88 'Civil power' was a misprint.

89 PP 1893, p. 395.

90 Such as that held at the Pontypridd Police Court on 11 November 1910.

91 Elias to War Office, 2 November 1910 in *Colliery Strike Disturbances in South Wales. Correspondence and Report*, PP 1911 (Cd. 5568), lxiv, 3.

92 Chief constable of Glamorgan to Home Office, Tuesday 8 November in ibid., 8.

93 Home Secretary to chief constable of Glamorgan, 8 November 1910 in ibid., 10.

94 PP 1908.

95 *The Times*, 9 November 1910, p. 10.

96 Macready (Report to Home Secretary) in PP 1911 (Cd. 5568), p. 17.

97 Home Secretary to chief constable of Glamorgan, 8 November 1910 in ibid., 16.

98 Home Office Press Release, 8 November 1910 in ibid., 20.

99 Home Secretary to Adjutant-General, 8 November 1910 in ibid., 11.

100 War Office to Macready, 8 November 1910 in ibid., 14.

101 MSWCOA to Home Secretary, 10 November 1910, in ibid., 40.

102 *The Times*, 10 November 1910, p. 10.
103 Chief constable of Glamorgan to Home Secretary, 14 November 1910, PP 1911 (Cd. 5568), 59.
104 Home Secretary to Macready, 8 November 1910 in ibid., 15.
105 Home Secretary to Macready, 9 November 1910 in ibid., 23.
106 *The Times*, 9 November 1910, p. 10.
107 Home Office to War Office, 5 January 1911, PP 1911 (Cd. 5568), 92.
108 Home Office to Macready, 22 November 1910 in ibid., 83.
109 Memo to Home Office, 13 November 1910 in ibid., 54.
110 MSWCOA to Home Office, 14 November 1910 in ibid., 61.
111 Memo to Home Office in ibid., 48.
112 Home Office to MSWCOA, 18 November 1910, in ibid., 62.
113 Messrs C. and W. Kenshole to Home Office, 11 November 1910 in ibid., 49.
114 Home Secretary to chief constable of Glamorgan, 8 November 1910 in ibid., 10.
115 Home Office to Messrs C. & W. Kenshole, 12 November in ibid., 50.
116 Moylan to Home Office, 22 November in ibid., 82.
117 Although Macready (1924, p. 155) was quite happy for captures to be handed over to the military for safe-keeping.
118 Home Secretary to Macready, 22 November, PP 1911 (Cd. 5568), 83.
119 Macready to Home Office, 24 November in ibid., 86.
120 *The Times*, 21 December 1910, p. 9.
121 Moylan to Home Office, 30 November in PP 1911 (Cd. 5568), 92.
122 *The Times*, 15 December 1910, p. 8.
123 *The Times*, 20 December 1910, p. 9.
124 Ibid.
125 The division of control between borough and county forces was severely censured by Macready (memorandum), PP 1911 (Cd. 5568), 48.
126 Home Office to Adjutant-General, 12 November 1910 in ibid., 44.
127 *The Times*, 24 November 1910, p. 12.
128 *The Times*, 14 November 1910, p. 6.

6 The army

1 Lord Weymouth to Chairman of Lambeth Q.S., 17 April 1768, quoted in Clode (1869, p. 628).
2 See Hayter (1978, pp. 47–8) for a more detailed exposition of this procedure.
3 Clarke to GOC N.E. District, York, 3 May 1893, HO/144/1494/X41472.135.
4 4 *Pltry. Debs.* lix, 14 June 1898, 230.
5 See Napier (1857, pp. 1–73) for similar incidents.
6 *Report of the Select Committee on the employment of the military in cases of Disturbances*, PP 1908 (236) vii, para. 13.
7 See Troup (1925, pp. 50–1) on the independence of the military authorities in 1911; and Pellew (1982, p. 92) on Troup and the Home Office's considerable reservations.
8 The Committee of Imperial Defence.

9 For example, the Industrial Unrest Committee (4 February 1919), the Supply and Transport Committee (October 1919), the Emergency Committee (25 November 1919), the Internal Protection Arrangements Committee (7 April 1919), the Preservation of Law and Order Committee (22 March 1925), and the Organisation for the Maintenance of Supplies (September 1925).

10 Close military/police support is at the heart of the 'Macready system'. It is worth comparing its operation in 1910 (Macready 1924, p. 152) with the almost identical strategy employed in 1919 (Reynolds and Judge 1968, p. 164). After the 1926 General Strike, senior police officers reported enthusiastically about co-operation (MEPO 2, 3135).

11 4 *Pltry. Debs.* 116, 29 May 1919, 1511.

12 Adjutant-General to DCIGS, 13 Oct 1919, WO 32/5611, quoted in Morgan (1987, p. 92).

13 Both Sir Robert Mark (1977, p. 28), the former metropolitan commissioner and Field Marshall Lord Carver (1983, p. 7), the former chief of UK land forces have asserted (somewhat inaccurately) that the army has not been used in Britain in a civil disorder role to any extent since 1918 and 1919, respectively.

14 The formation of a National Security Committee (renamed in 1975 the Civil Contingencies Committee) to co-ordinate police/military operations and formulate a gradated plan of military involvement certainly recalls the committee work of the 1910–26 period (Manwaring-White 1983, pp. 38–40).

15 See Chapter 8.

16 For examples of this alarming debate see *The Times*, 23 June 1972; Patrick Cosgrove in the *Spectator* 22 December 1973; *Guardian*, 8 January 1974; and *The Times*, 14 August 1974.

17 *State Research Bulletin* 13, August–September 1979, p. 132–3.

18 'Ulsterization' represented a further blow to the military conception of 'counter-insurgency'. On 12 January 1977, after a series of acrimonious disputes, a joint directive was issued transferring supreme authority in security matters from the military commander to the chief constable, Sir Kenneth Newman.

19 Lord Colville, 5 *Pltry. Debs.* (Lords), 17 January 1974, 1052.

7 The police

1 This practice was revived by Churchill in 1910 (see Chapter 5) and in 1969 35 officers were sent to the rebellious Caribbean island of Anguilla.

2 J.H. Hayes, 5 *Pltry. Debs.* 166, 12 July 1923, 1708.

3 2 & 3 Vict. c.93.

4 19 & 20 Vict. c.69.

5 Sir Rainald Knightly, Northampton Quarter Sessions, *The Times*, 5 April 1888, p. 5.

6 4 *Pltry. Debs.* cccxxiv, 16 April 1888, 1394.

7 *The Times*, 20 June 1888, p. 11.

8 4 *Pltry. Debs.* cccxxix, 6 August 1888, 1654.

9 Salisbury to Chamberlain, 11 March 1888.

10 *Pall Mall Gazette*, 29 March 1888, p. 4.

11 4 *Pltry. Debs.* cccxxix, 6 August 1888, 1655.

12 4 *Pltry. Debs.* cccxxiv, 16 April 1888, 1405.

13 *Daily News* 13 April 1888, p. 4. See also *Blackwood's Magazine*, 1888, p. 710, on the evils of 'dividing authority and weakening discipline'.

14 [1930] 2KB, 364.

15 In *Stanbury* v *Exeter Corporation* [1905] 2KB 838, a case concerning the sheep scab inspectorate.

16 *Fisher* v *Oldham Corporation* [1930] 2KB 364 at 372 and 377.

17 See *Edwards* v *Midland Rly Co.* (1881) Law Jo Reps 50, 281; *Lambert* v *G.E. Rly* [1909] 2KB, 776 at 781.

18 See *Bradford Corp & Anr.* v *Webster* [1920], 2KB 135, where a contract of service is assumed, and *Wallwork* v *Fielding* [1922] 2KB 66 at 74.

19 Captain Bourne, 5 *Pltry. Debs.* 314, 10 July 1936, 1554.

20 Cmnd. 1728.

21 Under their proposals, the police authorities would be responsible only for the provision of an 'adequate' force. *Royal Commission on the Police*, PP 1964 (Cmnd. 1728), para. 154.

22 *The Times*, 18 September 1984, p. 2; 19 September 1984, p. 2.

23 Barry Pain, in an address to the ACPO summer conference 1982.

24 'Chief Constable' to *Daily News*, 3 April 1888, p. 6.

25 John Kempster, *Report from the Select Committee on the Police Forces (Weekly Rest Day)*, PP 1908, ix, 679, Appendix xxii, p. 885.

26 Source: *Whitaker's Almanack*, 1951–90.

27 4 *Pltry. Debs.* cccxxix, 31 July 1888, 1656.

28 *Report of the Interdepartmental Committee on Riots*, PP 1895 (C.7650).

29 For further discussion of Regulation 39, see *Police Journal* xxix, no. 1, January–March 1946, p. 62.

30 David Hall, then President of ACPO, *Police*, July 1984, p. 14.

31 PP 1964, paras 118–51.

32 Anderton, *Police Review*, 16 November 1984.

33 Sir Phillip Knights, *Police Journal*, October–December 1981, pp. 331ff.

34 Committee for the co-ordination of organised action in civil emergencies and war planning.

35 The Home Secretary denied any knowledge of the operation in the House of Commons, despite having spent a large part of the previous day with the metropolitan commissioner. See 6 *Pltry. Debs.* 3, 13 April 1981, 30; see also Whitelaw (1989, p. 186).

36 PP 1964, para. 84.

8 The 1981 disorders

1 Pltry. Report, *The Times*, 25 March 1982; *New Society*, 3 December, p. 407.

2 See opinions of councillors Knight (*The Times*, 16 July 1981, p. 1), Simey (1982; 1988) and Judge in *Police* xiii, September 1981, pp. 8–12.

3 Deputy Clerk of Nottinghamshire City Council, Press Release, 16 September 1981.

4 See Scarman (1981, paras. 4.11–4.15); but see also Blom-Cooper and Drabble (1982).

5 *Guardian*, 11 July 1981, p. 1.

6 Home Office Statistical Department (HOSD) (Metropolitan) 20/82.

7 *The Times*, 16 July 1981, p. 1.

8 *The Times*, 13 July 1981, p. 1.

9 According to the *South London Press*, 200 defendants had appeared in Camberwell Green and South Western courts by Monday (see 14 July 1981, p. 1).

10 The Magistrates' Court Act 1980, s.43 empowered senior officers to grant, but not to refuse, bail to persons arrested without a warrant. Conversely, in the case of serious offences, where a custodial remand was sought, the defendant had to be produced before a court more or less immediately. See the corresponding powers under s.38 of the Police and Criminal Evidence Act 1984.

11 Lambeth magistrates' court has no territorial jurisdiction but processes the overflow from South London courts as well as high security cases.

12 Significantly later than that achieved by the West Indian community.

13 There was a history of somewhat racist utterances.

14 See 6 *Pltry. Debs.* 8, 6 July 1981, 21.

15 *The Times*, 4 July 1981, p. 1.

16 All of whom were produced by the police during the period 11–16 July.

17 *Justice of the Peace* 145, 15 January 1983.

18 HOSD 20/82 (Metropolitan) Table 2 shows that a greater proportion of the Southall defendants had previous convictions than any other group.

19 William Whitelaw, MP, 6 *Pltry. Debs.* 8, 8 July 1981, 189.

20 *Guardian*, 5 November 1981, p. 26.

21 Pooley, quoted in Ben-Tovim *et al.* (1980, p. 33).

22 Estimates by the Merseyside Community Relations Council.

23 *Liverpool Inner City Partnership Programme*, 1978, pp. 19–20.

24 *Guardian*, 6 July 1981.

25 All references in this section are to Oxford (1981a) (with paragraph numbers), unless otherwise stated.

26 For some reason, perhaps suggesting that the police deployment was in response to the barricade, the chief constable in his report to Lord Scarman, and in contradiction of his report to the Police Authority, times its construction at 7.00 pm (Oxford 1981b, p. 34).

27 *Guardian*, 7 July 1981, p. 1.

28 *Liverpool Echo*, 8 July 1981, p. 1.

29 Compare the figures given in 6 *Pltry. Debs.* 8, 9 July 1981, 189, with 6 *Pltry. Debs.* (Lords) 422, 16 July 1981, 1482, Oxford (1981b, p. 41); and *Liverpool Echo*, 15 July 1981, p. 7.

30 There was a slightly lower percentage (13 per cent) of white people arrested in 'Toxteth' and 5 per cent fewer unemployed. Of the defendants, 84 per cent lived locally in 'Toxteth' and 88 per cent of the Merseyside defendants also lived locally.

31 As one solicitor put it, 'we usually have a stipendiary and once he makes a decision it permeates to the others' (solicitor LG).

32 *Liverpool Echo*, 7 July 1981, p. 7.

33 Ibid.
34 These figures take no account, of course, of custodial sentences imposed by the Crown Court, which number 113. Unfortunately, HOSD (Liverpool) 20/82 Table 15 gives no breakdown of the lengths of sentences and, in any event, the sample used is much larger. The figure for custodial remand man-hours would also be increased *pro rata* bearing in mind the Crown Court waiting time.
35 See *Report on the Work of the Prison Department*, 1981, pp. 34–9.
36 *Liverpool Echo*, 13 July 1981, p. 1.
37 A history of conflict between the chief constable and the watch committee in Manchester had been resolved decisively in favour of the chief constable in the early century (Redford 1940, pp. 3–27).
38 Police spokesman in *Manchester Evening News*, 8 July 1981, p. 1.
39 Although 26 persons were later arrested for offences connected with this incident.
40 *Manchester Evening News*, 8 July 1981, p. 1.
41 *Police Review*, 8 September 1981, p. 1818.
42 Ibid.
43 Ibid.
44 *Manchester Evening News*, 9 July 1981, p. 9.
45 *Police Review*, 18 September 1981, p. 1818.
46 *Manchester Evening News*, 9 July 1981, p. 9.
47 Ibid., p. 10.
48 See remarks of Councillor Cox, *Manchester Evening News*, 10 July 1981, p. 27; and the rebuff to the militant group's call for an emergency meeting on policing, ibid., 13 July 1981, p. 1.
49 *Manchester Evening News*, 9 July 1981, p. 10.
50 Haldane Society, 20 July 1981, p. 1.
51 *Manchester Evening News*, 9 July 1981, p. 1.
52 An unfortunate phrase allegedly used by the chief constable, *Manchester Evening News*, 10 July 1981, p. 1.
53 *Manchester Evening News*, 9 July 1981, p. 8.
54 *Manchester Evening News*, 10 July 1981, p. 1.
55 Haldane Society, 20 July 1981, p. 1.
56 Ibid.
57 *Manchester Evening News*, 10 July 1981, p. 1.
58 This was alleged to involve *pro forma* charges which merely required the name of the defendant to be added.
59 Not all defendants were either arrested or produced immediately. At least 25 in Moss Side were released without charge.
60 *The Times*, 11 July 1981, p. 2.
61 Robert Carlyle, Chairman of the Manchester bench, *Manchester Evening News*, 5 August 1981, p. 4.
62 Haldane Society, 20 July 1981, p. 1.
63 Letter to Haldane Society, 9 October 1981.
64 HOSD 20/82 (Greater Manchester) Table 9.

9   Police and magistracy in contemporary civil disorder

1 See Chapter 1, and the submission by the Justices' Clerks to the Scarman Inquiry.
2 *The Times*, 14 July 1981, p. 13.
3 Quoted in *LAG Bulletin*, December 1981, p. 274.
4 See *Time Out*, 17 April 1981.
5 *The Times*, 13 July 1981, p. 2; Bunyan (1981b, p. 6).
6 See Nottingham Law Society *Report*, 1981, para. 8.
7 HOSD, 20/82, Table 6.
8 Riot, affray and unlawful assembly, ibid.

Bibliography

Adolphus, J. (1824). *Observations on the Vagrancy Act etc. and on the Powers and Duties of the Justices of the Peace.* Pamphlet.

Amey, G. (1979). *City under Fire: the Bristol Riots and Aftermath.* London, Lutterworth Press.

Anderson, Sir John (1929). The Police. *Public Administration*, **1**, 192–202.

Anderson, P. (1964). Origins of the Present Crisis. *New Left Review*, **23**, 26–59.

Anderton, J. (1981). *Report of the Chief Constable to the Greater Manchester Police Authority.* Manchester.

Anon. (1833). *Trial of Charles Pinney Esq.* Bristol, Gutch & Martin.

Applegate, R. (1969). *Riot Control – Materiel and Techniques.* Harrisberg, Stackpole Books.

Arnot, R.P. (1949). *The Miners.* London, George Allen & Unwin.

Arnot, R.P. (1967). *South Wales Miners.* London, George Allen & Unwin.

Ascoli, D. (1979). *The Queen's Peace. The Origins and Development of the Metropolitan Police 1829–1979.* London, Hamish Hamilton.

Babington, A. (1969). *A House in Bow Street. Crime and the Magistracy 1740–1881.* London, Macdonald.

Babington, A. (1990). *Military Intervention in Britain. From the Gordon Riots to the Gibraltar Incident.* London, Routledge.

Bailey, V. (1977). Salvation Army Riots. In A.P. Donajgrodski (ed.), *Social Control in Nineteenth Century Britain.* London, Croom Helm, 231–49.

Balbus, I.D. (1973). *The Dialectics of Legal Repression.* New York, Russell Sage.

Barnett, C. (1967). The Education of Military Elites. *Journal of Contemporary History*, **2**(3), 15–36.

Barnett, C. (1970). *Britain and her Army 1509–1970.* London, Allen Lane.

Beattie, J.M. (1986). *Crime and the Courts in England 1660–1800.* Oxford, Clarendon.

Bennett, G.J. and Ryan, C.L. (1985). Armed Forces, Public Disorder and the Law in the U.K. In P.J. Rowe and C.J. Whelan (eds), *Military Intervention in Democratic Societies*. London, Croom Helm, 166–96.

Bennett, T. (1983). *The Future of Policing*. Cambridge, Cropwood.

Bentham, J. (1825). *Observations on Mr. Secretary Peel's Speech Introducing his Police Magistrates' Salary Bill*. Pamphlet.

Ben-Tovim, G., Brown, V., Clay, D., Law, I., Loy, L. and Torkington, K. (1980). *Racial Disadvantage in Liverpool*. Liverpool, Merseyside Area Profile Group.

Besant, A. (1893). *An Autobiography*. London, T. Fisher & Unwin.

Bird, C. (1828). *Letter to the Right Hon, Robert Peel etc., with reference to the Expansion of the Jurisdiction of the Justices of the Peace*. Pamphlet.

Blackaby, R. (1979). *De-industrialisation*. London, Heinemann.

Blackstone, Sir William (1830). *Commentaries on the Laws of England* (4 vols). London, Thomas Tegg.

Blake, J. (1979). *Civil Disorder in Britain 1910–1939. The Roles of Civil Government and Military Authority*. DPhil dissertation, University of Sussex.

Blake, R. (1957). Great Britain. The Crimean War to the First World War. In M. Howard (ed.), *Soldiers and Governments*. London, Eyre & Spottiswoode, 27–50.

Blom-Cooper, L. and Drabble, R. (1982). Police Perceptions of Crime. Brixton, the Operational Response. *British Journal of Criminology*, **22**, 184–7.

Bowden, T. (1978). *Beyond the Limits of the Law*. Harmondsworth, Penguin.

Bowring, J. (1843). *The Works of Jeremy Bentham* (11 vols). Edinburgh, William Tait.

Boynes, T. and Baber, C. (1980). The Supply of Labour 1750–1914. In *Glamorgan County History*, Cardiff, University of Wales Press, 311–62.

Bramall, Sir Edwin (1985). The Place of the Army in Public Disorder. In P.J. Rowe and C.J. Whelan (eds), *Military Intervention in Democratic Societies*. London, Croom Helm, 68–84.

Brewer, J. (1989). *The Sinews of Power, War, Money and the English State, 1688–1783*. London, Unwin Hyman.

Brewer, J., Guelke, A., Hume, I., Moxon-Browne, E. and Wilford, R. (1988). *The Police, Public Order and the State*. London, Macmillan.

Bridges, L. (1981). Keeping the Lid on. British Social Policy 1975–81. *Race and Class*, **23**, 171–85.

Bridges, L. and Bunyan, T. (1983). Britain's New Urban Policing Strategy – The Police and Criminal Evidence Bill in Context. *Journal of Law and Society*, **10**(1), 85–107.

Brique, M. (1982). *We Want to Riot, Not Work*. London, Little A.

Broadbent, T.A. (1977). *Planning and Profit in the Urban Economy*. London, Methuen.

Brogden, M. (1977). A Police Authority – The Denial of Conflict. *Sociological Review*, **25**, 325–49.

Brogden, M. (1982). *The Police: Autonomy and Consent*. London, Academic Press.

Brown, J. (1978). *The Cranfield Papers*. London, Peel Press.

Brown, K.D. (1977). *John Burns*. London, Royal Historical Society.

BSSRS Technology of Political Control Group (1985). *TechnoCop. New Police Technologies*. London, Free Association Books.

Bunyan, T. (1977). *The History and Practice of the Political Police in Britain*. London, Quartet.

Bunyan, T. (1981a). The Police against the People. *Race and Class*, **23**, 153–70.

Bunyan, T. (1981b). The Growing Power of the Military. *Marxism Today*, **25**(6), 6–9.

Burgess, J. (1911). *John Burns. The Rise and Progress of a Right Honourable*. Glasgow, Reformers Bookstall.

Burgess, K. (1975). *The Origins of British Industrial Relations. The Nineteenth Century Experience*. London, Croom Helm.

Burney, E. (1979). *JP: Magistrate, Court and Community*. London, Hutchinson.

Burns, J.H. and Hart, H.L.A. (1970). *Works of Bentham*. London, Athlone Press.

Butler, J.E. (1879). *Government by Police*. London, Dyer.

Butler, R.A.B. (1974). The Foundation of the Institute of Criminology. In R. Hood (ed.), *Crime, Criminology and Public Policy*. London, Heinemann, 1–10.

Butler, Col. Sir William F. (1894). *Sir Charles Napier*. London, Macmillan.

Campbell, D. (1987). Policing: A Power in the Land. *New Statesman*, 8 May, 11–13.

Carlyle, T. (1988). *Critical and Miscellaneous Essays*, vol. VII. London, Chapman & Hall.

Carver, Field Marshall Lord C. (1983). The Army and the Police. *Police Studies*, **6**, 6–12.

Castells, M. (1975). Immigrant Workers and Class Struggles in Advanced Capitalism: The West European Perspective. *Politics and Society*, **5**(1), 33–66.

Chatwin, R. (1981). Brixton and After. *Marxism Today*, **25**(9), 26–7.

Churchill, R.S. (1967). *Winston S. Churchill. Vol. 11 Companion. Part 2. 1907–1911*. London, Heinemann.

Clark, D. (1981a). Oxford Must Go. But Will He? *Leveller*, **63**, 2–3.

Clark, D. (1981b). This is a Police City. *Leveller*, **63**, 8–9.

Clarke, J.C. (1955). *A History of Local Government in the United Kingdom*. London, Herbert Jenkins.

Clarke, S. (1977). Marxism, Sociology and Poulantzas' Theory of the State. *Capital and Class*, **2**, 1–31.

Clode, C.M. (1869). *Military Forces of the Crown. Their Administration and Government* (2 vols). London, Murray.

Clutterbuck, R.L. (1973a). *Riot and Revolution in Singapore and Malaya*. London, Faber & Faber.

Clutterbuck, R.L. (1973b). *Protest and the Urban Guerrilla*. London, Cassel.

Clutterbuck, R.L. (1974). A Third Force? *Army Quarterly*, **104**(1), 22–8.

Clutterbuck, R.L. (1975). *Living with Terrorism*. London, Cassel.

Clutterbuck, R.L. (1978). *Britain in Agony. The Growth of Political Violence*. Harmondsworth, Penguin.

Cobban, A. (1962). *Edmund Burke and the Revolt against the Eighteenth Century*. London, George Allen & Unwin.

Cockburn, C. (1977). *The Local State*. London, Pluto.

Cohen, R. (1987). *The New Helots*. Gower, Aldershot.

Cole, D. and Postgate, R. (1961). *The Common People*. London, Methuen.

Collison, M.G. (1983). *Law, the State and the Control of Labour in Eighteenth Century England*. PhD dissertation, University of Sheffield.

Colquhoun, P. (1806). *A Treatise on the Police of the Metropolis.* York, J. Mawman & Co.

Corrigan, P. (1980). The State as a Relation of Production. In P. Corrigan (ed.), *Capitalism, State Formation and Marxist Theory.* London, Quartet, 1–26.

Critchley, T.A. (1978). *A History of Police in England and Wales 1900–1966* (revised edn). London, Constable.

Darvall, F.O. (1969). *Popular Disturbances and Public Order in Regency England.* Oxford, Oxford University Press.

Davis, J. (1984). A Poor Man's System of Justice: the London Police Courts in the Second Half of the Nineteenth Century. *Historical Journal,* **27**(2), 309–35.

Deane-Drummond, Maj.-Gen. A.J. (1975). *Riot Control.* London, Royal United Services Inst.

Dear, M.J. and Clark, G.L. (1978). The State and Geographic Process: A Critical Review. *Environmental Planning,* **10**, 173–83.

Dearlove, J.N. (1973). *The Politics of Policy in Local Government: the Making and Maintenance of Public Policy in the Royal Borough of Kensington and Chelsea.* Cambridge, Cambridge University Press.

Debray, R. (1973). *Prison Writings.* London, Allen Lane.

De Castro, J.P. (1926). *The Gordon Riots.* Oxford, Oxford University Press.

Desmarais, R.H. (1971). The British Government's Strikebreaking Organisation and Black Friday. *Journal of Contemporary History,* **6**(2), 112–28.

Dobrovir, W.A. (1969). *Justice in Time of Crisis.* Washington, DC, US Government Printing Office.

Donajgrodski, A.P. (1977). *Social Control in Nineteenth Century Britain.* London, Croom Helm.

Dummett, M. (1980). *Southall 23rd April 1979. The Report of the Unofficial Committee of Enquiry.* London, Russell Press NCCL.

Dunbabin, J.P.D. (1963). The Politics of the Establishment of County Councils. *Historical Journal,* **6**(2), 226–52.

Duncan, S. and Goodwin, M. (1988). *The Local State and Uneven Development.* Cambridge, Polity Press.

Eagles, J. (1832). *The Bristol Riots.* London, Cadell.

Edwards, T. (1825). *A Letter to the Lord Lieutenant of the County of Surrey on the Misconduct of Licensing Magistrates and the Consequent Degredation of the Magistracy.* London, Butterworth & Son.

Emsley, C. (1983). *Policing in its Context 1750–1870.* London, Macmillan.

Emsley, C. (1987). *Crime and Society in England 1750–1900.* Harlow, Longman.

Engels, F. (1959). *Correspondence with Paul and Laura Lafargue 1868–1886* (vol. 1). Moscow, Foreign Language Publishing House.

Engels, F. (1960). *Correspondence with Paul and Laura Lafargue 1887–1890.* (vol. 2) Moscow, Foreign Language Publishing House.

Ensor, R.C.K. (1935). The Supercession of County Government. *Politica,* **14**, 425–47.

Evans, D. (1911). *Labour Strife in the South Wales Coalfield 1910–1911.* Cardiff, Educational Publishing Co.

Evans, E. (1977). *City in Transition.* Liverpool, Liverpool City Planning Dept.

Evelegh, R. (1978). *Peace Keeping in a Democratic Society. The Lesson of Northern Ireland*. London, Hurst & Co.

Field, S. (1982). Urban Disorders in Britain and America. A Review of Research. In S. Field and P. Southgate (eds), *Public Disorder*, Home Office Research Study 72. London, HMSO, 1–40.

Fine, B. and Millar, R. (1985). *Policing the Miners' Strike*. London, Lawrence and Wishart.

Finer, H. (1945). *English Local Government*. London, Methuen.

Foster, J. (1974). *Class Struggle and the Industrial Revolution*. London, Weidenfeld and Nicolson.

Foucault, M. (1977). *Discipline and Punish*. Harmondsworth, Penguin.

Foucault, M. (1980). *Power/Knowledge: Selected Interviews and Other Writings*. Brighton, Harvester.

Fox, K.O. (1973). The Tonypandy Riots. *Army Quarterly*, **104**, 72–8.

Fox, K.O. (1974). Public Order: the Law and the Military. *Army Quarterly*, **105**, 295–307.

Fraser, D. (1982a). *Municipal Reforms and the Industrial City*. New York, St Martin's Press.

Fraser, D. (1982b). The Agitation for Parliamentary Reform. In J.T. Ward (ed.), *Popular Movements c1830–1850*. London, Macmillan, 31–53.

Frobel, F., Heinrichs, J. and Kreye, O. (1980). *The New International Division of Labour*. Cambridge, Cambridge University Press.

Gattrell, V.A.C., Lenman, B. and Parker, G. (1980). *Crime and the Law. The Social History of Crime in Western Europe since 1500*. London, Europa Publications.

Geary, R. (1985). *Policing Industrial Disputes 1893–1985*. Cambridge, Cambridge University Press.

Gilroy, P. (1981). You Can't Fool the Youths . . . Race and Class Formation in the 1980s. *Race and Class*, **23**, 207–21.

Glassey, L.K.J. (1979). *Politics and the Appointment of Justices of the Peace 1675–1720*. Oxford, Oxford University Press.

Gorz, A. (1970). Immigrant Labour. *New Left Review*, **61**, 28–30.

Gramsci, A. (1971). *Selections from Prison Notebooks*. London, Lawrence and Wishart.

Gramsci, A. (1978). *Selections from Political Writings 1921–26*. London, Lawrence and Wishart.

Gray, R.Q. (1976). *The Labour Aristocracy in Victorian Edinburgh*. Oxford, Oxford University Press.

Griffith, J.A. (1966). *Central Departments and Local Authorities*. London, Allen & Unwin.

Gurr, T.R. (1976). *Rogues, Rebels and Reformers. A Political History of Urban Crime and Conflict*. Beverly Hills, CA, Sage.

Halévy, E. (1935). Before 1835. In H.J. Laski, W. Ivor Jennings and W.A. Robson (eds), *A Century of Municipal Progress 1835–1935*. London, George Allen & Unwin, 15–36.

Halévy, E. (1972). *The Growth of Philosophical Radicalism*. London, Faber & Faber.

Hall, S. (1980a). Nicos Poulantzas: State, Power, Socialism. *New Left Review*, **119**, 60–9.

Hall, S. (1980b). *Drifting into a Law and Order Society*. London, Cobden Trust.

Hall, S. (1985). Authoritarian Populism: A Reply to Jessop *et al. New Left Review*, **151**, 115–24.

Hall, S., Critcher, C., Jefferson, T., Clarke, J. and Roberts, B. (1978). *Policing the Crisis, Mugging, the State and Law and Order*. London, Macmillan.

Hamburger, J. (1963). *James Mill and the Art of Revolution*. New Haven, CT, Yale University Press.

Hamer, W.S. (1970). *The British Army. Civil Military Relations 1885–1905*. Oxford, Clarendon.

Hamnett, C. (1983). The Conditions in England's Inner Cities on the Eve of the 1981 Riots. *Area*, **15**(1), 7–13.

Harries-Jenkins, G. (1970). Professionals in Organisations. In J.A. Jackson (ed.), *Professions and Professionalization*. Cambridge, Cambridge University Press.

Harries-Jenkins, G. (1977). *The Army in Victorian Society*. London, Routledge & Kegan Paul.

Harring, S. (1981). The Taylorization of Police Work: Prospects for the 1980s. *The Insurgent Sociologist*, **11**(1), 25–31.

Harrison, B. (1965). The Sunday Trading Riots of 1855. *Historical Journal*, **8**, 219–45.

Harrison, B. (1982). *Peaceable Kingdom. Stability and Change in Modern Britain*. Oxford, Clarendon.

Hayter, T. (1978). *The Army and the Crowd in Mid Georgian England*. London, Macmillan.

Himmelfarb, G. (1986). *Victorian Minds*. New York, Alfred A. Knopf.

Hinton, J. (1965). The Labour Aristocracy. *New Left Review*, **32**, 72–7.

Hobsbawm, E.J. (1954). The Labour Aristocracy in 19th Century Britain. In J. Saville (Ed.), *Democracy and the Labour Movement*. London, Lawrence and Wishart, 201–39.

Hobsbawm, E.J. (1963). *Primitive Rebels. Studies in Archaic Forms of Social Movement in the 19th and 20th Centuries*. Manchester, Manchester University Press.

Hobsbawm, E.J. and Rudé, G. (1969). *Captain Swing*. London, Lawrence & Wishart.

Hogg, R. (1979). Imprisonment and Society under Early British Capitalism. *Crime & Social Justice*, **12**, 4–17.

Holloway, J. and Picciotto, S. (1977). Capital, Crisis and the State. *Capital and Class*, **2**, 76–101.

Holloway, J. and Picciotto, S. (1978). *State and Capital. A Marxist Debate*. London, Edward Arnold.

Holton, R.J. (1976). *Radical Syndicalism 1900–1917. Myths and Realities*. London, Pluto.

Hood, R. (1962). *Sentencing in Magistrates' Courts*. London, Stevens & Sons.

Howard, M. (1957). *Soldiers and Governments*. London, Eyre & Spottiswoode.

Howe, D. (1981). Brixton Before the Uprising. *Race Today*, **14** (2) 61–8.

Howe, D. (1982). From Bobby to Babylon. Blacks and the British Police. *Race Today*, February–March, 61–9.

Hume, L.J. (1981). *Bentham and Bureaucracy*. Cambridge, Cambridge University Press.

Hytner, B. (1981). *Report of the Moss-Side Enquiry to the Leader of the GMC*. Manchester, Greater Manchester Council.

Ivor Jennings, W. (1935). The Municipal Revolution. In H.J. Laski, W. Ivor Jennings and W.A. Robson (eds), *A Century of Municipal Progress 1835–1935*. London, George Allen & Unwin, 55–65.

Jackson, R.M. (1937). The Incidence of Jury Trial during the Past Century. *Modern Law Review*, **1**, 132–44.

Jefferson, T. (1990). *The Case Against Paramilitary Policing*. Milton Keynes, Open University Press.

Jefferson, T. and Grimshaw, R. (1982). Law, Democracy and Justice: the Question of Police Accountability. In D. Cowell, T. Jones and J. Young (eds), *Policing the Riots*. London, Junction Books, 82–117.

Jeffery, K. (1984). *The British Army and the Crisis of Empire 1918–1922*. Manchester, Manchester University Press.

Jeffery, K. (1985). Military Aid to the Civil Power in the U.K. An Historical Perspective. In P.J. Rowe and C.J. Whelan (eds), *Military Intervention in Democratic Societies*. London, Croom Helm, 51–67.

Jeffries, C. (1952). *The Colonial Police*. London, Max Parrish.

Jessop, B. (1982). *The Capitalist State*. Oxford, Martin Robertson.

Jessop, B. (1985). *Nicos Poulantzas: Marxist Theory and Political Strategy*. New York, St Martin's Press.

Jessop, B., Bonnett, K., Bromley, S. and Ling, T. (1984). Authoritarian Populism. Two nations and Thatcherism. *New Left Review*, **147**, 32–60.

John, G. (1982). *Moss Side Fighting Back*. Pamphlet.

Johnson, T.J. (1972). *Professions and Power*. London, Macmillan.

Joshua, H. and Wallace, T. (1983). *To Ride the Storm. The 1980 Bristol 'Riot' and the State*. London, Heinemann.

Keith-Lucas, B. (1960). The Independence of Chief Constables. *Public Administration*, **38**, 1–11.

Keith-Lucas, B. (1977). *English Local Government in the Nineteenth and Twentieth Centuries*. London, Historical Association.

Keller, L. (1976). *Public Order in Victorian London: the Interaction between the Metropolitan Police, the Government, the Urban Crowd and the Law*. PhD dissertation, University of Cambridge.

Kettle, M. (1982). The Keepers of the Queen's Peace. *New Society*, 25 March, 471–3.

Kettle, M. (1985). The National Reporting Centre and the 1984 Miners' Strike. In B. Fine and R. Millar (eds), *Policing the Miners' Strike*. London, Lawrence & Wishart, 23–33.

Kettle, M. and Hodges, L. (1982). *Uprising – The Police, the People and the Riots in Britain's Cities*, London, Pan.

Kirsch, B. (1981). Brixton and After. *Marxism Today*, **25**(7), 6–11.

Kitson, F. (1971). *Low Intensity Operations*. London, Faber & Faber.

Kushnick, L. (1981). Parameters of British and North American Racism. *Race and Class*, **23**, 187–206.

Lambert, B. (1806). *The History and Survey of London and its Environs etc*. London, T. Hughes.

Laski, H.J., Ivor Jennings, W. and Robson, W.A. (1935). *A Century of Municipal Progress 1835–1935*. London, George Allen & Unwin.

Law, I. and Henfry, J. (1981). *A History of Race and Racism in Liverpool 1660–1950*. Liverpool, Merseyside Community Relations Council.

Lee, J.M. (1963). *Social Leaders and Public Persons: a Study of County Government in Cheshire since 1888*. New York, Oxford University Press.

Le Vay, J. (1989). *Magistrates' Courts. Report of a Scrutiny 1989* (2 vols). London, HMSO.

Lewis, N. and Wiles, P. (1984). The Post Corporatist State. *Journal of Law and Society*, **11**(1), 65–90.

Lewis, R. (1980). *The Real Trouble. A Study of Some Aspects of the Southall Trials*. London, Runnymede Trust.

Lieberson, S. and Silverman, A. (1965). The Precipitants and Underlying Conditions of Riots. *American Sociological Review*, **30**, 887–98.

Little, B. (1967). *The City and County of Bristol*. London, Werner Laurie.

Lloyd, P.E. (1980). Manchester. A Study in Industrial Decline. In P.H. White (ed.), *The Continuing Conurbation*. Farnborough, Gower, 53–76.

Lock, J. (1980). *Marlborough Street. The Story of a London Court*. London, Robert Hale.

Lucas, P. (1962). Blackstone and the Reform of the Legal Profession. *English Historical Review*, **77**, 456–87.

Lunt, Maj.-Gen., J.D. (1974). Soldiers are not Policemen. *Army Quarterly*, **104**, 409–11.

Mace, R. (1976). *Trafalgar Square: Emblem of Empire*. London, Lawrence & Wishart.

Mack, M.P. (1969). *Jeremy Bentham. An Odyssey of Ideas 1748–1792*. London, Heinemann.

Macready, Sir Neville (1924). *Annals of an Active Life* (2 vols). London, Hutchinson.

Maitland, F.W. (1911). *The Shallows and Silences of Real Life*. Cambridge, Cambridge University Press.

Manchee, T.J. (1832). *The Origin of the Riots in Bristol*. Bristol, Pamphlet.

Mandel, E. (1975). *Late Capitalism*. London, New Left Books.

Manwaring-White, S. (1983). *The Policing Revolution*. Brighton, Harvester.

Mark, Sir Robert (1977). *Policing a Perplexed Society*. London, Allen & Unwin.

Mark, Sir Robert (1978). *In the Office of Constable*. London, Collins.

Marshall, G. (1965). *Police and Government*. London, Methuen.

Marshall, P. (1975). *Bristol and the Abolition of Slavery*. Bristol, Bristol Historical Association.

Marx, K. (1977). *Capital, Vol. 1*. London, Lawrence and Wishart.

Marx, K. (1980). *Collected Works, Vol. 14*. London, Lawrence and Wishart.

Mather, F.C. (1959). *Public Order in the Age of the Chartists*. Manchester, Manchester University Press.

Mathiesen, T. (1980). *Law, Society and Political Action: Towards a Strategy under Late Capitalism*. London, Academic Press.

McBarnet, D. (1981). *Conviction. The Law, the State and the Construction of Justice*. London, Macmillan.

McKenzie, I.K. and Gallagher, G.P. (1989). *Behind the Uniform. Policing in Britain and America*. Hemel Hempstead, Harvester Wheatsheaf.

McLean, I. (1975). *Keir Hardie*. London, Allen Lane.

McNee, Sir David (1983). *McNee's Law*. London, Collins.

Melville Lee, Capt. W.L. (1901). *A History of Police in England*. London, Methuen.

Midwinter, E.C. (1968). *Law and Order in Early Victorian Lancashire*. York, St. Anthony's Press.

Miliband, R. (1969). *The State in Capitalist Society*. London, Weidenfeld & Nicolson.

Miliband, R. (1970). The Capitalist State. Reply to Nicos Poulantzas. *New Left Review*, **59**, 53–60.

Mill, J.S. (1972). *Utilitarianism, Liberty, Representative Government*. London, Dent.

Milton, F. (1959). *In Some Authority. The English Magistrate*. London, Pall Mall Press.

Mingay, G.E. (1976). *The Gentry, The Rise and Fall of a Ruling Class*. London, Longman.

Moir, E. (1969). *The Justice of the Peace*. Harmondsworth, Penguin.

Moorhouse, H.F. (1978). The Marxist Theory of the Labour Aristocracy. *Social History*, **13**(1), 61–81.

Morgan, J. (1987). *Conflict and Order. The Police and Labour Disputes in England and Wales 1900–1939*. Oxford, Clarendon Press.

Morgan, J.V. (1918). *Life of Viscount Rhondda*. London, H.R. Allenson.

Morgan, K.O. (1973). The New Liberalism and the Challenge of Labour: the Welsh Experience 1885–1929. *Welsh Historical Review*, **6**, 288–312.

Morgan, K.O. (1981). *Rebirth of a Nation: Wales 1880–1980*. Oxford, Clarendon.

Morris, M. (1976). *The General Strike*. London, Journeyman Press.

Mosca, G. (1939). *The Ruling Class*. New York, McGraw-Hill.

Mullins, E. (1836). *Treatise on the Magistracy of England*. London, Richards.

Nairn, T. (1977). *The Break-up of Britain*. London, New Left Books.

Namier, Sir Lewis and Brooke, J. (1964). *History of Parliament. The Commons 1754– 1790* (3 vols). London, Parliamentary Trust.

Napier, Sir Charles (1837). *Remarks on Military Law and the Punishment of Flogging*. London, T. & W. Boone.

Napier, Sir William (1857). *The Life and Opinions of General Sir Charles James Napier* (4 vols). London, John Murray.

Nelson, W. (1718). *The Office and Authority of a Justice of the Peace*. London.

Newman, Sir Kenneth (1978). Prevention *in extremis* – The Preventative Role of the Police in Northern Ireland. In J. Brown (ed.), *The Cranfield Papers*. London, Peel Press.

Northam, G. (1988). *Shooting in the Dark. Riot Police in Britain*. London, Faber & Faber.

Oliver, I. (1987). *Police, Government and Accountability*. London, Macmillan.

Osborne, B. (1960). *Justices of the Peace 1361–1848*. Shaftesbury, Sedgehill Press.

Otley, C.B. (1968). Militarism and the Social Affiliations of the British Army Elite. In J. Van Doorn (ed.), *Armed Forces and Society*. The Hague, Mouton, 84–108.

Oxford, K. (1981a). *Public Disorders on Merseyside: July–August 1981*. Liverpool, Merseyside Police.

Oxford, K. (1981b). *Evidence to the Scarman Inquiry*. Liverpool, Merseyside Police.

Oxford, K. (1984). Policing by Consent. In J. Benyon (ed.), *Scarman and After*. Oxford, Pergamon, 114–24.

Page, L. (1947). *Justice of the Peace*. London, Faber & Faber.

Palmer, S.H. (1988). *Policing and Protest in England and Ireland 1780–1850.* Cambridge, Cambridge University Press.

Parker, H., Casburn, M. and Turnbull, D. (1981). *Receiving Juvenile Justice.* Oxford, Basil Blackwell.

Parris, H. (1961). The Home Office and the Provincial Police in England and Wales 1856–1870. *Public Law*, Autumn, 230–55.

Payne, R. (1968). *Marx.* London, W.H. Allen.

Peet, R. (1975). Inequality and Poverty: A Marxist Geographic Theory. *Annals of the Association of American Geographers*, **65**, 564–71.

Pellew, G. (1847). *Life etc. of First Viscount Sidmouth.* London, John Murray.

Pellew, J. (1982). *The Home Office 1848–1914. From Clerks to Bureaucrats.* London, Heinemann Educational.

Petras, J. and Gundle, J. (1982). A Critique of Socialist State Theorising. *Contemporary Crises*, **6**, 161–82.

Philips, D. (1976). The Black Country Magistracy 1835–60: a Changing Elite and the Exercise of its Power. *Midland History*, 161–96.

Philips, D. (1980). A New Engine of Power and Authority: The Institutionalisation of Law and Enforcement in England 1780–1830. In V.A.C. Gatrell, B. Lenman and G. Parker (eds), *Crime and the Law. The Social History of Crime in Western Europe since 1500.* London, Europa Publications.

Picciotto, S. (1979). The Theory of the State, Class Struggle and the Rule of Law. In B. Fine, R. Kinsey, J. Lea *et al.* (eds), *Capitalism and the Rule of Law.* London, Hutchinson.

Pocock, T. (1973). *Fighting General. The Public and Private Campaigns of General Sir Walter Walker.* London, Collins.

Poggi, G. (1978). *The Development of the Modern State.* London, Hutchinson.

Porter, B. (1987). *The Origins of the Vigilant State. The London Metropolitan Police Special Branch before the First World War.* London, Weidenfeld & Nicolson.

Poulantzas, N. (1969). The Problem of the Capitalist State. *New Left Review*, **58**, 67–78.

Poulantzas, N. (1974). *Classes in Contemporary Capitalism.* London, Verso.

Poulantzas, N. (1975). *Political Power and Social Classes.* London, New Left Books.

Poulantzas, N. (1976). *The Crisis of the Dictatorships. Portugal, Greece and Spain.* London, New Left Books.

Poulantzas, N. (1978). *State, Power, Socialism.* London, Verso.

Prince, M. (1988). *God's Cop. The Biography of James Anderton.* London, Frederick Muller.

Quinault, R. (1974). The Warwickshire County Magistracy and Public Order 1830–1870. In J. Stevenson and R. Quinault (eds), *Popular Protest and Public Order: Six Studies in British History 1790–1920.* London, Allen & Unwin, 184–214.

Radzinowicz, L. (1956a). *A History of the English Criminal Law and its Administration from 1750. Vol. 2. The Clash Between Private Initiative and Public Interest in the Enforcement of the Law.* London, Stevens & Sons.

Radzinowicz, L. (1956b). *A History of the English Criminal Law and its Administration from 1750. Vol. 3. Cross Currents in the Movement for the Reform of the police.* London, Stevens & Sons.

Radzinowicz, L. (1968). *A History of the English Criminal Law and its Administration from 1750. Vol. 4. Grappling for Control.* London, Stevens & Sons.

Reader, W.J. (1966). *Professional Men. The Rise of the Professional Classes in Nineteenth Century England.* London, Weidenfeld & Nicolson.

Redford, A. (1940). *The History of Local Government in Manchester.* London, Longmans, Green & Co.

Redlich, J. (1958). *The History of Local Government in England.* London, Macmillan.

Reilly, R. (1978). *Pitt the Younger.* London, Cassell.

Reiner, R. (1984). Is Britain Turning into a Police State? *New Society,* 2 August, 51–6.

Reiner, R. (1985). *The Politics of the Police.* Brighton, Wheatsheaf.

Reith, C. (1943). *British Police and the Democratic Ideal.* London, Oxford University Press.

Reith, C. (1956). *A New Study of Police History.* Edinburgh, Oliver & Boyd.

Rex, J. (1982). The 1981 Riots in Britain. *International Journal of Urban and Regional Research,* **6**(1), 99–113.

Reynolds, G.W. and Judge, A. (1968). *The Night the Police Went on Strike.* London, Weidenfeld & Nicolson.

Rhodes, R.A.W. (1986). 'Power Dependence'. Theories of Central–Local Relations: A Critical Re-assessment. In M. Goldsmith (ed.), *New Research in Central–Local Relations.* Aldershot, Gower, 1–33.

Rodrigues, J. (1981). The Riots of 1981. *Marxism Today,* **25**(10), 18–22.

Rogers, H.B. (1980). Manchester Revisited: A Profile of Urban Change. In P.H. White (ed.), *The Continuing Conurbation.* Farnborough, Gower, 26–45.

Rose, M.E. (1982). The Anti-Poor Law Agitation. In J.I. Ward (ed.), *Popular Movements.* London, Macmillan, 78–94.

Rosenblum, N.L. (1978). *Bentham's Theory of the Modern State.* Cambridge, MA, Harvard University Press.

Rosenhead, J. (1982). Soldier Blue. *New Socialist,* **5**, 7–9.

Roth, J.A. (1974). Professionalism – The Sociologist's Decoy. *Sociology of Work and Occupations,* **7**, 6–24.

Rudé, G. (1981). The Riots in History. *Marxism Today,* **25**, 23–4.

Ryan, A.P. (1956). *Mutiny at the Curragh.* London, Macmillan.

Saunders, P. (1979). *Urban Politics: A Sociological Interpretation.* London, Hutchinson.

Saunders, P. (1985). Space, the City and Urban Sociology. In D. Gregory and J. Urry (eds), *Social Relations and Spatial Structures.* London, Macmillan, 67–89.

Saunders, P. (1986). Reflections on the Dual Politics Thesis: the Argument, its Origins and its Critics. In M. Goldsmith (ed.), *Political Theory and the Management of Fiscal Stress.* London, Gower, 1–40.

Scarman, Lord (1981). *The Brixton Disorders, 10–12 April 1981. Report of an Inquiry,* Cmnd. 8427. London, HMSO.

Scott, I.R. and Latham, C.T. (1976). A Comment on the James Committee Report. *Criminal Law Review,* 159–74.

Scraton, P. (1982). Policing and Institutionalised Racism on Merseyside. In D. Cowell, T. Jones and J. Young (eds), *Policing the Riots.* London, Junction Books.

Scraton, P. (1985). *The State of the Police.* London, Pluto.

Silver, A. (1967). The Demand for Order in Civil Society: A Review of Some Themes in the History of Urban Crime, Police and Riot. In D.J. Bordua (ed.), *The Police. Six Sociological Essays*. New York, John Wiley, 1–24.

Simey, M. (1982). Police Authorities and Accountability: The Merseyside Experience. In D. Cowell, T. Jones and J. Young (eds), *Policing the Riots*. London, Junction Books, 52–7.

Simey, M. (1988). *Democracy Rediscovered. A Study in Police Accountability*. London, Pluto Press.

Simon, D. (1954). Master and Servant. In D. Saville (ed.), *Democracy and the Labour Movement*. London, Lawrence & Wishart, 160–200.

Singh, A. (1977). U.K. Industry and the World economy. A Case of De-Industrialisation. *Cambridge Journal of Economics*, 113–36.

Sivanandan, A. (1980). *Imperialism and the Silicon Age*. London, Race & Class.

Sivanandan, A. (1981). From Resistance to Rebellion. Asian and Afro-Caribbean Struggles in Britain. *Race and Class*, **23**, 111–52.

Skyrme, Sir Thomas (1979). *The Changing Image of the Magistracy*. London, Macmillan.

Smellie, K.B. (1963). *A History of Local Government*. London, George Allen & Unwin.

Smith, D. (1980). Tonypandy 1980: Definitions of a Community. *Past and Present*, **87**, 158–84.

Solicitor (1932). *English Justice*. London, George Routledge & Sons.

Somerton, H.W. (1832). *A Narrative of the Bristol Riots*. Bristol, Pamphlet.

Speck, W.A. (1977). *Stability and Strife*. London, Edward Arnold.

Spedding, J., Ellis, R.L. and Heath, D.D. (1861). *The Works of Francis Bacon* (vol. VII). London, Longman.

Spencer, S. (1985a). *Called to Account. The Case for Police Accountability in England and Wales*. London, National Council for Civil Liberties.

Spencer, S. (1985b). *Police Authorities during the Miners' Strike*. London, Cobden Trust.

Stammers, N. (1983). *Civil Liberties in Britain during the Second World War. A Political Study*. London, Croom Helm.

Stead, P.J. (1985). *The Police of Britain*. New York, Macmillan Publishing Co.

Stedman-Jones, G. (1975). Class Struggle in the Industrial Revolution. *New Left Review*, **90**, 35–69.

Steedman, C. (1984). *Policing the Victorian Community. The Formation of the English Provincial Police*. London, Routledge & Kegan Paul.

Stevenson, J. (1977a). Social Control and the Prevention of Riots in England 1789–1829. In A.P. Donajgrodski (ed.), *Social Control in Nineteenth Century Britain*. London, Croom Helm, 27–50.

Stevenson, J. (1977b). The Queen Caroline Affair. In J. Stevenson (ed.), *London in the Age of Reform*. Oxford, Blackwell, 117–48.

Stevenson, J. (1979). *Popular Disturbances in England 1700–1870*. London, Longman.

Stevenson, J. and Quinault, R. (1974). *Popular Protest and Public Order*. London, George Allen & Unwin.

Storch, R.D. (1975). The Plague of Blue Locusts. Police Reform and Popular Resistance in Northern England 1840–1857. *International Review of Social History*, **20**, 61–90.

Storch, R.D. (1976). The Policeman as Domestic Missionary. Urban Discipline and Popular Culture in Northern England. *Journal of Social History*, **9**, 481–509.

Sugarman, D. (1983). Law, Economy and the State in England 1750–1914. Some Major Issues. In D. Sugarman (ed.), *Legality, Ideology and the State*. London, Academic Press, 213–66.

Sweet, R. (1980). *Real Trouble, a Study of Aspects of the Southall Trials*. London, Runnymede Trust.

Tarling, R.C. (1979). *Sentencing Practice in Magistrates' Courts*, Home Office Research Study 56. London, HMSO.

Taylor, A.J.P. (1965). *English History 1914–1945*. Oxford, Clarendon.

Thirlwall, A.P. (1982). De-industrialisation in the United Kingdom. *Lloyds Bank Review*, **144**, 22–37.

Thomas, B. (1930). The Migration of Labour into the Glamorgan Coalfield 1861–1911. *Economica*, **10**, 275–94.

Thomas, S. (1974). *The Bristol Riots*. Bristol, Bristol Historical Association.

Thomis, M.I. and Holt, P. (1977). *Threats of Revolution in Britain 1789–1848*. London, Macmillan.

Thompson, E.P. (1963). *The Making of the English Working Class*. London, Victor Gollancz.

Thompson, E.P. (1965). The Peculiarities of the English. *Socialist Register*, **2**, 311–62.

Thompson, E.P. (1971). The Moral Economy of the English Crowd in the Eighteenth Century. *Past & Present*, **50**, 76–130.

Thompson, E.P. (1975). *Whigs And Hunters*. Harmondsworth, Penguin.

Thompson, E.P. (1977). *William Morris. Romantic to Revolutionary*. London, Merlin Press.

Thompson, E.P. (1978). *The Poverty of Theory*. London, Merlin Press.

Thompson, F.M.L. (1963). *English Landed Society*. London, Routledge and Kegan Paul.

Thurston, G. (1967). *The Clerkenwell Riot. The Killing of Constable Culley*. London, George Allen & Unwin.

Tobias, J.J. (1967). *Crime and Industrial Society in the Nineteenth Century*. London, Batsford.

Townshend, C. (1982). Martial Law and the problems of Emergency in Britain. *Historical Journal*, **25**(1), 167–95.

Traill, J. (1839). *A Letter to the Right Hon Lord Brougham and Vaux on the Police Reports and the Police Bills*. Pamphlet.

Troup, Sir Charles Edward (1925). *The Home Office*. London, G.P. Putnam's Sons Ltd.

Tugendhat, C. (1971). *The Multinationals*. London, Eyre & Spottiswoode.

Turner-Samuels, D. (1981). *Final Report of the Working Party into Community–Police Relations*. Lambeth, Lambeth Borough Council.

Uglow, S. (1988). *Policing Liberal Society*. Oxford, Oxford University Press.

Unsworth, C. (1982). The Riots of 1981: Popular Violence and the Politics of Law and Order. *Journal of Law & Society*, **9**(1), 63–85.

Van Doorn, J. (1975). *The Soldier and Social Change: Comparative Studies in the History and Sociology of the Military*. Beverly Hills, CA, Sage.

Vogler, R.K. (1982). Magistrates and Civil Disorder. *LAG Bulletin*, November, 12–15.

Vogler, R.K. (1983). The Changing Nature of Bail. *LAG Bulletin*, February, 11–15.

Vogler, R.K. (1990). Magistrates' Courts and the Struggle for Local Democracy. In C.S. Sumner (ed.), *Censure, Politics and Criminal Justice*. Milton Keynes, Open University Press, 59–92.

Waddington, P.A.J. (1985). *The Effects of Police Manpower Depletion during the N.U.M. Strike 1984–5*. London, Police Foundation.

Weatheritt, M. (1986). *Innovations in Policing*. London, Croom Helm.

Webb, S. and Webb, B. (1963). *English Local Government* (4 vols). London, Frank Cass.

Western, J.R. (1965). *The English Militia in the Eighteenth Century*. London, Routledge & Kegan Paul.

Whelan, C.J. (1981). The Law and the Use of Troops in Industrial Disputes. In R. Fryer, A. Hunt, D. McBarnett (eds), *Law, State and Society*. London, Croom Helm, 160–76.

Whelan, C.J. (1985). Armed Forces, Industrial Disputes and the Law in Great Britain. In P.J. Rowe and C.J. Whelan (eds), *Military Intervention in Democratic Societies*. London, Croom Helm, 110–29.

Whitelaw, W. (1989). *The Whitelaw Memoirs*. London, Aurum Press.

Williams, D. (1967). *Keeping the Peace: The Police and Public Order*. London, Hutchinson.

Williams, D. (1974). Offences against the State. *Criminal Law Review*, November, 634–41.

Williams, D. (1981). The Brixton Disorders. *Cambridge Law Journal*, **41**(1), 1–6.

Williams, J. (1980). The Coal Mining Industry 1750–1914. In *Glamorgan County History*. Cardiff, University of Wales Press, 311–62.

Williamson, P.J. (1985). *Varieties of Corporatism*. Cambridge, Cambridge University Press.

Wise, E. (1907). *The Law Relating to Riots and Unlawful Assemblies*, 4th edn. London, Butterworth.

Zangerl, C.H.E. (1971). The Social Composition of the County Magistracy in England and Wales, 1831–1887. *Journal of British Studies*, 113–25.

Zelditch, M. (1962). Some Methodological Problems of Field Studies. *American Journal of Sociology*, **67**, 566–78.

UK Official Papers

Parliamentary Papers

Report from the Select Committee appointed to inquire into the state of the Police of the Metropolis, PP 1816 (510) v.

Report of the Select Committee on (Policemen as Spies) etc., PP 1833 (627) xiii.

Report from the Select Committee appointed to inquire into the conduct of the Metropolitan Police on the 13th May last in dispersing a Public Meeting in Coldbath Fields, PP 1833 (718) xiii.

Report from the Select Committee on the Police of the Metropolis etc., PP 1834 (600) xvi.

Report from the Select Committee appointed to inquire into the (Metropolis Police Offices) with a view to the further improvement of the same, PP 1837 (451) xii.

Report from the Select Committee on Metropolis Police Offices, PP 1837–8 (578) xv.

First Report of Her Majesty's Commissioners appointed to Inquire into the Execution of the Criminal Law, especially respecting Juvenile Offenders and Transportation, PP 1847 (447) vii.

Report of Her Majesty's Commissioners appointed to Inquire into the alleged Disturbance of the public peace in Hyde Park on Sunday 1st July 1855 and the conduct of the metropolitan police in connection with the same, PP 1856 (2016) xxiii.

Report of the Committee to Inquire and Report as to the Origin and Character of the Disturbances which took place in the Metropolis on Monday 8th February, PP 1886 (C.4665) xxxiv.

Report of the Departmental Committee appointed to inquire into the Disturbances at Featherstone on 7th September 1893, PP 1893/4 (C.7234) xvii.

Report of the Interdepartmental Committee on Riots appointed by the Home Secretary, PP 1895 (C.7650) xxxv.

Report of the Select Committee on the Employment of the Military in Cases of Disturbances, PP 1908 (236) vii.

Report of the Royal Commission on the Selection of Justices of the Peace, PP 1911 (Cd.5250) xxxvi (minutes) 1910 (Cd.5358).

Colliery Strike Disturbances in South Wales. Correspondence and Report, PP 1911 (Cd.5568) lxiv.

Report of the Royal Commission on Justices of the Peace, PP 1946/8, 1947/8 (Cmd. 7463) xii.

Royal Commission on the Police, PP 1964 (Cmnd.1728).

Parliamentary Proceedings

Parliamentary History, vols i–xxvi, 1625–1803.
Parliamentary Debates, First Series, vols i–xli, 1803–1820.
Parliamentary Debates, New Series (2), vols i–xxv, 1820–1830.
Parliamentary Debates, Third Series, vols i–ccclxvi, 1830–1891.
Parliamentary Debates, Fourth Series, vols 1–199, 1891–1908.
Parliamentary Debates, Fifth Series, vols 1–1000, 1908–1981.
Parliamentary Debates, Fifth Series, from 1981.

Index

Thurston, G., 96
Times, The, 31–2, 36, 40–41, 45, 61, 63–5, 72, 79, 81–2, 151, 163
Tindall, L.C.J., 37
Tonypandy (1910), 53, 54, 89
  power relations (shifts), 74–82
Tories, 29–31, 46, 98
Tory Democrats, 99
Townshend, C., 83
Toxteth riots, *see* Liverpool riots (1981)
Trafalgar Square (1887), 55, 97
  power relations (shifts), 60–69
Traill, James, 27
Trenchard, Lord, 97, 108
Triple Alliance strike (1911), 89
Troup, Charles, 51, 52, 55, 106
Turner-Samuels, S., 116

Uglow, S., 107, 109, 110, 111
unemployment
  Liverpool, 131
  Manchester, 144
  1981 riots, 113, 114, 115
  Trafalgar Square, 55, 60–69
United Services Journal, 36
Unsworth, C., 115, 134
Urban Aid, 131
urban renewal scheme, 145

Van Doorn, J., 87, 90
Vaughan, Mr (magistrate), 55, 62, 63, 67

Vogler, R.K., 52, 57, 100, 164, 167

Walker, General Sir Walter, 91
Wallace, T., 114
War Office, 53, 71, 73, 75–6, 78, 80, 84, 86, 97
Warren, Sir Charles, 61–4, 67–8, 97, 108
watch committees, 101, 105
Weatheritt, M., 10, 110
Webb, B. and S., 14, 33, 34, 46, 98
Wellington, Duke of, 14
Westminster Police Bill (1785), 16–19
Wetherell, Sir Charles, 32–3, 36–7
Weymouth, Lord, 84
Wharncliffe, Lord, 31
Whelan, C.J., 56, 84, 88, 89, 91, 93
Whig Party, 19, 26, 28–9, 30, 31, 46
Whitelaw, W., 107, 109, 133
Wilkinson, General, 84–5
Wilkite riots (1763), 45
Williams, D., 56, 91, 94
Williams, J., 71, 74
Williams, L., 52
Williams, Mr Justice, 72
Willink Royal Commission, 101, 111
Wilson line, 52
Wise, E., 13
working class, 47, 57, 96

Zangerl, C.H.E., 47, 48